# PERSPECTIVES ON NUCLEAR STRATEGY OF INDIA AND PAKISTAN

# PERSPECTIVES ON NUCLEAR STRATEGY OF INDIA AND PAKISTAN

Editor

Mohammed Badrul Alam

KALPAZ

Perspectives on Nuclear Strategy of India and Pakistan



ISBN: 978-81-7835-963-2



Published in 2013 in India by
Kalpaz Publications,
C-30 Satyawati Nagar
Delhi-110 052.

E-mail: Kalpaz@hotmail.com

*Laser Typesetting* : Awadhesh Computers, Delhi

*Printed at:* G. Print Process,Delhi

# Contents

# Preface

The primary purpose of this book is to analyse, examine, evaluate and critique contemporary works on South Asian security order encompassing aspects of nuclear strategies of India and Pakistan, impact of nuclear South Asia in the regional and technological context as well as the viability of various confidence-building measures both in the conventional and non-conventional areas. The book offers a number of scenarios under which a stable (and, unstable) security regime may evolve in South Asia in the not so distant future.

With the nuclear explosion conducted by India in 1998 to be subsequently followed up by its neighbour, Pakistan and the escalation of conflict over Kashmir, the nuclear debate in the sub-continent has become a live issue. Although, India tested in 1974, what it termed as a "peaceful nuclear explosions", India has proclaimed itself to be a nuclear weapon state with the declaration of a nuclear doctrine in August 1999. This edited volume will examine and evaluate India's and Pakistan's nuclear doctrines and other current measures that are geared towards developing a sound nuclear strategy in consonance with paradigm shift in their respective foreign policy orientations in recent years. The book will also discuss and analyse various confidence-building measures, both military as well as non-military between India and Pakistan. As India and Pakistan shape and fine tune their nuclear doctrine, which type of weapon system these countries will prefer to and adopt and why? What will be the outcome of such a nuclear strategy in the foreign policy arena in the regional sector as well as in the global scene? Is there a possibility for the emergence of a stable nuclear proliferation regime in South Asia based on nuclear deterrence? The book will attempt to provide answers to the above questions in addition to forecasting a probable scenario, should nuclear deterrence fails.

Chapter One deals with key elements of nuclear doctrines of India and Pakistan including the changes and transformations that have taken place within the last few years. Mohammed Badrul Alam also analyses and examines the following aspects: (a) Conceptualising risk paradigm and situating Pakistan's fragile regime, (b) Nuclear First Strike Option versus No First Use, (c) Institutional arrangements related to setting up of nuclear command, (d) Delineating the notion of nuclear threshold and, (e) Examining viability of Limited Wars.

Chapter Two looks at Pakistan's nuclear strategy. Manpreet Sethi examines Pakistan's nuclear doctrine and strategy. Divided into four main sections, it first outlines the role that the country envisages for its nuclear weapons. The second section identifies the main attributes of the nuclear doctrine as can be extrapolated from statements of military and civilian elite. The third segment outlines some of the current developments in its nuclear capability. The chapter concludes with some suggestions on how India should respond to these developments.

Chapter Three focuses on the hype by the nuclear complex in South Asia and how the nationalist media around the tests demonstrated a blind spot, amounting to a veritable black hole, in the nuclear imaginings of the respective security elites. Ali Ahmed highlights this deficit in strategic thinking to conclude that, firstly, the nuclear complex needs stringent oversight, and, secondly, that a nuclear peace movement needs to be energised expeditiously in order to bring about that oversight.

Chapter Four examines and evaluates various confidence-building measures, military as well as non-military, that were initiated between India and Pakistan. Mohammed Badrul Alam also addresses and delineates definition and conceptual notion as well as some of the pertinent aspects of ongoing peace process including Track-II diplomacy and nuclear risk reduction measures being undertaken by India and Pakistan.

Chapter Five addresses the ways through which a terrorist or any radical group could perpetrate a nuclear strike using either a nuclear bomb with the aim of causing mass casualties and widespread destruction or disperse radioactive contamination through a radiological dispersion device to simply provoking mass fear with both environmental and economic disruptions. Animesh Roul suggests that the evident efforts by jihadist terrorists in the South Asian context to acquire nuclear and radiological weapons continue to be among the key challenges.

Chapter Six analyses the following puzzle: what are the thresholds beyond which Pakistan would respond with nuclear weapons, what role Pakistan ascribes to tactical and strategic nuclear weapons and whether Pakistan considers nuclear first strike as a viable option? Yogesh Joshi suggests that for real confidence-building in the nuclear sphere, apart from Pakistan, must India also explain the rationale of the current technological drive in India's nuclear strategy and must also understand the consequences for regional balance of power through the eyes of others specially Pakistan.

Chapter Seven examines how Pakistan's National Disaster Management Agency (NDMA) in consultation with the experts of the Pakistan Nuclear Regulatory Authority (PNRA), Pakistan Atomic Energy Commission (PAEC) and the Strategic Plans Division (SPD) devises a Nuclear Emergency Response Plan (NERP). Tughral Yamin surmises that it will include guidelines not only for the rescue and relief organisations but also for the general public to follow in a nuclear emergency.

Chapter Eight analyses the nuclear doctrine in the framework of Deterrence and Compellance theories keeping in view the crises between India and Pakistan. Sannia Abdullah throws light on the strategic stability of South Asia after the induction of the Cold Start phase in India-Pakistan relations.

Chapter Nine highlights as to why it became imperative for Pakistan to acquire nuclear weapons despite external and internal pressures. It examines the significance of Pakistan's nuclear weapon tests in May 1998 in the backdrop of India's initiative. Zafar Khan identifies the factors that helped the proponents of Pakistan's nuclear weapon tests, which this writer calls Pakistan's security epistemic community (SEC), to succeed against the external and internal opponents of Pakistan's nuclear deterrence and outweigh their case for Pakistan maintaining a non-nuclear stance.

Chapter Ten explains how the Pakistani leaders realised that given the disparity in size and resources it would be impossible for Pakistan to defend itself conventionally against India and it needed an equaliser in the shape of nuclear capability to safeguard its territorial integrity. Naeem Salik analyses the context under which Pakistan was, therefore, left with no option but to pursue its own military nuclear programme.

Chapter Eleven looks at the challenges faced by Pakistan in light of India's sustained assistance from Russia in developing and operating nuclear submarines. Muhammad Azam Khan advocates that Pakistan should chart a course to train, lease and if possible, acquire nuclear submarines from China so as to maintain its hard earned and deftly protected strategic potential.

This book attempts to provide a balanced, objective assessment of nuclear strategies of India and Pakistan, and offers a state and non-state centric paradigms in a post-Cold War unipolar world. The book also discusses the impact of nuclearisation on security relationship and the delicate, problematique balance of power between India and Pakistan. The book outlines in cogent details various critical viewpoints of prominent scholars who have tried to address South Asian nuclear discourse using content, empirical, technological and analytical approaches.

***Mohammed Badrul Alam***

# Acknowledgements

This book has its origin from teaching a wide range of students in India, the USA and Japan. My students at Nimapara College (Utkal University, Bhubaneswar, India) were the early inspirations for sharpening my writing skills. Later in New Delhi where I earned my M.Phil degree in American Studies at Jawaharlal Nehru University, my professors, Dr. B.K. Shrivastava, Dr. M.S.Venkatramani and Dr. R.P. Kaushik taught me aspects of nuclear security studies and its implications. My long stint working at the American Center library and Indian council for World affairs (Sapru House) in New Delhi opened up my eyes to the scope and breadth of literature on almost all important facets of security studies.

In the United States, where I attended Cornell University in Ithaca, New York, I earned my M.A. and Ph.D degrees in International Studies. While at Cornell, many professors instilled in me the various intricacies and complexities of issues related to nuclear proliferation and their impact in the shaping of South Asian society. The professors are: Dr. Richrad Polenberg, Dr. Mary Fainshod Katzenstein, Dr. Milton Jacob Esman, Dr.Walter Lafeber, Dr. Martin Shefter, Dr. Benjamin Ginsburg, Dr. Peter Katzenstein, Dr. Richard Rosecrance, Dr. Ami Ayalon, Dr. Stewart Blumin, Dr. Joel Silbey, Dr. Myron Rush, Dr. George Kahin, Dr. Norman Uphoff, Dr. Steven Jackson. From the Cornell University Library, Mr. Ved Kayastha was of invaluable help in providing input and feedback whenever needed.

I am grateful to Dr. Bryan Reddick, Dean of Elmira College, New York, Dr. Anthony Layng, Professor of Anthropology, Dr. Robert Park, Professor of Political Science, Dr. Myra Glenn, Professor of History and Prof. Peter Ladley,

Department of English, all from the same institution, for encouraging me at all times. Dr. Frank Czerwinski of the State University of New York at Cortland offered me useful advice whenever I sought it. My colleagues at Midway College, Kentucky, namely, Dr. Robert Miller, Professor of Religion, Dr. Judith Hatchet, Professor of English, provided me with useful research assistance.

In Japan, where I have been teaching at Miyazaki International College in Southern Kyushu since January 1998, the following people helped me in shaping my ideas and bringing in the right focus on South Asian security discourse. Among the colleagues who helped me are: Dr. Kate Greenfield, Dean; Dr. Getachew Felleke, Professor of Economics; Prof. Jun Maeda, Professor of Japanese Literature; Prof. Amanda Bradley, Professor of English Language; Dr. Jeong Pyong-Hong and Dr. Yasu Izumikawa, Professors in Political Science. My students at the Miyazaki International College in the course, "South Asian Societies and Cultures", provided interesting glimpses from the security literature as India and Pakistan evolved the nuclear security doctrine. My friend working at other institutions in Japan also offered useful comments on this book project. Among those are: Dr. Joel Campbell (Professor of Political Science, Osaka University), Dr. Mika Mervioe (Professor of Political Science, University of Shimane), Dr. Jeffrey Folks (Professor of American Literature, Doshisa University at Kyoto), Dr. Wilhelm Vosse (Professor of Political Science, International Christian University, Tokyo).

At Jamia Millia Islamia University, Delhi, where I am presently a Professor of Political Science, a number of my colleagues in the Department of Political Science including Prof.Rumki Basu, Prof. Nisar Ul Haq, Prof. Furqan Ahmad, and from the Economics department, Prof. Shahid Ashraf, were great source of inspiration and motivation. A number of doctoral scholars including Sarish Sebastian, Kuldeep Singh, Reyaz Ahmad Ganie, Muzaffar Ahmad Ganie, Akhilesh Tiwari, Digvijay Singh Sekhawat, were of immense help in collecting the source materials.

I am extremely grateful to Shri Amit Garg and his highly competent and capable associates at the Kalpaz Publications Delhi, who not only showed keen interest but also agreed to publish the manuscript and put it on a fast track.

I am also deeply appreciative and grateful to Dr.Maqsudul Hasan Nuri, Acting President, Islamabad Policy Research Institute (IPRI) and Visiting Professor Department of Defence and Diplomatic Studies, Fatima Jinnah Women University, Rawalpindi, for granting me the necessary permission to re-print articles published in the recent issues of Islamabad Policy Research Institute Journal and authored by Tughral Yamin, Sannia Abdullah, Zafar Khan, Naeem Salik and Commander Muhammad Azam Khan.

The greatest gratitude is owed to my mother, Mrs. Hedatun Nisa and brothers:

Dr. Mohammed Shamsul Alam and Mohammed Aminul Alam, and sisters: Dr. (Mrs.) Swaleha Khatun, Mrs. Rahima Khatun, Mrs. Sofia Khatun, my wife: Mrs. Gahartaj Rokeya and my children: Saira Alam, Zubair Alam, Sadaf Alam and Munawar Alam. Although quite demanding and at times frustrating, everyone allowed me the time and necessary emotional support I needed to complete my work. Much of my success is due to their love and affection at all times.

**Mohammed Badrul Alam**

# List of Contributors

**Mohammed Badrul Alam,** Professor, Dept. of Political Science, Faculty of Social Sciences, Jamia Millia Islamia University, New Delhi.

**Manpreet Sethi,** Project Leader, Nuclear Security, Centre for Air Power Studies, New Delhi.

**Ali Ahmed,** Assistant Professor, Nelson Mandela Center for Peace and Conflict Resolution, Jamia Millia Islamia University, New Delhi.

**Animesh Roul,** Executive Director of Research Society for the Study of Peace and Conflict (SSPC). New Delhi.

**Yogesh Joshi,** is a Doctoral Research Scholar at the Center for International Politics, Organisation and Disarmament (CIPOD), School of International Studies, Jawaharlal Nehru University, New Delhi.

**Tughral Yamin,** Deputy Chief Manager, Centre for MCW Technologies, National Engineering and Scientific Commission, Islamabad.

**Sannia Abdullah,** Lecturer, Defence and Strategic Studies (DSS), Quaid-i-Azam University, Islambad.

**Zafar Khan,** Doctoral Scholar, Department of Politics, University of Glasgow, United Kingdom.

**Naeem Salik,** Advisor, Faculty of Contemporary Studies, National Defence University (NDU), Islamabad.

**Muhammad Azam Khan,** Research faculty member in Pakistan Navy War College, Lahore.

# 1

# Grand Nuclear Strategy of India and Pakistan: A Comparative Study

*Mohammed Badrul Alam*

Analysing South Asian security scene in the post-Cold War involves overt back to back nuclearisation by India and Pakistan in 1998 and the changing perceptions of national security as reflected in the policy formulations of both countries on nuclear strategy. For Pakistan, comprehensive deliberations on security problematique is addressed within the gambit of its newly acquired nuclear weapons and in the shaping of its nuclear doctrine.

The chapter analyses, evaluates and investigates Pakistan's nuclear doctrine by critically examining the following aspects: (a) Conceptualising risk paradigm and situating Pakistan's fragile regime, (b) Nuclear First Strike Option versus No First Use, (c) Institutional arrangements related to setting up of nuclear command, (c) Delineating the notion of nuclear threshold, (d) Examining viability of Limited War. Specific proposals floated by Pakistan toward strategic restraint regime will also be analysed. Finally, the article will address the current peace dialogue between India and Pakistan and how that could affect latter's strategic perspective in the long term.

## Within Risk Paradigm: Is Pakistan a Risk?

Whether to risk – a taste for it or an aversion to it – is a meaningful way to explain decision making since it links the strategic and the psychological conceptions of choice.[1] It portrays leaders as calculating goal-seekers while allowing them to have different personal decision making styles. One can call Khruschev risk-acceptant or risk-seeking and Brezhnev risk-averse without implying either one was more rational than the other. In the same vein, one can argue that governing elites of Pakistan are risk takers perhaps to the point of brinkmanship. According to Utility theory suggested by De Finetti (1952) and developed by Arrow (1964), Pratt (1964), Goldgeier/Tetlock (2001), Berejikian(2002), Herrmann/ Fischerkeller (1995), Hymans(2006), Mercer (2005), Hashmi/Lee (2004), etc., the risk averse person will prefer not to gamble too hard and accept the best outcome at face value while risk taker will try to push the envelope too far to the point of brinkmanship for deriving maximum advantage or leverage. Risk acceptance was attributed to Britain and France in their intervention in Suez (Richardson, 1992) and to Eisenhower in his deception about the U-2 over-flight (McDermott, 1998); while a cautious decision was the United States staying out of the Suez crisis (McDermott, 1998). This association of risk acceptance with riskier choice appears in Bueno de Mesquita's revised expected utility theory of war (1985) and its development by Morrow (1987). The idea is that a risk-averse state is one that chooses policies that reduce others' incentives to attack it. Jervis (1992) presents a prospect theory interpretation of crisis instability and suggests that because decisions are being made among losses in territory, reputation or domestic support, a leader intends to order a pre-emptive strike in cases in which the standard expected utility model would predict the actor to cut his losses to the minimum. Under this model, it is possible to argue that under extreme provocation and in an asymmetrical strategic environment vis-a-vis India, Pakistan's ruling elite may adopt a policy of pre-emption as it may determine that it(Pakistan) has nothing more to lose by not going in for the first use of nuclear weapons.

## Contextualising the Concept of Deterrence

Concept of deterrence assumes significance in military strategic discourse when one or the other state in the same regional neighbourhood acquires nuclear weapons. Within deterrence literature, deterrence by denial, according to Glen Snyder, is premised on the failure of deterrence and the preparedness by the other party to this eventuality.[2] The other version of the deterrence by denial is by denying the adversary the specific military advantage it might want to respond through an overwhelming force of its own. Michael Howard has defined deterrence as a policy that seeks to persuade an adversary, through the actual threat of military retaliation, that the costs of using military force to resolve political conflict will outweigh the benefits derived from it.[3] Deterrence theory assumes that there is a certain measure of transparency of interests and capability inherent in a state's action and in its response in a given strategic situation that are of supreme national importance.

In contrast, the theory of deterrence by punishment seeks to prevent aggression by threat of punitive retaliation. US strategic policy in the 1950s with its emphasis on massive retaliation and assured destruction are examples of deterrence by punishment.[4]

In the context of South Asia, Pakistan's nuclear doctrine relies in part on both of these components: deterrence by denial as well as deterrence by punishment. What makes Pakistan's strategic policy bit ambiguous is neither of these concepts been articulated or explored fully to its operational limits vis-a-vis India's nuclear strategy.

## India's Nuclear Doctrine and Compare/Contrast with Pakistan

In 1974, India conducted a nuclear test that it termed a 'peaceful nuclear explosion'. However, in 1998, India conducted a full scale nuclear test and subsequently claimed to attain nuclear capability which was followed soon after by its neighbour, Pakistan, also opting for the same nuclear route. A year later, the draft on nuclear doctrine was presented in August 1999 to the Indian Prime Minister and the Cabinet and was subsequently released for public debate by the National Security Advisory Board.

The nuclear doctrine of India was perhaps the first of its kind among the known nuclear weapon states of the world, and India prepared the expansive nuclear doctrine document before obtaining capability mentioned in it. This draft, with minor alternations, effectively become India's nuclear doctrine on January 4, 2003 when the Cabinet Committee on Security Affairs (CSA) reviewed the operationalisation of India's nuclear doctrine. The following are some of the highlights of India's and Pakistan's nuclear doctrine on a comparative note.[5]

- India's strategic perspective for its nuclear doctrine encompasses wider latitude than South Asia in keeping with its strategic potential. Pakistan's perspective as presently evident seems to be India-specific.
- India proclaims 'no-first-use' as a matter of principle. Pakistan is averse to it and disinclined to give any such guarantees, feeling that a bland 'no-first use' policy invalidates its deterrence advantage against India.

- India's nuclear weapons system will be 'TRIAD' (land based ballistic missiles, sea based assets and air borne platforms). Pakistan's current capacity in this regard is limited to land based and aircraft delivery systems.
- India and Pakistan's nuclear doctrines emphasise a 'credible minimum deterrent.' However, Pakistan's capabilities in this direction may be questionable.
- India has revised its nuclear doctrine in 2003 by including any chemical, biological and nuclear attack on its territory to be responded through massive nuclear retaliation. Pakistan has not made any such formulations so far.
- India's nuclear arsenal will be under civil political control at all times. Pakistani's nuclear arsenal will be under defacto control of the Army Chief.
- India will not resort to use or threat of use of nuclear weapons against non-nuclear weapon states or those not aligned with nuclear weapon powers. Pakistan has not made any such explicit pledge in its nuclear policy.
- 'Kargil'(1999) and 'Operation Parakram'(2001-02) crises demonstrated that Mutually Assured Destruction deterrence is operating in South Asia, and that both sides have fairly recessed red lines for launching a nuclear strike on the other side. But it remains unclear how much of their restraint is not a fallout of direct deterrence, rather a lack of political will or external intervention.
- India and Pakistan seem to be eager to engage in dangerous brinkmanship. Elite leadership of both countries are acutely aware of the utility of nuclear weapons as a political tool rather than their military implications. Provocative statements are being made,

often for consumption of domestic or third-party audiences, which has the potential of sending mixed signals to the adversary.

- On the positive side, recent crises have shown three potentially stabilising trends between India and Pakistan: a growing sense of restraint in each country's crisis management behaviour, growing transparency and openness in their strategies, and growing US involvement in crisis resolution.
- The incentives to persist with unconventional and low intensity conflict in the form of state-supported terrorism, state-supported insurgency and cross-border terrorism are likely to continue at the lower end of the conflict spectrum as large scale conventional wars remain risky. This may result in conventional deterrence stability even though the stability might be construed as 'ugly' and less than perfect peace.

## Evolution of Pakistan's Nuclear Program and Z.A. Bhutto

The key decision whether Pakistan should embark on a 'coherent nuclear program' was discussed for the first time in 1963, though its deterrence value was emphasised by Zulfikar Ali Bhutto publicly for the first time in 1965.[6] To quote him, "All wars of our age have become total wars and it will have to be assumed that a war waged against Pakistan is capable of becoming a total war...and our plan should, therefore, include the nuclear deterrent."[7] After China's nuclear tests in 1964, Pakistan was apprehensive that India would go nuclear. Bhutto, who was then a member in Ayub Khan's cabinet stated, "If India developed an atomic bomb, we too will develop one 'even if we have to eat grass or leaves or to remain hungry' because there is no conventional alternative to the atomic bomb."[8] Two aspects of his statement are noteworthy—first, its linkage to India, and second, his emphasis on atomic bomb as the ultimate weapon.

The secession of East Pakistan in 1971 and the subsequent 1974 tests by India led to a serious rethinking among Pakistan's nuclear security elite which ultimately paved the way for paradigm shift in South Asian security enclave.

## Pakistan's Nuclear Command

With Pakistan opting for the nuclear weaponisation in the summer of 1998, it also established the Nuclear Command Authority (NCA) in February 2000 with three components: an Employment Control Committee, the Development Control Committee and the Strategic Plans Division. Pakistan also set up a nuclear regulatory authority to bring proper coordination in its nuclear program. NCA is responsible for policy formulation, employment and development control over all strategic nuclear forces and strategic organisations. Besides the President, the NCA includes foreign affairs, defense and interior ministers, chiefs of all military services and heads of strategic organisations. At a review session in November 27, 2000, the NCA reviewed the strategic and security environment facing Pakistan and took important decisions on nuclear policy matters that included, amongst others, strategic threat perception, restructuring of the strategic organisations and export control mechanisms.[9]

## Pakistan's thinking on No First Use (NFU)

Pakistan has thus far shown little interest in the idea of NFU. Perhaps the closest Pakistan has officially come to accepting the language of no first use was in the summer of 2002 when India and Pakistan confronted each other in the wake of the Kaluchak massacre in Jammu and Kashmir. In response to India's threats to retaliate conventionally to the massacre,

Pakistan stated that it would respond forcefully in turn, hinting that it was prepared to use nuclear weapons as a first choice. Shortly thereafter Islamabad publicly clarified, apparently under US pressure, that responding to an Indian attack did not mean nuclear use, presumably first use, against India.

Among non-officials in Pakistan, those who oppose weaponisation as well as those who support a minimum deterrent would probably support NFU, the former as an interim confidence-building measure in the transition to nuclear disarmament and the latter in order to keep the nuclear arsenal minimal and to signal moderation and restraint. Most prominently, Pervez Hoodbhoy has suggested that India and Pakistan should, as part of a bilateral nuclear treaty, agree to a no first use policy. Hoodbhoy argues that NFU would actually benefit Pakistan. NFU would be an investment in stability and survival. In case of nuclear war, Pakistan would have much more to lose than India since New Delhi can inflict much greater nuclear damage (and presumably absorb much greater loss).[10]

Pakistani skepticism or opposition to NFU seems to arise from the following concerns. In contrast to India, Pakistan's thinking on a no first use/first use policy is almost completely military-strategic and country specific (India). First of all, as in India and elsewhere in the world, there are those in Pakistan who doubt the efficacy and practicality of an NFU. Now, the question arises, can Pakistan rely on India's leadership to abide by a no first use commitment? Also, are there any way of verifying in absolute sense that an adversary (India) is committed to no first use?

Secondly, even if NFU were credible, acceptance of it would mean permanent Pakistani strategic inferiority and widening the window of vulnerability. Given Pakistan's inferiority in conventional forces vis-a-vis India, the threat of first use is vital to its (Pakistan's) deterrence against India, while the actual use of nuclear weapons first may be vital to Pakistan's defense and its survival if and when deterrence fails.

Thirdly, there is a line of more offensive-minded Pakistani thinking that vehemently opposes an NFU. As per this line of reasoning, first use of nuclear weapons is intrinsic to Pakistan's exploitation of the asymmetrical conventional situation in South Asia. Protected under the umbrella of nuclear weapons, Pakistan is free to choose sub-conventional conflict with India. For example, in Kashmir fearing Pakistan's first use, India cannot cross the Line of Control in Kashmir valley or the international boundary further south. These strategists regard Pakistan's support of cross-border terrorism in Kashmir since the late 1980s, the Kargil war in 1999, and the crisis of May-June 2002 as validating the correctness of their hypothesis. In spite of Pakistani provocations, as these thinkers surmise, India chose not to retaliate across the Line of Control or cross the international boundary.

## Pakistan's First Strike Option

In order to maintain 'strategic balance', Pakistan taking note of India's overwhelming superiority in conventional arms and manpower may be tempted to go in for rapid escalation with a first strike option. Pakistan is very likely to exercise this option to counter India should the latter pose a serious and credible threat to Pakistan's territorial integrity leading to its dismemberment and further fragmentation.[11] Pakistan's President Pervez Musharraf while proclaiming to be in full control of his nation's strategic assets did not hesitate to threaten India to use nuclear weapons in the event of latter violating the 'Line of Control or the international border.'[12] In this context, it is worth mentioning the comments made by General Khalid Kidwai, Head of the Strategic Plan Division of the Pakistan's Army.

"Nuclear weapons are aimed solely at India. In case, deterrence fails, they will be used, if,

(*a*) India attacks Pakistan and conquers a large part of its territory (space threshold),

(*b*) India destroys a large part either of its land or air forces (military threshold),

(*c*) India proceeds to the economic strangling of Pakistan (economic threshold),

India pushes Pakistan into political destabilisation or creates a large internal subversion in Pakistan (domestic destabilization)"[13]

Pakistan, however, is acutely aware of profound asymmetry in military balance in South Asia. Even Pakistan resorting to a limited war with salami slicing tactics have the potential of backfire. In the words of General Jehangir Karamat, a former Chief of Army of Pakistan, "Pakistan accepts the imbalance inherent in the equation with India and will not seek to match capabilities. Pakistan, will, therefore, modernise and upgrade its military power in carefully selected areas so that its deterrent and defense capability are not degraded and it never faces a scenario of overwhelming strategic superiority from India. This deterrence is the best guarantee of stability because an unacceptable imbalance can have serious implications."[14] According to Zafar Iqbal Cheema, Pakistan's deterrence can be further augmented by its decision to assemble rapidly a small nuclear force, to diversify weapons by using designs that rely on both uranium and plutonium, to develop wide ranging missile programs, and to take steps to miniaturise nuclear warheads.[15] To supplement this line of thinking, Zafar Nawaz Jaspal emphasises more on capability and less on the number of warheads. According to him, "In the present strategic scenario, Pakistan possesses enough strategic weaponry... to provide it with a minimum nuclear deterrence. The basis of this perception is that in nuclear deterrence, parity between opponents is not based on numerical equality of the number of nuclear delivery systems, or of the number of warheads or in the yield of megatons available to each opponent. Parity requires assured destruction capability."[16]

Pakistan's interest in first use may in part be supported by a calculation that there are first uses of nuclear weapons against India that would not necessarily invite nuclear retaliation. Stephen P. Cohen, an internationally renowned security analyst, suggests that the Pakistani army has conceived of an escalation ladder.[17] Four of these possible scenarios involve the threat of first use or actual first use:

- Private and public warnings to India not to move its forces threateningly,
- A demonstration explosion on Pakistani territory to deter India from a conventional attack,
- The use of a 'few' nuclear weapons on Pakistani territory against intruding Indian forces and
- Nuclear strikes against 'critical' Indian military targets, preferably in areas with low population and without much by way of infrastructure.

Of these four, according to Cohen, the first two could well avoid Indian retaliation altogether since they would be carried out inside Pakistan and would not target Indian assets. The second two, Pakistani planners might calculate, would be more provocative but might still not cause India to unleash a full scale retaliatory strike.

In this context, Shireen Mazari argues 'The first generation of nuclear weapons that Pakistan would deploy would have large CEP (circular error probability) that is, would not be too accurate; therefore, at least initially Pakistan would have to evolve a counter-value strategy: that is, targeting Indian economic leadership and population centers rather than hardened military targets."[18]

Mirza Aslam Beg, on the issue of Pakistan's nuclear option, says, The strategy of deterrence, through flexile response is applicable, based on minimum number of weapons. What comprises minimal nuclear deterrence, is a national issue, a function of the political and military judgment, related to adversary's capability."[19]

On the assured nature of Pakistan's nuclear capability, there are two divergent views. Lt. Gen. Asad Durrani states, "Neither of us relishes the prospect of ever using them, especially when the other side could match the response. India could consider taking out our nuclear arsenal, to deny us its use in practice, it is an extremely risky proposition. Even on odd weapon that survived the so-called 'first strike', could cause irreparable damage."[20] On the other hand, Ayesha Siddiqa-Agha argues, "The idea is to ensure that in case of hostilities, Islamabad can manage to deliver two to three nuclear weapons to the adversary's territory. For the time being, this would be achieved with land-based missiles."[21] In the same vein, Ejaz Haidar considers, "Pakistan is in a better position to challenge India through low intensity conflict. This meant that India could now be denied the luxury of expanding the conflict and capitalising on the conventional symmetries."[22]

## Viability of Limited War

Some analysts have raised specter of limited war in the context of India and Pakistan going nuclear due to miscalculation and misperception. Even limited war, in conventional sense, between India and Pakistan can rapidly escalate into nuclear conflict. Traditionally, a limited war is likely to have the following key features:

1. It is likely to be limited in a geographical sense, although in terms of numbers of personnel involved, types of weapons used and duration of conflict, it might be unlimited in scope and actual use;

2. It is also likely to be limited in terms of its objectives within a strategic space using calibrated use of force, i.e., between initiating an armed conflict and an all-out war.

3. It may be limited from the perspectives of the initiator of the conflict, though this may not necessarily be the case with the defender.

However, four factors can turn any conventional conflict, however 'limited' in nature, into acquiring a nuclear dimension:[23]

(*a*) The politico-military objectives which India considers limited, might be deemed unlimited and unacceptable by Pakistan. Islamabad plans to use nuclear weapons in the event of a deep military offensive by India. How 'deep' would be deep enough for India to obtain its objective, and how 'deep' would be too much for Pakistan to absorb, is vague and unclear and will always remain so. Issue of extent of loss of territory, image, legitimacy, is important.

(*b*) Pakistan's military has shown a greater inclination towards a possible use of nuclear weapon. In Pakistan, nuclear command and control are exclusively in the hands of the military. Faced with significant conventional asymmetry and seeming evidence of a conventional attack by India, Pakistan's decision makers may be tempted to threaten the first use of nuclear weapons;

(*c*) In the case of India and Pakistan, inadequate command and control structures, deficient early warning arrangements and perceptions about a doubtful capacity to launch a retaliatory 'second strike' send mixed signals which enhance the risk of a nuclear exchange;

(*d*) A possible reappraisal of India's operational doctrine can further encourage Pakistan to take recourse to atomic weapons even in conventional warfare.

In this context, it is worth noting, analyst Bharat Karnad's 'Sialkot Grab' published in the inaugural issue of *Center for Land Warfare Studies* (*CLAWS*), *Army 2020*. Karnad visualises "India cutting off a thirty mile deep swathe of territory all along the border, threatening Pakistan's center of gravity located in the urban centers at around that depth. His assessment is that this would not entail a nuclear war since it would not threaten Pakistan's survival. Since Indian mechanised forces would be within fallout distance of urban concentrations and Pakistani forces, Pakistan would also be deprived of nuclear targets. Indian deterrence would preclude city busting as an option."[24] Karnad's thesis is that success in a nuclear confrontation is predicated on confronting the adversary with impossibly tough choices he cannot risk taking. There are practical problems with the 'Sialkot Grab' scheme of fighting a limited war. The area encompassed in the thirty mile deep stretch would be quite inhospitable like the US finds areas outside its 'green zones' in Iraq. Since it is densely populated, it could lead to several Fallujas. Collateral damage resulting from conventional war would also be considerable, thereby providing the rationale for Pakistan to up the ante. Contrary to Karnad's thinking, the Indian flirtation with Pakistan's self-defined nuclear threshold is likely to push the conflict up in the escalatory ladder. [25]

## Issue of Nuclear Command and Control and Hot Line

On the crucial issue of nuclear command and control in Pakistan nuclear establishment, the key component is who actually is in - charge. According to Lt. Gen. (Retd.) Sardar F.S. Lodi, the following basic guidelines have to be met in this regard:[26]

- The final orders to use nuclear weapons must come from the highest executive authority in the country;
- The decision must be based on a deteriorating military situation after the enemy's conventional attack is likely to break through or has already breached the main defence line;
- In case of a pre-emptive strike, it must be ensured that the enemy was preparing to launch a nuclear attack, which could cripple Pakistan's nuclear ability to strike back.

Some of Lodi's other recommendations are:

(*a*) Our standard of communication from the Chief Executive right down to the missile launch pad and the air base concerned must be perfect and not be susceptible to interruption at all times;

(*b*) Intelligence gathering agencies must be able to provide accurate, up-to-date and timely information about enemy's additional troop deployments and likely intentions;

(*c*) Our final decision to employ the nuclear option must be based entirely on the security and integrity of the country, when other conventional means of defence have proved inadequate;

(*d*) Our close friends and allies abroad must be kept abreast of the latest situation on the ground and eventually the urgent requirement to employ nuclear weapons;

(*e*) It must be kept in mind that the nuclear option would be a weapon of last resort which may eventually produce no winners or losers and must therefore be employed with the greatest of care and caution after discussing all the pros and cons of the situation, its impact in the region and beyond and its international ramifications.'[27]

Another aspect related to Pakistan's nuclear doctrine is the issue of 'Hot Line' that has restarted among the leaders at the highest level in both Islamabad and New Delhi following a 20-year gap in 1997 is in disuse now. Although some movement has been made in this regard during the June 19-20, 2004 meeting at the foreign secretaries level, yet no firm time table been set as to when the Hot Lines might be activated and become operational. According to Pervaiz Hoodbhoy, Professor of Physics at the Quaid-e-Azam University in Islamabad, Pakistan, "Should a nuclear war occur, it may well be that the order is not given by the Chief Executive or the Prime Minister or whoever. That decision may be taken by a Brigadier, who will decide whether you and I live or die. Any missiles fired by India or Pakistan would take four to eight minutes to hit its target. This means both countries are prepared to launch a nuclear strike on the basis of a warning. In a few hundred seconds, the credibility of the warning must be gauged. Is it the blip on the radar screen really a missile? If so, is it likely to be carrying a nuclear warhead? An alert must then be flashed to the strategic command center. And, if necessary, a launch order transmitted to the missile site."[28]

It is hoped that in the near future, a decision to activate Hot Line at the highest level be taken as has been done already at the area commander level along the entire stretch of India-Pakistan border.

## Possibility of Threats or Diversion of Fissile materials

Like in any nuclear weapon state, multiple vulnerabilities exist in a nuclear weapons complex.[29] In the case of Pakistan, it is possible that groups or individuals may violate security rules for a variety of reasons, including profit making, settling a vendetta, or religious or ideological motives. Rogue elements may try to gain control over sensitive items for their own use or to transfer these items to another state or to other non-state actors for financial or ideological reasons. A special concern is that Pakistan, as its history suggests, may suffer another military coup at some point of time. A new leadership, in that case, can be expected to place a high priority on seizing the country's nuclear assets.

The threat of theft or diversion of fissile material or nuclear weapons falls into three general areas:

- Outsider Threat—The possibility that armed individuals or groups from outside a facility may gain access and steal nuclear weapons, weapons, components or fissile material.
- Insider Threat - The possibility that individuals who work inside the facility will remove fissile material, nuclear weapon's or weapons components without proper authorisation.
- Insider/Outsider Threat - The possibility that insiders and outsiders conspire together in connivance to obtain fissile materials, weapons, or weapon components.

If Pakistan suffers extreme instability or civil war, additional threats to its strategic nuclear assets are also possible. This may happen, as Muthiah Allagappa comments, due to military's inherent struggle to attain legitimacy and in "military's inability to construct an acceptable political framework for the management of the state, including the acquisition and exercise of state power"[30] and in facilitating the emergence of a viable civil society:

- ***Loss of Central Control of Storage Facilities***—Clear lines of communication code and control over weapons, weapon's components, and fissile material may be broken or lost entirely.
- ***Coup***—In the most extreme case, a coup takes place and the new regime attempts to gain control of the entire nuclear complex. A New York Times report suggested US policy makers envisioning alternatives for Pakistan after Musharraf. Under this scenario, the Vice-Chief of the Army, Ahsan Saleem Hyat, took over from General Musharraf as head of the military and former banker Mohammedmian Soomro installed as president, with General Hyat wielding most of the power.[31] In this context, Sydney J. Freedberg writes, "He is just the latest leader to stand precariously atop Pakistan's three ever-shifting tectonic plates - generals, politicians and mullahs. Sooner, not later, he will lose his footing. To understand what might happen next, it's important to understand the three major power centres at work in Pakistan."[32] It is also possible that foreign government(s) may intervene to prevent hostile entity from seizing the strategic nuclear assets.

In the current Post-Bin Laden scene when Al Qaeda has vowed to take revenge and the fragility of President Asif Ali Zardari's regime, Pakistan must also increasingly worry that experts from the nuclear complex could steal sensitive information or assist nuclear weapons programs of other countries or terrorist groups. The information could include highly classified nuclear weapons data, exact storage locations of weapons or fissile material, access control arrangements, or other sensitive, operational details about these weapons.

**Issue of Disaster Management**

There is no reference in Pakistan's nuclear doctrine as to the appropriate disaster control system, should a potential accident does occur. Pakistan, at the present time, does not have anything even close to the capabilities of managing a nuclear disaster, should it occur either from a nuclear first strike or from a retaliatory strike by the adversary.

In a chilling report published by Britain based *NEW SCIENTISTS* in 2002, it was reported that a massive loss of men and materials would occur should a nuclear exchange take place between India and Pakistan. As per this report, "At least 2.9 million people would be killed and another 1.4 million severely injured. This report is based on 10 Hiroshima type bombs, 5 in India (Bangalore, Mumbai, Kolkata, New Delhi, Chennai) and 5 in Pakistan (Karachi, Lahore, Faisalabad, Islamabad, Rawalpindi). India sides with an estimated 1.5 million people dead and 900,000 injured. And, from Pakistan side 1.2 million dead and 600,000 injured. If the bomb explodes on the ground instead of in the air, resulting radioactive dust could kill more people. Due to prevailing winds from west to east, India would incur more casualties than Pakistan. This is just ten bombs, which is 1/10th of estimated number of nuclear bombs both countries are believed to have possessed"(33, See, Table 1.1)

Another report provided even a scarier picture. "Nuclear exchange could kill up to 12 million people at one stroke plus injury up to 7 million. Even a so-called limited war' would have cataclysmic effect overhauling hospitals across

Asia and requiring vast foreign assistance to battle radioactive contamination,

Table 1.1

***Estimated nuclear casualties for attacks on 10 large Indian and Pakistani cities***

| *City Name* | *Total Population Within 5 Kilometers of Ground Zero* | *Number of Persons Killed* | *Number of Persons Severely Injured* | *Number of Persons Slightly Injured* |
|---|---|---|---|---|
| **India** | | | | |
| Bangalore | 3,077,937 | 314,978 | 175,136 | 411,336 |
| Bombay | 3,143,284 | 477,713 | 228,648 | 476,633 |
| Calcutta | 3,520,344 | 357,202 | 198,218 | 466,336 |
| Madras | 3,252,628 | 364,291 | 196,226 | 448,948 |
| New Delhi | 1,638,744 | 176,518 | 94,231 | 217,853 |
| Total India | 14,632,937 | 1,690,702 | 892,459 | 2,021,106 |
| **Pakistan** | | | | |
| Faisalabad | 2,376,478 | 336,239 | 174,351 | 373,967 |
| Islamabad | 798,583 | 154,067 | 66,744 | 129,935 |
| Karachi | 1,962,458 | 239,643 | 126,810 | 283,290 |
| Lahore | 2,682,092 | 258,139 | 149,649 | 354,095 |
| Rawalpindi | 1,589,828 | 183,791 | 96,846 | 220,585 |
| Total Pakistan | 9,409,439 | 1,171,879 | 614,400 | 1,361,872 |
| **India and Pakistan** | | | | |
| Total | 24,042,376 | 2,862,581 | 1,506,859 | 3,382,978 |

famine and disease. More deaths would occur later caused by urban firestones, ignited by the heat of a nuclear exchange, deaths from longe term radiation, or the disease and starvation expected to spread."[34]

In this regard, India's Home Ministry is currently raising several battalions to tackle natural disasters and combat nuclear, biological and chemical warfare. In all likelihood, Pakistan is expected to follow India's path in having a National Emergency Response Force battalions so as to be deployed in strategic locations under the supervision of the Director-General of Civil Defence, should such consequence management contingencies arise.

## Pakistan's Current Missile Capability and India's Cold Start Strategy

According to *Jane Intelligence Review,* Pakistan has nearly completed development of a solid fuel missile that could strike key Indian cities from deep within Pakistan territory through Ghauri-series of liquid propelled missiles in an offensive operation and Shaheen-series weapons as defensive measures.

On May 24, 2002, (and very recently on April 19, 2011), Pakistan also tested Intermediate Range Ballistic Missile *Hatf-V (Ghauri)* that has a range of 1,500 kilometers (1,000 miles) that can hit most populous cities of Northern, Central and Western India. The father of the Pakistan nuclear bomb, Dr. A. Q. Khan, in a declaration has asserted that Ghauri missiles could "wipe out thrice, all the big cities of India."[35] On June 4, 2004, Pakistan also successfully test-fired *Hatf*-V and *Ghauri*-1. In addition to it, Pakistan is now equipped with ballistic missiles like: *Abdali-1,* Hatf-V, Ghaznavi (SRBM), Shaheen series of MRBM (750-2500 km) and Ghauri series of MRBMs and IRBMs ranging between 1,300 to 3,500 km. India, on the other hand, on June 13, 2004, has successfully test fired Brahmos, the supersonic cruise missiles that can travel at Mach 2.823 and which has been configured to be launched from either land, ship, submarine and aircraft using liquid ramjet technology. Furthermore, India has test fired Agni-III longest-range missile successfully on April 12, 2007, which can hit objects from a range of 3000 miles and thus the entire territorial space of Pakistan (in addition to those of China's mega metropolis of Beijing and Shanghai) can be within India's missile range. Agni-III's successful test is likely to put additional pressure on Pakistan's nuclear establishment as the former can claim to have attained minimum credible deterrence and which can form crucial component of India's nuclear doctrine. Agni-IV was tested on November 15, 2011, with a range of 3500 km. Furthermore, on April 19, 2012, India testfired its mostambitious strategic missile, the over 5,000-km range Agni-V, in a bid to join the super exclusive ICBM (intercontinental ballistic missile) club that counts just US, China, France, and UK as its members. In coming years, India is also opting for nuclear submarines, with nuclear-tipped ballistic missiles, for assured and effective second-strike capabilities and nuclear-tipped cruise missiles (LACMs) to provide India a definitive strategic edge. In addition, India's Armed forces have formulated joint war doctrine to ensure that individual combat capabilities of Army, Navy and Air Force can come together in the event of war. It remains to be seen whether and when Pakistan will match India's cruise missile and related capabilities so as not to provide its rival a strategic edge.

Similarly, India's new *Cold Start* Strategy that became operational with major military exercise *VAJRA SHAKTI* in May 2005 has been of real concern to Pakistan's nuclear establishment. Under the Cold Start Strategy, India could retaliate with nuclear weapons if its armed forces were subjected to nuclear, chemical or biological strikes and this could have profound strategic impact on Pakistan's nuclear doctrine. Although Cold Start Strategy was in place under the North Atlantic alliance, a similar replication in the South Asian context might have serious implications thus further endangering the strategic environment of the region.

## Towards a Strategic Restraint Regime

Perhaps, what is needed is a level of transparency and credible approach. To Pakistan's credit, at the October 1998 talks at the foreign minister level, Pakistan proposed a framework for what was called a strategic restraint regime[36] The framework included:

- a non-aggression pact;
- the prevention of a nuclear weapons and ballistic missile race;
- risk reduction mechanisms such as nuclear risk reduction centers;
- avoidance of nuclear conflict;
- formalising moratoria on nuclear testing;
- non-induction of anti-ballistic missile systems and submarine-launched ballistic missiles; and
- formal nuclear doctrines of minimum deterrent capability.

Pakistan also proposed mutual and balanced reduction of forces in the conventional field. India matched these proposals by offering a framework consisting of:

- no-first-use pledges;
- agreement on preventing nuclear war, including through accidental or unauthorised use of nuclear weapons;
- extension of agreements prohibiting attack against nuclear installations;
- advance notification of ballistic missile tests; and;
- verification of nuclear related data exchange.

In this context, Michael Kreppon, South Asia strategist at the Washington DC based Henry Stimson Center has outlined a viable ten key commandments to reduce the risks of nuclear escalation:[37]

- Don't change or alter the territorial status quo in sensitive areas by use of force;
- Avoid nuclear brinkmanship on both sides;
- Avoid dangerous and threatening military practice;
- Put in place special reassurance measures for ballistic missiles and other nuclear forces;
- Implement properly mutual and international treaty obligations, risk-reduction and confidence-building measures;
- Agree on verification arrangements, including intrusive and comprehensive monitoring;
- Establish reliable lines of communication, between political leaders and between military leaders;
- Establish conventional and reliable command and control arrangements as well as intelligence-gathering capabilities to know what the other side is up to, especially in a crisis;
- Keep working hard on these arrangements, improve them, don't take anything for granted; and
- Hope for plan dumb luck or divine intervention.

Along this line, Hassan Askari Rizvi and Rajesh M.Basrur[38] have suggested eight measures, which in their viewpoint could substantially enhance the safety and security of nuclear facilities in India and Pakistan:

1. Track down the groups and the individuals engaged in violent activities and terrorism;
2. Extensive surveillance of the borders and coastlines to contain the movement of goods and people;

3. More use of modern technology to enhance the physical protection of nuclear weapons, material and installations;
4. Thorough scrutiny of the personnel handling the nuclear programmes of the two countries;
5. Acquisition of latest technologies for the transportation of fissile and radioactive materials;
6. Highly trained manpower may be employed for the protection of nuclear facilities;
7. Extensive coordination network amongst all the set-ups dealing with the nuclear infrastructure and in addition, there should be an independent body to ensure an oversight and accountability; and
8. Finally, a disaster management body may be established to handle a security alarm systems, and the actual nuclear-terrorist incidents and emergencies.

## Conclusion

In the shadow of Pakistan's nuclear doctrine lies the perennial issue of Kashmir which is the bone of contention between India and Pakistan since 1947. Since volatility over Kashmir may yet provide a flash point, that possibility may induce both countries to come to a negotiating table and to opt for nuclear deterrence and quick implementation of 'enforceable and verifiable' confidence-building measures which may include simultaneous signing of CTBT and other international safeguards and ushering in of citizens diplomacy. The statement made by Gen. Pervez Musharraf on December 18, 2003 to be flexible on Kashmir issue and be ready to bend on his UN Kashmir baggage by keeping aside UN Security Council Resolution was a welcome sign and could have been explored further. Elaborating his vision for the resolution of the long tangled Kashmir problem, Musharraf had outlined a four-step approach. It involved recognition of the centrality of Kashmir for the settlement of all disputes between India and Pakistan, commencement of a dialogue on that basis, elimination of solutions not acceptable to India, Pakistan and people of Kashmir, and initiating the process for finding a solution acceptable to all parties.[39]

Along with it, the following confidence-building measures at the non-military level could be pursued in right earnest:

- Unofficial dialogue through Track-II should be encouraged by the two governments to assist official-level talks between India and Pakistan;
- Commerce and trade such as having a Free Trade Agreement, Granting Most Favored Nations status, Open Visa Regime, Evolving a common currency etc.; and
- Along with Lahore-Amritsar route, bus service between Srinagar and Muzafarabad linking both Indian and Pakistan sides of the Line of Control across the Kashmir valley that began in April 2005 to continue for the foreseeable future.

Similarly, on Siachen glacier along the Kashmir front, the world's highest battlefield, CBM talks could be initiated geared toward demilitarisation and firm commitment made by both India and Pakistan to stop aggressive maneuvers, avoid lateral movement of troops on the glacier and declare Siachen as a mountain of peace. In this context, a positive development has taken place on April 6, 2007, when the Indian Defence Secretary and his Pakistan counterpart met in Rawalpindi and later on May 30, 2011 in Delhi as part of the fourth and fifth round of Composite Dialogue process. Under this ongoing dialogue, Pakistani has softened its stance from total opposition to authentication of troops. It has offered India a package deal under which it (Pakistan) has agreed to the Indian demand but has asked India for a time bound withdrawal of its troops to the pre-conflict positions as a quid-pro-quo.[40]

Second, India's ex-foreign minister, Mr. K. Natwar Singh's proposal to evolve and study the feasibility of a common nuclear doctrine between India, Pakistan and China in order to bring peace and stability to the region could be explored further. Third, CBMs and related negotiations including the feasibility of common pipeline between Iran, Pakistan and India for enhanced energy cooperation could be pursued more aggressively. Another measure that could be tried was a concerted effort on the part of the permanent members of the UN Security Council to act as honest facilitators "to help in ushering a common, strategic dialogue and language on arms control in South Asia"[41] and foster open communications among the parties concerned. But then, the concept of nuclear deterrence for two South Asian rival countries with deep rooted historical animosities and regional ambitions might be an uphill task unlike the case of the United States and former Soviet Union during the Cold War years when both the countries stayed broadly within the perimeter of deterrence. With the shaping of nuclear doctrines of Pakistan and India in place, it was hoped a peace constituency could hopefully take firm hold in South Asia in making sure the proactive peace process currently underway between India and Pakistan was irreversible.

Six elements are critical to sustain this process of dialogue.[42] One, preservation of agreements and CBMs (military and non-military) instituted so far between India and Pakistan. Two, promoting resolution of disputes so that peace-process gains momentum into a conflict resolution mode. Three, a problem-solving proactive approach be applied by both sides. Four, principle of reciprocity and goodwill to guide the dialogue process. Five, political contacts sufficiently at high level to the highest level are needed to discuss issues critically and keep the engagement process moving. Six, there is a need to evolve a convergent vision for a future of peace and cooperation in the entire South Asian region. What is more important in this regard is the perception of risk which appear to be only limited regional perceptions of the shared bilateral risks of nuclear war and avoidance of possible catastrophe.[43] In short to intermediate term, viable solution(s) has to be evolved for solving the various, bilateral intractable issues so as to have saleability and acceptability by all stakeholders. There is also a compelling need to recalibrate other national strategic priorities – national defence, Kashmir, convert 'trust deficit' into 'trust surplus' etc.[44] The issue is complicated further by the profound asymmetry between Pakistan's obsession with India in its security thinking and India's focus on a range of security imperatives of which Pakistan is but one.

## References

1. O'Neil, Barry, "Risk Aversion in International Relations Theory", International Studies Quarterly, Vol. 45, No. 4, March 2001, p. 617-640.
2. Snyder, Glenn, Deterrence and Defence, Princeton, Princeton University Press, 1961.
3. Howard, Michael, "Reassurance and Deterrence: Western Doctrine in the 1980s", Foreign Affairs, Vol. 61, No. 1, 1982/83, p. 315; also, see Rajain, Arpit, Nuclear Deterrence in Southern Asia, London: Sage Publishers, 2005, p. 63.
4. Dulles, John Foster, "Challenge and Response in US Policy", Foreign Affairs, Vol. 36, No. 1, 1968, pp. 62-64; also see McNamara, Robert S., The Essence of Security: Reflections in Office, London: Hodder and Stoughton, 1968, p. 52.
5. Kapila, Subhash, "India and Pakistan Nuclear Doctrine: A Comparative Analysis", Article No. 260, New Delhi: Institute of Peace and Conflict Studies, September 15, 1999; also available at http://www.ipcs.org/newKashmirLevel2.jsp?action=showView&k Value=573&subCatID=null&mod=null; see also, "Limited War Under the Nuclear Shadow in South Asia", Article No. 1623, New Delhi: Institute of Peace and Conflict Studies, 29 January,

2005, available at http://www.ipcs.org/Nuclear_articles2.jsp?action=showView&kValue=1636 & issue=1015 & status=article &mod=a; also see Tellis, Ashley J., Stability in South Asia, Santa Monica, CA: Rand Corporation, 1997, p. 77.

6. Refer Bhutto's statement in the National Assembly of Pakistan, see The National Assembly of Pakistan Debates, 3 (1-13), May 30, 1974, third session of 1974, pp. 304-5.

7. Bhutto, Z.A. Myth of Realities, Karachi: Oxford University Press, 1969, p.153.

   Cited in Cheema, Pervez Iqbal "Nuclear Development in Pakistan: Future Directions", in P.R. Chari et al Nuclear Non-Proliferation in India and Pakistan, Manohar, Delhi, 1996, p.105; also see Smruti S. Pattnaik, "Pakistan's Nuclear Strategy", *Strategic Analysis,* New Delhi, January-March 2003, Vol. 27, No. 1, pp. 94-114; see, Ganguly, Sumit (2011), 'The Road from Pokhran II,' in Bhumitra Chakma (ed) The Politics of Nuclear Weapons in South Asia (Surrey: Ashgate), pp. 29-37.

8. See www.stratfor.com, December 7, 2000; also see "Pakistan sets up N-arms Command", *The Times of India,* New Delhi, November 28, 2000; also, "Musharraf to head Pak Nuclear Command", *The Statesman,* Kolkata, February 4, 2000.

9. Pugwash Meeting No.279, Kanti Bajpai, "No First Use of Nuclear Weapons", available at www.pugwash.org/reports/nw/bajpai.htm, Bajpai, Kanti (2009), 'To war or not to war: The India-Pakistan crisis of 2001-2,' in Sumit Ganguly and S. Paul Kapur (eds.), Nuclear Proliferation in South Asia: Crisis behaviour and the bomb (London: Routledge), pp. 162-182.

10. "India's Nuclear Command to be in place", *The Times of India,* New Delhi, India, May 23, 2002

11. "Pakistan's Nuclear Gamble: A Deadly Ploy", Institute of Peace and Conflict Studies, January 17, 2003, New Delhi, available at www.ipcs.org

12. Lieutenant General Sardar Lodhi, F.S. (Retd. Pakistan Army), "Pakistan's Nuclear Doctrine", Pakistan Defense Journal, 1999; See also Brigadier Ismat, Saeed (Retd. Pakistan Army), "Strategy for Total Defense: A Conceptual Nuclear Doctrine", *Pakistan Defense Journal,* March 2000; also see Zafar Iqbal Cheema; "Pakistan's Nuclear Use Doctrine and Command and Control" in

Peter R. Lavoy, Scott D. Sagan, and James J. Wirtz, Planning the Unthinkable: How New Powers Will Use Nuclear, Biological, And Chemical Weapons, London: Cornell University Press, 2000.

13. General Jehangir Karamat, "South Asian Stability- A Pakistan Perspective", Pugwash Meeting No.277, Pugwash Group on South Asian Security, Geneva, Switzerland, November 1-3, 2002.
14. Cheema, Zafar Iqbal, "Pakistan's Nuclear Use Doctrine and Command and Control", in Peter R. Lavoy, Scot D. Sagan and James J.Wirtz (eds), Planning the Unthinkable: How New Powers will Use Nuclear, Biological, Chemical Weapons. London: Cornell University Press, 2000.
15. Jaspal, Zafar Nawaz, "Reassessing Pakistan's Nuclear Strategy", available at http://www.defencejornal.com/2001/july/reaass-ening.htm
16. Cohen, Stephen P., The Pakistan Army, Karachi: Oxford University Press, 1998, pp.177-79.
17. "Formulating a Rational Strategic Doctrine", 1999, a paper available on the website of the Pakistan institute of Air Defence Studies, http://www.piads.com.pk/users/piads/mazari3html
18. "Deterrence, Defence and Development", 2001, available at http://www.piads.com.pk/users/piads/beg2.html
19. "Doctrinal Doublespeak", Paper presented at Pugwash Meeting no.280, Avoiding an India-Pakistan Nuclear Confrontation, Lahore, Pakistan, March 11-12, 2003, available at: http://www.pugwash.org/reports/rc/sa/march2003/pakistan2003-durrani.htm
20. Siddiqa-Agha, Ayesha, "Nuclear Navies", Bulletin of Atomic Scientists, Vol. 56, No. 5, 2000.
21. Haidar, Ejaz, "Stable Deterrence and Flawed Pakistani Nuclear Strategy', *The Friday Times*, February 2, 2002.
22. Albright, David, "Securing Pakistan's Nuclear Weapons Complex", October 2001, www.isis-online/publications/terrorism/stanleypaper.html. Also, see, Landau Network. http://www.mi.infn.it/~landnet and cotta@mi.infn.it; See, Sumit Ganguly and Kent Biringer; "Nuclear Crisis-Stability in South Asia", in Lowell Dittmer, eds, South Asia's Nuclear Security Dilemma: India, Pakistan, and China, New York, M.E.Sharpe, 2005, p. 32, also see, Rajain Arpit, *ibid*, No. 2, p.90.

23. Ahmad, Firdaus, "Pakistan's Possible Nuclear Game Plan", Institute of Peace and Conflict Studies, New Delhi, Article No.1683, March 28, 2005, available at: www.ipcs.org
24. *Ibid*, No. 24.
25. Lodi, Lt. Gen. (Retd) Sardar F.S., "Pakistan's Nuclear Doctrine", available at http://www.defencejournal.com/apr99/pak-nuclear-doctrine.htm
26. *Ibid*, No. 26.
27. Quoted by M.V.Ramana and C.Rammanohar Reddy(ed.), Prisoners of the Nuclear Dream, London, Orient Longman, 2003, p.21.
28. David Albright, *Ibid.*15
29. Alagappa, Muthiah, "Investigating and Explaining Change", in Muthiah Alagappa (ed.), Coercion and Governance: The Declining Political Role of the Military in Asia, Stanford: Stanford University Press, 2001, p.51.
30. Mazzetti, Mark, "One Bullet Away from What",? *The New York Times,* March 11, 2007.
31. Freedberg, Sydney J., "After Musharraf", *National Journal,* December 16, 2006, Vol. 38, Issue 50-52, p. 38.
32. www.sify.net, May 25, 2002, also see *New Scientist,* England, May 24, 2002.
33. "The Day After in India,Pak:12 million dead", *Indian Express,* New Delhi, India, May 28, 2002.
34. See, www.rediff.com, October 5, 2001; also see *The Times of India,* New Delhi, November 10, 2003 also see *The Times of India,* New Delhi, April 13, 2007.
35. Farah Zahra, "Pakistan's Road to a Minimum Nuclear Deterrent", *Arms Control Today,* Washington, DC, July/August 1999; also available at http://www.armscontrol.org/act/1999_07-08/fzja99.asp?print
36. For more details on Ten Commandments, see Michael Kreppon, 'The Stability-Instability Paradox, Misperception, And Escalation Control In South Asia,' The Henry L. Stimson Center, May 2003, p. 8.
37. Hassan Askari Rizvi and Rajesh M. Basrur, Nuclear Terrorism And South Asia, Occasional Paper No. 25, Albuquerque, NM: Sandia National Laboratories, February 2003, p. 79.

38. See *Indian Express,* New Delhi, December 19, 2003; also see *The Hindu,* Chennai, December 19, 2003.
39. See www.rediff.com, April 6, 2007.
40. Statement by Ambassador Akram, Munir; Pakistan in the Conference on Disarmament, August 19, 1999, available at http://www3.itu.int/pakistan/CD-Indian%20Nuclear%20Doctrine-19%20August%2099.htm
41. See Maleeha Lodhi, "Nuclear Cloud over South Asia", *The Times of India,* New Delhi, May 1, 2006.
42. See Shaun Gregory, "A Formidable Challenge: Nuclear Command and Control in South Asia", Disarmament Diplomacy, The Acronym Institute, Issue No. 54, February 2001.
43. See Shaukat Aziz's statement, "Result-oriented Talks must", The Tribune, April 4 , 2007, www.tribuneindia.com

# 2

# Pakistan's Nuclear Doctrine and Strategy

*Manpreet Sethi*

Chagai hills in Pakistan reverberated with the sound of six nuclear explosions on 28 and 30 May, 1998 after India had conducted its own tests at Pokhran on 11 and 13 May the same year. However, it is widely believed that Pakistan had acquired a nuclear weapon capability in 1984 itself when AQ Khan claimed that Khan Research Laboratories (KRL)[1] was "in a position to detonate... a nuclear device on a week's notice."[2] By 1986, the US National Intelligence Estimate had concluded that Pakistan was only "two screwdriver turns" away from a nuclear weapon,[3] and the same was proudly acknowledged by Pakistan in 1987.[4]

India is the *raison d'etre* of Pakistan's nuclear weapons. Its nuclear doctrine and strategy is wholly and solely India centric, designed to address perceived conventional and nuclear threats from India. Consequently, the nature of the Pakistani nuclear deterrent (including delivery mechanisms), as also its rules of employment and deployment, are all tailored to meet this one requirement.

This article examines Pakistan's nuclear doctrine and strategy. Divided into four main sections, it first outlines the role that the country envisages for its nuclear weapons. The second section identifies the main attributes of the nuclear doctrine as can be extrapolated from statements of military and civilian elite. The third segment outlines some of the current developments in its nuclear capability and examines the rationale for them given the role of Pak nuclear weapons and its doctrine. The chapter concludes with some suggestions on how India should respond to these developments.

## Role of Pakistan's Nuclear Weapons

Pakistan considers its nuclear weapons as its most precious strategic asset. The country's leadership is extremely conscious of their value as the ultimate guarantor of the nation's existence as a sovereign entity. This was avidly brought out in one of the writings of Gen. Mirza Aslam Beg, former Chief of Army Staff. In an article entitled 'Pakistan's Nuclear Imperatives', he wrote, "Some safety against extinction is the inalienable right of an individual or a nation. Oxygen is basic to life, and one does not debate its desirability, nuclear deterrence has assumed that life-saving property for Pakistan."[5]

Its nuclear weapons are used for six specific tasks by Pakistan. These are enumerated in the following paragraphs.

## Strategic Equaliser of Power Asymmetry

Since independence, Pakistan has looked for ways to equalise the power asymmetry with India either through alliance building with USA, China and other Muslim countries, or through acquisition of modern conventional weaponry. However, it was in the acquisition of nuclear weapons that Pakistan discovered the best and most effective equaliser. It was with this clear objective that Zulfikar Ali Bhutto as prime minister of the country embarked on the nuclear weapons programme in January 1972, within three weeks of its defeat in the 1971 war. He was clear that Pakistan's development of nuclear weapons would serve to effectively and more holistically counter-balance India's pre-eminence in the sub-continent, and demonstrate national technological capabilities.

In yet another use of its nuclear weapon for bridging the gap with India, Pakistan has intelligently manipulated the US for conventional arms and economic assistance. For instance, after India's peaceful nuclear explosion in 1974, Bhutto warned the US that if his country was unable to get "sufficient conventional weapons" to bridge the disparity, Pakistan "would forego spending on conventional weapons and make a big jump forward for concentrating all its energy on acquiring the nuclear capability."[6] Pakistani leaders have always tried to justify nuclear weapons as the only means available to "preserve a broad strategic equilibrium with India, to neutralise Indian nuclear threats or blackmail, and to counter India's large conventional forces".[7] And, the US was easily convinced since it anyway perceived India as part of the Soviet constellation in the Cold War, while Pakistan was their ally against the Communist bloc.

## Deterrent against Conventional War

Islamabad believes that notwithstanding its conventional inferiority, the nuclear weapon provides it an "infrangible guarantee of its independence and physical integrity"[8] even as it pursues provocative and offensive revisionist policies. Keen to avoid a full-scale conventional conflict with India, but desirous of altering the status of Kashmir, Pakistan reckons this possible through nuclear weapons. Without them in its quiver, it is certain that Pakistan's proxy war would have breached the limits of India's tolerance and led to a conventional offensive. This eventuality, Pakistan perceives, is blocked by its nuclear weapons. As explained by Benazir Bhutto in an interview in 2004, nuclear weapons ensured that "India could not launch a conventional war, knowing that if it did, it would turn nuclear, and that hundreds of millions would die... suicide not just for one, but for both nations."[9]

Evidently then, Pakistani leaders, even civilian, have believed that the danger of nuclear escalation insulates Pakistan from Indian conventional attack, allowing Pakistan not only to ensure its own security, but to also pursue blatantly an aggressive strategy in Kashmir. For the Pakistani security establishment, nuclear weapons provide a shield to deter conventional aggression, even as it pursues covert aggression through sub-conventional means.

This linkage became starkly evident when there was a significant spurt in insurgency and terrorism in J & K from 1988 onwards, soon after the acquisition of nuclear weapons capability by Pakistan. The trend continued through the 1990s and was interspersed by statements by AQ Khan in 1992, and other political and military leaders in 1995-96 threatening India from taking decisive military action against Pakistan.[10] The idea was to allow Islamabad the freedom to manage escalation at a desirable level. According to one analyst, "Islamabad is convinced that the mere threat of approaching the nuclear threshold will prevent India from seizing the strategic initiative and military dominance of events, permitting Pakistan to escalate the crisis at will without the fear of meaningful Indian retribution."[11] It was hardly surprising, therefore, that even amidst fighting in Kargil, Pakistani army leaders insisted, "there is no chance of the Kargil conflict leading to a full-fledged war between the two sides."[12] Pakistani military counsel to the civilian government dismissed chance of a total war because nuclear deterrence afforded it greater impunity and immunity.

## Means for Nation Building and Prestige

Apart from security, Bhutto's push for nuclear weapons was

also motivated by a desire to "divert the nation's attention from the humiliation it had suffered as a result of its defeat in the East..."[13] and his yearning for Pakistan "to walk tall".[14] Indeed, over the years, the country's nuclear achievements have proved to be an effective rallying point for national pride. Not surprisingly therefore, Kahuta that houses the uranium enrichment plant has been described as the 'symbol of our national defiance' and the mastery of the enrichment technology as the "symbol of national pride, scientific and technical modernity and independence from foreign powers."[15] This has been explained thus by Brahma Chellaney:[16]

> *"The rapid technological advances by Pakistan in recent years are a symbol of nationalistic pride in a country which has overcome major political, technical, and industrial challenges to mount a program with a team of dedicated scientists. Pakistan is showing the world—as China did in the sixties—how a country with limited technical resources and a narrow industrial base can acquire nuclear weapons and ballistic missile capabilities by riding a wave of nationalism".*

## Instrument to Legitimise Military Power

Ironically enough, Zulfikar Ali Bhutto originally intended Pakistan's nuclear programme to serve as a civilian counterweight to the military. The programme was launched by his civilian government and the military evinced little interest in the same. But, it was during Zia ul Haq's tenure as President, that the programme came under military control and direction. And there it has remained ever since. In fact, the Pakistani Army, keeping even the Air Force and Navy out,[17] has effectively honed it as a 'trump card'[18] against the civilian politicians and not allowed their influence in nuclear decision-making. Benazir Bhutto had openly admitted her limited participation in the country's nuclear decisions, including that she was allowed to be Prime Minister under the tacit agreement that she would not interfere with the military's control of the nuclear programme. Meanwhile, by constantly retaining the domestic focus on rivalry with India, Pak Army has conditioned the nation's public to believe that there is a constant threat from India, which can only be effectively addressed by allowing the military a free hand with the country's economy, polity and nuclear policy.

### Tool for Gaining Leadership of the Islamic World

Besides using it as a rallying point for national pride, Pakistan has also used the idea of 'Islamic Bomb' to acquire support for and leadership of the Islamic countries. By portraying its nuclear weapons capability as belonging to the larger Muslim community, especially in the earlier decades of its nuclear programme, Pakistan was able to garner material and moral support from other Muslim countries such as Saudi Arabia, Libya and Iran. President Zia said in 1978 that Pakistan's possession of the nuclear weapon "would reinforce the power of the Muslim world".[19] Twenty years later, after the nuclear tests in Chagai, PM Sharif said, "Not only the whole nation, but the whole Islamic ummah hailed Pakistan for its great achievement and expressed happiness over the decision."

### Nuclear Deterrence

Traditionally, nuclear weapons have been used to establish nuclear deterrence to safeguard a nation from nuclear coercion or blackmail from the nuclear weapons of the adversary. But for Pakistan, deterrence of Indian nuclear weapons is the least important, or the most prosaic, of the number of tasks they perform. The nuclear weapons, instead, are seen as more relevant to checkmate India's conventional capability so that Pakistan can pursue its policy of 'bleeding India through a thousand cuts' without fear of reprisal from a superior conventional military.

## Pakistan's Nuclear Doctrine

The Pakistani nuclear doctrine is not available as a written document. Whether as a matter of deliberate policy, or purely by default, but probably because of a bit of both, Pakistan's nuclear doctrine is shrouded in ambiguity. As a former Pakistani Foreign Minister, Agha Shahi wrote in 2000:

> "*...a policy of ambiguity would appear to be best for Pakistan's security. Spelling out its nuclear doctrine would detract from the imperative of uncertainty about when a nuclear strike as a last resort would... reinforce maximally credible nuclear deterrence by raising the threshold of Indian calculation of unacceptable risk.*"[21]

Despite the lack of transparency, however, it is possible to identify some attributes of the Pakistani nuclear doctrine from statements of civilian and military leaders and from the writings on the subject by Pakistani strategic community.

## Minimum Nuclear Deterrence

One year after the conduct of its tests, in May 1999, PM Nawaz Sharif, in a lecture to the officers of Pakistan's National Defence College described minimum nuclear deterrence as "one of the principles guiding Pakistan's nuclear policy".[22] However, Islamabad has maintained that the 'minimum' cannot be defined and is in fact a dynamic concept based on calculations of the number of nuclear weapons estimated with the adversary, the manner of their deployment, and other technological imperatives such as missile defence.

Pakistan's calculation of minimum is closely linked to its perception of India's nuclear numbers, and its ability to inflict unacceptable damage on India. The problem, however, arises in defining what would constitute unacceptable damage for a geographically bigger, and an institutionally and economically stronger India. Gen. Mahmud Durrani sought to resolve this problem by suggesting, "overkill would by necessity be built into the response."[23] Over the last decade, Pakistan is known to have steadily increased its nuclear arsenal and most current Western estimates place it at between 95-110 warheads.[24]

## Nuclear First Use

Pakistan's main concern has always been to offset India's superior conventional military and its own lack of strategic depth that constraints its ability to pursue a defensive strategy. The nuclear doctrine is aimed at addressing these limitations and hence, it is not at all illogical that Islamabad retains the option of first use of nuclear weapons. Fearful of the possibility of finding itself at the receiving end in a conventional conflict,[25] Pakistan projects its nuclear arsenal as a weapon of last resort. As argued by Air Cmde. (retd.) Tariq Mahmud Ashraf:

> *"Being on a weaker military footing... Pakistan's nuclear employment doctrine should assert that since she would be fighting for her very survival as an independent nation state in any future war,... Pakistan... must reserve the right of first use of nuclear weapons and this assertion should be made as part of her nuclear employment doctrine."*[26]

Viewing 'first use' as an "option enhancing policy,"[27] Pakistan dismisses India's offers for a mutual no first use agreement. As explained by Lt. Gen. (retd.) Sardar Lodi,

> *"India's offer of a treaty to be signed by the two countries, agreeing not to be the first to use nuclear weapons against*

*each other is one-sided and would benefit India only, as it has a superior conventional force. It may be more apt for both countries to sign a mutual test ban treaty to start with, followed by a no-war pact."*[28]

This posture of a low nuclear threshold stems from a national compulsion because Pakistan's offensive strategy at the sub-conventional level keeps it in a state of perpetual conflict.[29] This is meant to reinforce its deterrence since nuclear weapons become an effective shield even against conventional attack. It seeks to deter India with the thought that Pakistan would not hesitate to use nuclear weapons if pushed against the wall.

But, how far back would be too far back has obviously not been clearly identified. In 1999, an op-ed by three prominent Pakistani leaders stated that Pakistan would resort to nuclear strike only in the event of comprehensive military defeat, threat to large population centers, or lines of communication.[30] Subsequently in 2002, Gen. Khalid Kidwai, head of Strategic Plans Division (SPD) that manages Pakistan's nuclear assets and operations, spelt out four distinct thresholds for nuclear use: loss of large parts of territory (space threshold); destruction of large part of land or air forces (military threshold); economic strangulation (economic threshold); and political destabilisation or large scale internal subversion (domestic destabilisation threshold). Since then, however, Pakistan has been quieter on its red lines. In fact, Gen. Asad Durrani even said in 2003, Pakistan should not "identify those core interests that, if threatened, could trigger a nuclear retort... These are elements of operational planning and stating them could betray a country's conventional limits."[31] By vaguely articulating a range of thresholds likely to trigger nuclear first use, Pakistan has sought to strengthen its strategy of continuing sub-conventional conflict while checkmating India's superior conventional capability.

## Offensive Defence

Given the above, it is natural that Pakistan's nuclear doctrine should be no different from its overall military doctrine of offensive defence. The nuclear weapon is projected both as an offensive instrument that holds out the threat of nuclear strike right at the beginning of every crisis, irrespective of its nature and scale, and at the same time also a defensive weapon against India's punitive action. This is meant to give Pakistan an opportunity to conduct a swift, sub-conventional assault, mostly in Kashmir, and then use the nuclear shield to prevent/mellow/checkmate an Indian response.

Pakistan seeks to derive deterrence by propagating the nuclear weapon for 'total defence', to deter both nuclear and conventional attack, and against counter force and counter value targets. Lt. Gen. (Retd.) Kamal Matinuddin had written in 2002 "(Indian) population centers, industrial assets, resources, and nuclear or conventional forces of the enemy can all be targeted... While giving primacy to counter value targets, the enemy's concentration of armoured formations in the rear should also be considered as targets for a nuclear strike."[32]

## Recent Developments in Pakistan's Nuclear Capability

To checkmate a possible conventional attack from a superior Indian force, Pakistan's nuclear deterrence needs to be sufficiently credible. Its capability, force posture and force structure must convey the message that it is capable of using the nuclear weapon first and yet somehow denying the choice of retaliation to India. Seen from this perspective, one can see some method in the trajectory being followed by Pakistan's nuclear capability development.

## Tendency to Increase Warhead Numbers

Despite professing minimum nuclear deterrence, Pakistan is cautious not to build too small a nuclear force since "small forces would presumably be easier to destroy in a first strike and, therefore, have less credibility as a deterrent because the surviving forces may not be able to retaliate."[33] In fact, though immediately after the tests, Pakistan was satisfied with existential deterrence based on uncertainty, it now believes that development of a second strike capability is critical for credible deterrence.

This desire could expectedly grow as India acquires and deploys some form of a limited ballistic missile defence (BMD). Pakistan strongly believes that an Indian BMD, coupled with Pakistan's lack of strategic depth, would destabilise its deterrence. Islamabad fears that such a capability would "provide an elated sense of security and prompt pre-emptive impulses from India."[34]

Pakistan's response to this is likely to be to go in for its own BMD systems as well as building up its offensive forces to overwhelm Indian defences. It is not a stray coincidence that the rate of nuclear and missile activity in Pakistan has risen manifold over the last few years. Former President Musharraf admitted as much in July 2005 when he said the country's nuclear programme is progressing "ten times faster than before".[35] The pace has certainly not lessened since then. In fact, Pakistan today has the dubious distinction of having the world's fastest growing nuclear stockpile. This is evident in the estimates available in the public domain on the numbers of warheads, nuclear facilities, and fissile material stockpile.

**Table 2.1 – Number of Warheads**

| *Year* | *No. of wares* | *Source* |
|---|---|---|
| *2007* | *60-80* | *International Panel on Fissile Material, 2007 (IPFM)* |
| *2009* | *70-90* | *Federation of American Scientists (FAS)* |
| *2011* | *90-110* | *Nuclear Notebook, Bulletin of Atomic Scientists (BAS)* |
| *2020* | *150-200 (estimated)* | *Same as above* |

**Table 2.2 – Plutonium (Pu) Production**

| ***Nuclear Facility** (Pu Production)* | ***Status*** | ***Capacity*** | ***Production of fissile material*** | ***Source*** |
|---|---|---|---|---|
| Khushab I | Operationl | 40-50 MW | 6-12 kg per year | BAS |
| Khushab II | Believed to be operation | 40-50 MW | 6-12 kg per year | BAS |

| Khushab III & IV | Under construction | 40-50 MW | Likely same as above | IPFM, 2011 |
|---|---|---|---|---|
| Reprocessing | One Operational + one under construction | | | |

**Table 2.3 — Fissile Material Stockpiles**

| *Year* | *Type of FM* | *Estimated Stockpile* | *Source* |
|---|---|---|---|
| 1999 | WGPu | 2-13 kg | ISIS (institute for Science & International Security) |
| 2006 | WGPu | 90 kg | IPFM, 2010 |
| 2010 | WGPu | 100 kg | IPFM, 2010 |
| 1999 | HEU | 585-800 kg | ISIS |
| 2011 | HEU | 2600 kg | FAS |

## Diversified Weapons based on Highly Enriched Uranium and Plutonium Designs

Initially, Pakistan opted for the plutonium (Pu) route to nuclear weapons. With the natural uranium-heavy water moderated reactor, Karachi Nuclear Power Plant (KANUPP) becoming critical in 1971, Pakistan believed that by acquiring a reprocessing plant, it could access plutonium. This, however, proved to be infructuous. Not only did KANUPP prove to be inefficient and under IAEA safeguards, but Pakistan's contract with France for the reprocessing plant was jettisoned by US non-proliferation concerns and stood cancelled in June 1978. Meanwhile, as a hedging strategy, Pakistan had already begun active pursuit of the uranium enrichment technology with a formal launch of a project the same year. In this it met with far greater success since AQ Khan surfaced at just the right time with the stolen designs of centrifuges to procure enriched uranium,[36] and today Pakistan's nuclear weapons are primarily based on HEU. The main enrichment facility exists at the KRL at Kahuta and is being supplemented with a new enrichment facility near Wah (Gadwal uranium enrichment plant). Meanwhile, smaller pilot scale enrichment facilities exist at Chaklala, Sihala and Golra.

Pakistani nuclear tests in 1998 were of low yield, HEU fission weapons of varying designs, yields and sizes. Pakistani officials themselves have provided different yields of the five devices tested on the first day with some suggesting it to be of 25 and 12 kt, besides three sub kiloton devices, and AQ Khan claiming that one of the devices was a boosted fission device of 30-35 kt and the other four being tactical weapons.[37] The sixth device tested on 30 May, 1998 is believed to have been a plutonium weapon, though there is no consensus on this.[38] In any case, in recent times, it is evident that Pakistan has devoted greater attention to plutonium weapons since these would be lighter, more compact and more easily deliverable.

## Tactical Nuclear Weapons (TNW)

Development and deployment of atomic artillery weapons has been denied by Gen. Kidwai,[39] but some others like Brig. Saeed Ismat have written in favour of tactical nuclear weapons.

> *"Our aim should be the destruction of the invading military forces only and not his civilian population. We should aim to strike with tactical nuclear weapons at the base of enemy offensive... Some standard artillery guns, rockets, and missiles can deliver these, so can helicopters and aircraft. Such low yield, high radiation nuclear*

> *weapons can quickly and decisively alter the entire course of battle. Though tactical in characteristics these can produce strategic effect.*"[40]

According to this viewpoint, given Pakistan's lack of geographical depth and inferior military resources, TNW are the only possible tools for tilting the balance in favour of Pakistan by threatening enemy intruders with a planned employment of these weapons. Also given that Pakistan projects its nuclear weapons as militarily usable, this 'conventionalisation' of its nuclear weapon appears natural.

It is in this context that Pakistan has been testing very short range ballistic missiles. In April 2011, the Hatf IX or Nasr, a nuclear capable missile, with a range of no more than 60 kms was first test fired. More such tests have been conducted in the year since then. The press release on this event explained the development of the Nasr as a measure "to add deterrence value to Pakistan's strategic weapons development programme at shorter ranges." It also cryptically described the missile as being able to carry "nuclear warheads of appropriate yield with high accuracy, and shoot and scoot attributes."

Obviously, such a system could only be a battlefield weapon and many strategic analysts, within Pakistan as also in the US, have described it as a measure to specifically counter the Indian Cold Start strategy. The Pakistani official statement itself clarifies, "This quick response system addresses the need to deter evolving threats." The premise is that if Indian troops were to make any shallow thrusts into Pakistani territory in case of a terrorist strike, then they could face the possible use of a small nuclear weapon mounted on such a missile. Some of the possible purposes to undertake such an attack could be to shock, create a sense of further danger, signal initiative, determination or even recklessness so as to intimidate India, make it pause and dare it to react with escalation.

Considering the active missile programme of the country, Pakistan's keenness to equip itself with a credible deterrent delivery capability based on a variety of ranges and payload capacities. Pakistan's desire to have very short range as well as medium range missiles in its arsenal is quite evident from the pattern of missile testing that the country has followed over the last five years. In fact, the consistent pursuit of missiles of ever longer ranges may be explained for two reasons: one, to be able to hit deeper into India; and secondly, to base its own missiles in more remote and less accessible mountainous areas in order to enhance survivability and ensure second strike capability. Meanwhile, at the other end of the spectrum, the very short range missiles give it the capability to project a low nuclear threshold and thus deter any attempt by India to undertake even a conventional attack.

## Conclusion

Pakistan has an intelligent and rational nuclear policy best suited to its national security needs. Its nuclear weapons play an important role in enhancing its defensive capability to meet the perceived threat from India and are designed to deter both conventional and nuclear aggression. The first use nuclear doctrine makes a deliberate attempt to demonstrate irrationality and heighten the nuclear danger for two audiences: one, to instill fear in India that it has a low nuclear threshold; and secondly, to attract international intervention on Kashmir.

Six conclusions on Pakistan's nuclear doctrine and strategy are evident:

(*a*) Nuclear weapons occupy a central role in Pakistani national security and will continue to do so;

(*b*) Till such time as Pakistan finds it prudent to abandon its proxy war against India, or give up its revisionist designs, it will retain first use doctrine;

(*c*) Despite large-scale modernisation of conventional forces, Pakistan will seek deterrence against an Indian conventional attack by projecting first use of nuclear weapons.

(*d*) Given the continued focus on nuclear weapons, Pakistani priorities in the next 10-15 years will be to improve survivability, penetrability and improvements in its C-3I capabilities. This will be achieved through creation of hard and deep buried storage and launch facilities, air defence around strategic sites, mobile missile units, concealment and deception, and a strategic triad;

(*e*) Acquisition of missile defence to nullify India's advantage in this field and the simultaneous development of counter measures would be undertaken, with significant Chinese help; and

(*f*) Pakistan will seek to deter India by projecting its readiness to engage in nuclear use of its low yield nuclear weapons against Indian military targets. This would be based on the assumption that such an act may not invoke nuclear retaliation from India because one, the international community would stop India from nuclear retaliation; and secondly, because a 'soft' nation like India would rather settle for war termination than raise the level of escalation to risk more Pakistani attacks on Indian cities.

So, what should be India's response to these Pakistani developments? First of all India has to understand the role that nuclear weapons play in Pakistan's national security. This has been highlighted in the first section of this paper with the clear objective of liberating India from being self-deterred by the Pakistani nuclear doctrine. In fact, the recent developments in Pakistani nuclear arsenal that brook a tilt towards tactical nuclear weapons do not necessitate any changes in the Indian doctrine or nuclear arsenal. India has long maintained that it has no interest in nuclear war fighting —whether with small yield weapons on the battlefield or with large bombs on cities.

The purpose of the Indian nuclear weapon is narrow and limited to safeguarding the country against nuclear coercion, blackmail or its possible use. The path it has chosen to achieve this is through the suggestion of deterrence by punishment. This strategy seeks to deter nuclear use by conveying a certainty of retaliation in response to a first use, irrespective of its yield or choice of target. In that sense, the threshold for Indian nuclear use is very clearly stated as any kind of first use "on Indian territory or on Indian forces anywhere." The response from India has been described in the Cabinet Committee on Security's Review of Operationalisation of India's Nuclear Doctrine as being 'designed to inflict unacceptable damage'. For India, therefore, any use of the nuclear weapon would have strategic implications and would invoke a punitive response. The focus of the Indian nuclear arsenal must hence continue remain on ensuring credibility through survivability of reliable delivery systems of adequate ranges.

In nuclear strategy, it is not essential to respond to every move of the adversary. While the developments certainly need to be monitored, the initiative must be retained by self, while responding to them instead of it becoming an automatic response to follow the trends set in motion by the other side. India is not interested in fighting a nuclear war, whether of the limited and tactical variety or a larger strategic exchange. This is the message that should go out loud and clear.

## References

1. Inaugurated in July 1976, it was then known as Engineering Research Laboratories (ERL) until May 1981 when President Zia ul Haq changed the name to Khan Research Labs in honour of A Q Khan's service to Pakistan's nuclear programme.

2. IISS Strategic Dossier, *Nuclear Black Markets: Pakistan, A Q Khan and the Rise of Proliferation Networks – A Net Assessment,* (London: International Institute for Strategic Studies, May 2, 2007), p. 22.
3. *Ibid,* p.22.
4. Gen Aslam Beg, "Pakistan Nuclear Propriety", *National Security,* FRIENDS, 2000, as cited in Paolo Cotta-Ramusino and Maurizio Martellini, Nuclear Safety, Nuclear Stability and Nuclear Strategy in Pakistan, Landau Network - Centro Volta report, Jan 21, 2002. Gen. Beg, Vice Chief of Army in 1987 and Chief from 1988-91, claims that Pakistan had six nuclear devices by 1989 and 15 delivery systems by 1991.
5. General Mirza Aslam Beg, "Pakistan's Nuclear Imperatives", *National Development and Security,* vol.3, no.10, Nov 1994, pp. 29-41.
6. S. Paul Kapur, "India and Pakistan's Unstable Peace" Why Nuclear South Asia is not like Cold War Europe", *International Security,* Vol. 30, no. 2 (Fall 2005), pp. 127-152.
7. For more on these linkages see JN Dixit, *India-Pakistan in War and Peace* (New Delhi: Books Today, 2002).
8. Yossef Bodansky, "Pakistan's Nuclear Brinkmanship", Freeman Centre for Strategic Studies, Israel. Available at http://www.freeman.org
9. Ihtasham ul Haque, "Peace Linked to Kashmir Solution", *Dawn Weekly Wire Service,* 26 June 1999, as cited in Peter Lavoy, n.7, pp. 248-49.
10. Savita Datt, To Chagi and Beyond: Nuclear Developmetns in Pakistan (New Delhi: IK International Private Ltd, 2003), p. 42.
11. Steve Weissman and Herbert Krosney, *The Islamic Bomb* (New York: Times Books, 1981), pp. 17-18.
12. IISS Strategic Dossier, n.2, p. 20.
13. Brahma Chellaney, "South Asia's Passage to Nuclear Power." *International Security, Vol.* 16, Issue 1, 1991, p. 43.
14. The Army has monopolised the post of Chairman, Joint Chiefs of Staff since the 1998 nuclear tests, abandoning the tradition of all the three services holding the position by rotation.
15. Ashley Tellis, *India's Emerging Nuclear Posture: Between Recessed Deterrence and Ready Arsenal* (Santa Monica: RAND, 2001).

16. Smruti Pattanaik, "*Pakistan's Nuclear Strategy*", *Strategic Analysis,* Vol 27, no.1, Jan-Mar 2003.
17. *Summary of World Broadcast, Part 3* (Asia Pacific), FE/3241, June 1, 1998, p. A 1. Emphasis added.
18. Agha Shahi, "Command and Control of Nuclear Weapons in South Asia", *Strategic Issues,* March 2000, p.56, as cited in Rifaat Hussain, n. 16, p.13.
19. Rajesh Rajagopalan, *Second Strike: Arguments About Nuclear War in South Asia* (New Delhi: Penguin, 2005), p. 51.
20. Maj. Gen. Mahmud Durrani, "Pakistan's Strategic Thinking and Role of Nuclear Weapons," *Cooperative Monitoring Centre Occasional Paper,* SAND 2004, available at http://www. cmc. sandia.gov.
21. Nuclear Notebook, *Bulletin of Atomic Scientists,* 2011.
22. Pakistani strategists point out that India's capture of just 140 kms would wipe out the state because its communication, irrigation, industry and population are all together within that depth. See Syed Rifaat Hussain, "War Against Terrorism: Pakistan's Perspective", *IPRI Journal,* Vol. 4, no.1, 2004.
23. As cited in Rifaat Hussain, n. 7, p.11.
24. Stephen Cohen, The Pakistan Army (London: Oxford University Press, 1998).
25. Sardar Lodi, "Pakistan's Nuclear Doctrine", *Defence Journal,* vol.3, no.4, April 1999.
26. Ajay Behera, "On the Edge of Metamorphosis" in Ajay Behera and Joseph C. Mathew ed. *Pakistan in a Changing Strategic Context* (New Delhi: Knowledge World, 2004), p. 36. Emphasis added.
27. Agha Shahi, Zulfiqar Ali Khan and Abdul Sattar, "Securing Nuclear Peace", *The News* (Islamabad), 5 Oct., 1999.
28. As cited in Varun Sahni, "The Stability-Instability Paradox: A Less than Perfect Explanation" *in* E. Sridharan ed., *Undeeterred? Deterrence Theory and the India-Pak Conflict* (New Delhi: Routledge, 2006).
29. As cited in Rifaat Hussain, n. 7, p. 13.
30. Zafar Nawaz Jaspal, "Reassessing Pakistan's Nuclear Strategy", http://www.defencejournal.com, July 2001.
31. Fear as stated by no less than Director Arms Control and Disarmament Affairs, Strategic Plans Division, Khalid Banuri,

"Missile Defences in South Asia: The Next Challenge", *South Asian Survey*, 2004, p.197.

32. "Pak Strategic Missiles can Penetrate Proposed Indian BMD Shield: Gen. Musharraf", http://www.pakistanidefence.com, 26 July, 2005.
33. For details on A Q Khan's operations see Gordon Corera, Shopping for Bombs: Nuclear Proliferation, Global Insecurity and the Rise and Fall of AQ Khan Network (New Delhi: Foundation Books, 2006), p. 150.
34. IISS Dossier, n.2, p. 33.
35. The American Los Alamos lab had claimed it to be a plutonium device on the basis of environmental sampling. But the report was contested by Lawrence Livermore labs. It may also be recalled that after the North Korean nuclear test in October 2006, which was believed to be a plutonium weapon, President Musharraf had denied any Pakistani role since he claimed Pakistan did not have a plutonium weapon.
36. Paulo Cotta-Ramusino, n.4.
37. Brig. (Retd.) Saeed Ismat, "A Conceptual Nuclear Doctrine", *Defence Journal*, Vol. 3, no. 8, March 2000.

# 3

# The Nuclear Domain : In Irreverance

*Ali Ahmed*

## Introduction

The back-to-back tests, as has been the wont in South Asia since May 1998, of the Agni-V and Shaheen-1 respectively in early summer 2012 have brought out the manner of perception management indulged in by the two states, India and Pakistan, regarding nuclear developments. The hype by the nuclear complex and the nationalist media around the tests demonstrated a blind spot, amounting to a veritable black hole, in the nuclear imaginings of the respective security elites. This paper highlights this deficit in strategic thinking to conclude that, firstly, the nuclear complex needs stringent oversight, and secondly, that a nuclear peace movement needs to be energised expeditiously in order to bring about that oversight.

While the effects of nuclear exchanges have been dwelt on in literature to demonstrate how horrendous will be the outcome, what is missing is engagement with the social and political fallout of such exchange(s). This is the blind spot the paper seeks to dispel. In doing so it demonstrates that the opportunity provided by the distasteful manner the nuclear complex sought to present its questionable wares must prompt appropriate attitudinal corrections towards nuclear weapons. The paper challenges the nuclear doctrine in vogue, maximally of 'massive' punitive retaliation and minimally of imposing 'unacceptable damage' through such retaliation. It concludes that since India will not be able to sustain 'unacceptable damage' and survive as we know it, it must not think of inflicting this on others unless warranted by the nature of the enemy nuclear first use. This implies a move towards a nuclear doctrine ending nuclear exchanges at the lowest levels possible. Arguing towards this, the paper first brings out the current scope of nuclear strategic thinking in India and then dwells on the aspects that seem to have escaped nuclear strategy, specifically, the aftermath of a nuclear exchange. Lastly, it sets about dispelling the blind spot by recommending a change in nuclear doctrine.

## Nuclear doctrine

Nuclear doctrine can be both declaratory and operational. There may or may not be a convergence between the two. The declaratory doctrine may be distinct from operational doctrine, even though in light of the connection between transparency and deterrence, they may be the same. In India's case, the declaratory doctrine is the one in the open domain. There is also presumably an operational doctrine. Whether the two are the same or distinct is a matter of conjecture. However, as this section will seek to demonstrate, the irrationality endemic in the declaratory doctrine suggests that the operational doctrine could possible be different.

India's declaratory nuclear doctrine is that in case of nuclear first use by an adversary in any manner against India and its forces anywhere, India will retaliate with a 'massive' counter to inflict 'unacceptable damage'. Firstly, as to whether it requires a 'massive' strike to inflict 'unacceptable damage' is moot. Secondly, in case of Chinese nuclear first use against India, for India to go 'massive' in retaliation makes little sense. As to how India will mount a 'massive' counter strike has not been explicated since Agni-V will not be in serial production for another half a decade. Also in case India were to inflict 'unacceptable damage' on China, it can be assured of receiving the same right back and with some interest. This implies that going 'massive' against China is irrational. In case Chinese first use has been 'massive' or of first strike proportions, then it is not understood how India can mount a 'massive' counter. India would require breaching the 'minimum' in the popular formulation of its nuclear doctrine — 'credible minimum deterrence' - in case it is to acquire the number necessary to survive a 'massive' Chinese strike and then to counter with an equivalent salvo.

In respect of Pakistan, 'massive' nuclear retaliation against its nuclear first use of higher order proportions makes eminent sense. After all a higher order nuclear attack would certainly have damaged India enough to make India exact an appropriate if not proportionate price. However, in case of nuclear first use by Pakistan restricted to a lower order strike then if India was to go 'massive' in retaliation, Pakistan could be incentivised to retaliate similarly. Given that its nuclear numbers are reportedly in the range of lower three figures, it has the arsenal to inflict unacceptable damage on India.

This brief dismissal of the intent of 'massive' nuclear retaliation is necessary to demonstrate that though India had overtly had the bomb for over three years by the time the doctrine was officially endorsed by the Cabinet Committee on Security, India had not been able to cope doctrinally. The term was an unnecessary introduction, suggestive of the other aims the declaratory doctrine had set out to achieve, such as for instance, political muscle flexing by India in wake of Operation Parakram. That the declaratory doctrine, despite widespread criticism on this score and more, has remained unchanged implies that there is a possible disconnect between declaratory and operational doctrine. It is infeasible that operational doctrine can be coincident with declaratory doctrine that is so bereft of strategic logic.

However, in case the term 'massive' is disregarded, then the retaliation criterion left is 'unacceptable damage'. Is retaliation with a quantum of force to inflict unacceptable damage sensible in all manners of nuclear first use? When nuclear first use by the enemy is of such an order as to result in unacceptable damage to oneself, then it makes eminent sense to consider retaliation that inflicts like damage on the enemy. However, in case the damage caused by the nuclear first use is not of an unacceptable order, such as when it is a single warhead of low kilo-tonnage on a tactical level target, then inflicting unacceptable damage in return would lay India open to receiving a like counter strike. This means escalation is inevitable. The logic behind the doctrinal threat is that deterrence involves promising just such an escalation. It will make first use considerations more fraught, leading to abandonment of the nuclear option. However, where an enemy has the capacity for strike back in equal measure, as does China unquestionably and arguably even Pakistan in light of higher numbers now available to it, then default escalation to unacceptable levels of damage is not sensible as an operational doctrine, howsoever persuasive its deterrence logic may be. Therefore, even the much haloed term, 'unacceptable damage', sanctified as dogma exam in the Draft Nuclear Doctrine, cannot be taken as gospel.

What then is left of retaliation criteria? It emerges that in India's case declaratory doctrine is very likely to be distinct from operational doctrine. Absence of articulation of operational doctrine is only superficially understandable. While nuclear secrecy has its place, nuclear transparency has significance for deterrence. For instance, if India's declaratory doctrine in all its imperfection was indeed its operational doctrine then the fallout would be as follows. The enemy knowing that India would launch a 'massive' counter to any form of first use, would take care to launch a first strike attempt so as to degrade India's retaliatory strike to the extent possible. This would surely be of unacceptable order many times over. In other words, promising a massive counter only serves to make India insecure. After receiving enemy first use of a massive order, India would unlikely be in a position to launch a massive counter, even if it is still able to inflict unacceptable damage. In other words, the enemy may be materially less set back than India in such an exchange. Given this transparency that operational doctrine is not as irrational as declaratory doctrine is necessary. In other words, nuclear secrecy is not always an altogether good thing.

In the consideration so far, the 'massive' criterion has been decisively negated and 'unacceptable damage' stays on. In the latter case it has been seen that inflicting unacceptable damage as counter to first use not of levels of unacceptable damage amounts to escalation and is also escalatory. Therefore, unacceptable damage in retaliation for first use exacting unacceptable damage makes sense and little sense otherwise. This implies that for lower order strikes, lower order retaliation makes more sense. The criterion that emerges then is a 'tit for tat' nuclear response. Tit for tat implies massive to counter massive first use, unacceptable damage in return for unacceptable damage and lower order retaliation for lower order first use. This may be how operational doctrine, that needs to be notably rational, is configured.

The advantages are several. Assured retaliation is in place in that there would be no question of self-deterrence since the retaliation would be equivalent, militarily feasible, politically justifiable and diplomatically sustainable. It will enable a negotiated end to both the exchange and to the conflict, the latter under the shock effect of multiple nuclear blasts. It negates escalation, enabling termination at the lowest level of nuclear use possible. It limits both the exchange and damage received, since inflicting equivalent damage in return would not incentivise a counter strike. A seemingly disproportionate counter will likely see a continuing exchange and higher cumulative damage at the end of it all. It is the closest equivalent in tacit bargaining which incentivises limitation while conveying an implacable intent to match the enemy 'tooth for tooth, eye for eye'. The latter assures deterrence. Given these advantages, it is well nigh possible that a 'tit for tat' nuclear doctrine may well be the operational doctrine.

The 'tit for tat' strategy makes sense for reacting to nuclear first use and to the initial exchange(s). Beyond a point, there may be a need to limit damage to oneself by indeed going 'massive' to take out the enemy's ability to continue exchanges. The understanding is that the nuclear blast in its effects can have the fallout of awakening the strategic leadership to the consequence of its use that exercises and war games simply cannot replicate. Therefore there is hope for ending an exchange at the lowest level, but in case that proves to be false in the context of unfolding reality, then 'tit for tat' can be abandoned. This brings out the criterion of circumstance dependent strategic choice.

The argument against such calculation— 'tit for tat' strategic choice— presumes that nuclear war can be kept limited. A critique would have it that this may be a false notion, given escalatory tendencies in nuclear use. In this logic, escalation being inevitable, it is better to shoot off what one has prior to the enemy resorting to this, while one still has the capability to do so. The 'in case I don't he will and since he will, I must...' logic will lead to higher order strikes sooner than later. In other words, nuclear war can only be Total War and reaching this speedily at that. Such thinking possibly is behind the terms 'massive' and 'unacceptable damage'. It does have deterrence value in the faet that an enemy contemplating nuclear moves would be compelled to rethink in face of inevitability of receiving such damage. However, an enemy may well be compelled to go first due to military circumstances at the conventional level of the conflict. This conventional nuclear interface requires being brought onboard nuclear strategic thinking. Inadvertent escalation could occur, as also accidental crossing of the threshold; war, after all, being a game of chance, fog and friction. Therefore, recourse to inevitable escalation and suffering the resulting damage makes less sense in case push comes to shove, taking the realm beyond nuclear deterrence to nuclear employment.

Given this seemingly self-evident logic, why does the term 'unacceptable damage' have such credence? That the term is associated with distinguished nuclear experts lends it currency. However, the term was relevant a decade ago, when the state of the arsenal perhaps permitted only such an option. Having few warheads and limited means of delivering them, there were fewer options in terms of operational employment of nuclear weapons in counter strikes. Even then it was not necessary to 'go' with all or majority of them straight off. However, using even a few of them would amount to a greater proportion being used since they were fewer then than now. The term unacceptable damage was euphemism for counter city or counter value strike. The few weapons would be put to good use and not 'wasted' on tactical targets. This makes 'massive' understandable, in that if for instance ten are used of an arsenal comprising 25 weapons, it would be over a third of the weapons being used. That these number would wreak unacceptable damage is a given. However, even then it was possible to use, say, three weapons in reply to a nuclear first use with a single warhead by the enemy. In such a case neither would the strike necessarily be massive nor would it inevitably cause unacceptable damage. It would only be so in case of counter value targeting. Since fewer weapons were available and delivery systems were not as variegated and accurate, they were more likely to be employed in such a manner.

Additionally a buffer existed then at the conventional nuclear interface. India's conventional doctrine was a defensive one of counter offensive in wake of Pakistan's taking to the offensive first in keeping with its military doctrine of offensive defence. In such a case, a nuclear first use threat would only have developed after Pakistan had struck first conventionally and India had replied with a counter offensive using its strike corps. Given the strategic possibility of being torn into two at the midriff in the well known scenario of a dash to the Sukkur barrage at Rahim Yar Khan, the possibility of Pakistan going nuclear was immanent. The situation then was of recessed deterrence with both states only a screw's turn away from deployable warheads. The nuclear threat would only develop well into the conflict, one in which Pakistan was against the ropes.

This situation has changed drastically in light of a changed conventional doctrine in India. India no longer sees itself as a defensive power. Its military doctrine is one of proactive, offensive operations, albeit in keeping with a Limited War concept. India is ready to be off the blocks in case of subconventional provocations, believing that its readiness helps deter such provocations. This means that the threat for Pakistan reaching the nuclear button could develop in quick time, the buffer of India first awaiting and then reacting to Pakistani conventional military moves having long gone. India is intent on making Pakistan react. The nature of the reaction is only partially in Indian hands, in that India can preclude nuclear reaction by ensuring that its military operations keep below the nuclear threshold. However, Pakistan has demonstrated a capability for tactical nuclear employment that is suggestive of early nuclear first use in a low nuclear threshold mode. This means that a nuclear outbreak can be in fairly short order.

Such an outbreak need not necessarily, as earlier, be in a higher order strike in that earlier it was so since, as mentioned, the bombs were fewer and the delivery systems less well developed. Therefore, higher order first use was ruled in, to which India's promise of unacceptable damage in return, made eminent sense. Now that is not the case. Firstly, India is on the offensive. Secondly, Pakistan has the ability for a lower order strike. Thirdly, India has a variegated capability that includes lower order nuclear responses. Therefore, there is no need to persist with the term 'unacceptable damage', leave alone 'massive'. Given the change at the conventional level to the offensive, there needs to be a corresponding change at the nuclear level. Being more offensive at the conventional level, India needs to be more restrained at the nuclear level. This means that India could threaten anything, but does not need to carry out the promise in exact. Some would say that this would impact credibility in that it would negate India's image of promise keeping, making it more prone to and vulnerable against nuclear threats. However, promise keeping has to be weighed against damage avoidance (to be tackled in the next section). By keeping the promise escalation is assured into the unacceptable domain since even if unacceptable damage is caused, and perhaps more because such damage is inflicted, the enemy counter will be to inflict like damage right back. This is now within its capability. In effect, what starts out as a subconventional provocation demanding of conventional punishment ends up as a nuclear conflagration, unacceptable damage on both sides amounting to as much. This is strategic imbecility, a blind spot aggravated by the discussion on possible damage scenarios discussed in the next section.

## Mutual assured destruction?

The problem with nuclear strategic thinking is that it restricts itself to deterrence. However, nuclear strategy is also about employment of nuclear weapons once deterrence of first use has proven to be wanting in the introduction of nuclear weapons into a conflict. In effect, once deterrence is no longer the chief factor, what are the criteria for nuclear weapons employment? For deterrence there is a need to make threats believable through stating it, having the capability, demonstrating a will to follow through to make the threat credible and communication of both the intent and capability to the adversary. Nevertheless in case of break down in deterrence, then contemplating nuclear weapon's employment requires a fresh framework. While deterrence will continue to have a role, such as how to deter escalation, the deterrence logic has it that the threat having been made, follow through is all that needs being done so as to reinforce credibility into the future. This is a blind spot in nuclear strategic thinking that can prove a black hole, as the remainder of this section will attempt to bring out.

In case of enemy nuclear first use of a higher order, there is a stronger case to go proportionately high in retaliation. Higher order nuclear first use would have exacted unacceptable damage. In order to punish the enemy and make him desist, it may be necessary to inflict on it like damage so that it's strategic elite returns to strategic rationality. However, for lower order nuclear first use against India or its forces, going for higher order retaliation will lay India open to a similar counter. This is avoidable escalation in light of the consequences of unacceptable damage. What are the possible consequences?

The material aspect of the damage from the physical effects of nuclear weapons such as their blast, heat, radiation etc. effects has been competently assessed elsewhere. The social, psychological and political consequence has not found reflection in literature. This requires imagining for ensuring the operation of self-deterrence on political decision makers. In case unacceptable damage is taken as euphemism for counter value targeting then receiving such attacks may prove a telling blow on the socio-political fabric of the nation-state, fragile as it is at the best of times. While defence technologists boast of an ability to defend at least two urban concentrations against missile strikes, their credibility is too well known to dwell on in any detail here. Therefore, their words can be taken as instance of information warfare meant for the putative enemy or self-aggrandisement, the likelier explanation, rather than for informing nuclear choices of a political decision maker. The boast in any case brings out the vulnerability of the remainder of the country. The statement is to imply that the command and control assets of the state will be preserved by anti missile defences and therefore the state will be able to survive. While this may be so, it is difficult to imagine that it would be able to cope with the immediate and long term social turmoil that could result.

The precedence of having coped with Partition can be trotted out to establish that India can, and will, survive. On the other hand, precedence of the anti Sikh riots of 1984, the Babri Masjid demolition and Gujarat carnage suggests that the state will not be able to re-establish itself for at least some time. In the interim the social fabric will disintegrate, preventing the state from recreating state and society in its pre-nuclear incidence image. All consequences will be compounded by the environmental disaster. The extant social and economic inequality will exacerbate, enabling attempts at take over of the state and society by forces currently located at both extremes of the political spectrum. The well-honed suppressive powers of the state may require exercising and in the process changing India. In effect, while India may re-emerge it would not be as we know it. This means that the assumption that informs nuclear strategy that India can survive while Pakistan will be finished is untenable. India as we know it will be 'finished'. In other words, Pakistan has 'assured destruction' capability, with assured destruction being redefined not in the percentages of Cold War vintage but in terms more suited to India's reality of a subcontinental state in size, diversity and resulting complexity. The possibility of an unraveling of India, not unknown in history, is the foremost political level consideration in nuclear decision making. The decision imperative is therefore how to avoid this.

The nuclear security establishment and the nuclear complex operate on the strategic level and not the political level. They may tender advice that is leavened with political factors, but would retain its strategic level bias. Therefore, it would likely be pitched at the implications for in-conflict deterrence rather than on wider national security. It is therefore the prerogative of the political head to accede to the advice to the extent required or override it in its entirety. While the political head and the civil-military nuclear complex share the goal of security, the principal-agent problem arises when there is divergence between the two. Bridging this gap bottom-up cannot be done by the nuclear complex since that would amount to usurpation of political functions. Instead, civilian political masters need to take on the bridging function. The charge of 'meddling' can be managed under the principle of civilian supremacy. The nuclear complex, as represented by its expert civil-military leadership, has little claim to socio-political expertise, and therefore cannot dictate strategy.

The political level consideration in circumstance of nuclear use is therefore not deterrence focused but based on the socio-political outcomes of nuclear exchange(s). The overriding consideration in such a circumstance for a political decision maker is therefore preservation of a given socio-political order. This imperative must inform the choice made from among retaliation alternatives. The option that best provisions this is the one to alight on, irrespective of the deterrence oriented dictates of nuclear doctrine. Nuclear strategy is therefore not about the threat of damage to the enemy and carriage of it to fulfillment, but of preserving the state and society from such damage.

The criterion for nuclear employment is different from the criterion for nuclear deterrence. While the latter has threat and its delivery at heart, the former is about self-preservation. In a situation in which the enemy has a capability to set back state and society, even if not an assured destruction capability, avoiding nuclear escalation to such levels is the prime consideration. A strategic level argument that can be anticipated could be that this can be done by damage limitation strikes to take out the enemy's retaliatory capability. Such reasoning carries the kernel of first strike. However, the enemy even if recipient of either a first strike or damage limitation strike has the capability of broken backed retaliation that can prove telling for state and society, even if, as mentioned, it is not of assured destruction levels. Pakistan has taken care to proliferate vertically with just such an intention in mind. This must be a message for India to recalibrate its doctrine, or at a minimum arrive at an operational doctrine that concedes Pakistan assured destruction capability, defined as an ability to set India back inordinately.

## Directions in nuclear strategy

The blind spot having been identified, it needs plugging. The first step must be to recognise what's the current direction for what it is. This is not necessarily coincident with what the nuclear complex and nuclear security establishment purports it to be. Their projection is that India's is a deterrent doctrine. It is a 'retaliation only' doctrine. However, the nature of the retaliation, as seen in the previous sections, is not in Indian security interests. It makes India doubly insecure. Firstly, it invites nuclear first strike since the enemy would want to degrade India's nuclear might to the extent possible so that the promised 'massive' retaliation is less than it would otherwise be. Second, in case first strike is not resorted to in first use and instead the enemy settles for a lower order strike, then upping the ante to unacceptable levels is, as brought out in the previous section, suicidal besides being self-admittedly genocidal. Therefore, 'retaliation only' may be good, but is not good enough as doctrine. A doctrine needs to optimally secure India and minimally not make India any more insecure. A reformulation of the doctrine is therefore necessary.

It is important to do so since from a doctrine emerge force structures, command and control and arsenal size and composition etc. From the direction of India's deterrent it is clear that India is going in for 'something of everything'. Arguably this would be acceptable in case the 'minimal' in the formulation 'credible minimum deterrent' is maintained inviolate. Is this the case? India is going in for a nuclear triad. It is also working towards a ballistic missile shield. These are advertised as reinforcing its No First Use pledge in that the enhanced survivability will help with assured retaliation. The numbers to inflict unacceptable damage need to be able to survive. These would be for both adversaries. In addition there is to be a reserve. The intention of having multiple warheads in the Agni. Vs suggests a larger arsenal. The nuclear submarines armed with ballistic missiles too will require to be self-contained. This would make the numbers climb, impinging on 'minimal'. Numbers will tend to stabilise only when assured destruction capability is perceived to have been reached after absorbing a first strike. This in its interaction with two adversaries will be incessantly upward. Besides, depending on how the missile shield shapes up, India, with its additional numbers, could position itself well to even consider abandoning No First Use at will. First strike considerations will not be far away, especially when faced with two foes in the 'two front' scenario, subscribed to earlier by the military and now acceded to even by a government that should know better.

This possibility in a conflict with a nuclear backdrop will enhance the 'Will he, won't he?' apprehension on both sides, building in a tendency to preemption by either. The suggestion in nuclear strategic counsels could well be a change from NFU to the inadvisability of waiting for the enemy to strike. Such a strike if of first strike proportions could deflate India's promise of 'massive' and even 'unacceptable damage'. Therefore, an Indian first strike could well be on its way, with a preventive or pre-emptive rationale. Pakistan's nuclear numbers indicate that it will not spare India irrespective of the damage it receives. Clearly, while Pakistan may 'cease to exist', as is put in some gleeful perspectives, so will India as we know it, as seen in the previous section.

This direction in India's deterrent needs arresting. This is easier said than done. The record of India's nuclear complex and nuclear security establishment has been one of an avid political player. The two are cognizant of institutional interests and are adept at playing the bureaucratic and perception management game. They have taken undue advantage of their 'brahmanical' position and the 'holy cow' status of high science. Politicians have for their part been debilitated by a seeming political necessity of not appearing 'soft' on defence. Therefore, there has been little check and oversight of the direction and pace of nuclear developments. The nuclear peace lobby has always been marginal, and increasingly perhaps sidetracked in combating the advance of nuclear power across the country. Therefore, there has been little challenge to nuclear verities. This has allowed blind spots to be inherited by succeeding generations of strategists. It is time the pied piper be called to attention and the emperor revealed to have no clothes on.

What then needs to be the direction? Firstly, there needs to be an over-watch by a parliamentary committee. Just as war is too serious a business to be left to generals alone, likewise the nuclear complex cannot dictate in what is essentially an issue in the political domain. The manner a state provisions security for itself is a political decision. It is time political India resurrects itself to take command of the strategic heights. The nuclear complex is peopled by technologists, while the nuclear security establishment has strategists. Neither is intellectually equipped, leave alone authorised, to intrude into the political domain. The insights of military sociology on civil-military relations, specifically the control of the military, need to expand beyond the uniformed military to include the military technological sphere.

An instrument of control is doctrine. An expansively phrased doctrine, as India's has been shown up here, is at root of the tendency towards nuclear expansionism. A reworking of the doctrine can limit and thereby help re-establish control over the civilian-military nuclear sphere. This reworking, as noted, must move beyond the deterrence domain to deal employment. This means the criterion of limiting both the risk of and damage received for self-preservation must inform doctrine. The current emphasis is on punishment. The converse as demonstrated makes more sense. Therefore, the formulation should be to end nuclear exchange(s) at the lowest level possible. This has advantages of preserving the 'minimal' under threat in case of autonomy for the nuclear sector from institutional compulsions. The formulation is in keeping with deterrence in that the escalatory threat is held out in case the exchange is not terminated. The shift to self-preservation incentivises the enemy to shift likewise. This does not need to await the outbreak of nuclear exchange. Restricting nuclear use to the lowest level necessarily implies building mechanisms in peace time robust enough to withstand the buffeting of war. This can serve to reconcile doctrines and arsenals in peacetime. Such a mechanism should be self-annihilating: the more used, the less needed.

## Conclusion

The celebrations of technological prowess such as an ability to 'take out' Beijing obscures the insecurity such ability brings with it. Strategists play as much a part in this obfuscation as technologists. While the latter's motivations are sufficiently transparent, centered as they are on institutional interest, those of strategists are less so. These could range from nationalism and its variant, cultural nationalism, to narcissism. This contaminates their output. Therefore, leaving the nuclear strategic space to the nuclear complex and the nuclear security establishment is an abdication of political responsibility by the political leadership. Recouping would involve political examination of the doctrinal sphere afresh. A blueprint for such examination has been laid out here. It now awaits political attention and will.

## References

Ahmed, A. (2008), "The Need for Clarity in India's Nuclear Doctrine", New Delhi: IDSA, http://www.idsa.in/publications/stratcomments AliAhmed111108.htm

Ahmed, A. (2010), "Pakistani Nuclear Use and Implications for India", Strategic Analysis, 34 (4): 531-544.

Ahmed, A. (2010), *Reconciling Doctrines: Prerequisite for Peace in South Asia,* IDSA Monograph Series No. 3, 2010

Ahmed, A. (2011), Reviewing India's Nuclear Doctrine, April 24, 2009, Issue Brief, IDSA.

Badri-Maharaj, S. (2000), The Armageddon factor: Nuclear Weapons in the India-Pakistan Context, New Delhi: Lancer Publishers.

Bajpai, K. (2009), "The BJP and the Bomb", in Sagan, S. (ed.), *Inside Nuclear SouthAsia,* Stanford: Stanford University Press.

Bajpai, K. (2012), "Missiles Missiles every where", *The Times of India,* 28 April 2012.

Basrur, R. (2006), Minimum Deterrence and India's Nuclear Security, Stanford: Stanford University Press.

Basrur, R. (2008), South Asia's Cold War: Nuclear Weapons and Conflict in Comparative Perspective, London: Routledge.

Clark, I. (1982), Limited Nuclear War: Political Theory and War Conventions, Oxford: Martin Robertson

College of Combat (1981), "Effects of Nuclear Asymmetry on Conventional Deterrence", *Combat Paper No. 1,* Mhow: College of Combat.

Hoodbhoy, P. (2012), "Let us become - proudly - bayghairat", *The Express Tribune,* 6 May, 2012.

Joint Statement (1998), "Joint Statement by Department of Atomic Energy and Defence Research and Development Organisation", Press Release, http://www.indianembassy.org/pic/PR_1998/May98/prmay1798.htm

Joshi, M. (2012), "DRDO being needlessly boastful", *India Today,* 20 April, 2012.

Kanwal, G. (2008), Indian Army Vision 2020, New Delhi: Harper Collins.

Kapur, S.P. (2007), Dangerous Deterrent: Nuclear Weapons Proliferation and Conflict in South Asia, Stanford: Stanford University Press

Karnad, B. (2002), Nuclear Weapons and Indian Security: The Realist Foundations of Strategy, New Delhi: MacMillan.

Ladwig, W. (2008), "A Cold Start for Hot Wars? The Indian Army's new Limited War Doctrine", International Security, 32 (3): 158-190.

Lodhi, F.S. (1999), "Pakistan's Nuclear Doctrine", *Defense Journal,* http://www.defencejournal.com/apr99/pak-nuclear-doctrine.htm.

Narang, V. (2009), "Strategic Weapons Behavior in South Asia", in Sagan, S. (ed.), Inside Nuclear South Asia, Stanford: Stanford University Press.

Pandit, R. (2010), "Future War on Two-and-a-Half Fronts?", *The Times of India,* New Delhi, 31, May 2010.

Rajagopalan, R. (2005), Second Strike: Arguments of Nuclear War in South Asia, New Delhi: Penguin.

Sagan, S. (1996-97), "Why do States Build Nuclear Weapons? Three Models in Search of a Bomb", *International Security,* 21 (3): 73-85.

Sagan, S. (2000), "The Origins of Military Doctrines and Command and Control Systems" in Lavoy, P., S. Sagan, and J. Wirtz (eds.), Planning the Unthinkable: How New Powers Will Use Nuclear, Biological and Chemical Weapons, Cornell: Cornell University Press.

Sagan, S.D. (2009), "The Evolution of Pakistani and Indian Nuclear Doctrine" in Sagan, S.D. (ed.), Inside Nuclear South Asia, Stanford: Stanford University Press.

Sethi, M. (2009), Nuclear Strategy: India's March Towards Credible Deterrence, New Delhi: Knowledge World

Singh, J. (2000), "A Nuclear Strategy for India", *Strategic Analysis,* XXIV (9): 1212-1225.

Subrahmanyam, K. (1986) (ed.), India and the Nuclear Challenge, New Delhi: Lancers.

Subrahmanyam, K. (1986), "Nuclear Deterrence" in his (ed.), India and the Nuclear Challenge, New Delhi: Lancers.

Sundarji, K. (1992), "Nuclear Deterrence Doctrine for India", Part 1 and 2, *Trishul,* V (1): n.d. and V (2): 42-60.

*Suo Motu Statement (1998), "Suo Motu* Statement by Prime Minister Shri Atal Bihari Vajpayee In Parliament on 27th May, 1998"; http://www.indianembassy.org/pic/pm-parliament.htm.

Tellis, A. (2001), India's Emerging Nuclear Posture: Between Recessed Deterrent and Ready Arsenal, Santa Monica: RAND.

■■■

# 4

# In the Shadow of Nuclear Weapons: India, Pakistan and Confidence Building Measures

*Mohammed Badrul Alam*

Peace Process in the shape of confidence-building measures (CBMs) are recognisable as "arrangements designed to enhance...assurance of mind and belief in the trust-worthiness of states...confidence is the product of much broader patterns of relations than those which relate to military strategy. In fact the latter have to be woven into a complex texture of economic, cultural, technical and social relationships."[1] This suggests military and non-military initiatives undertaken by antagonistic states to reduce tensions and enhance mutual confidence. This article will examine and evaluate various confidence-building measures, military as well as non-military, that were initiated between India and Pakistan. The article will also address and delineate definition and conceptual notion as well as some of the pertinent aspects of ongoing peace process including Track-II diplomacy and nuclear risk reduction measures being undertaken by India and Pakistan.

CBMs are designed essentially to increase understanding by reducing suspicions. They are separable into military and non-military CBMs and into those having a unilateral, bilateral or international content. Military CBMs are also classifiable into transparency, communications and constraint measures to perform the related functions of information, notification, observation and stabilisation. (2) CBMs can further be catalogued into provisions enabling information exchange, mutual access to observation or arrangements to handle incidents and crises. (UN 1982)

A counsel of perfection suggests their pursuit in all these separate directions. But, negotiating and implementing "CBMs requires political will, but only modest amounts of capital need be expended to begin the process... [CBMs] have met the minimal requirements of not worsening any state's security and not increasing existing levels of hostility."[3]

## Challenges to CBMs in South Asia

Synthesising 'security consensus' in South Asia has proved difficult since four seminal factors lie at the roots of insecurities in the region.[4] They are:

Firstly, the bitter hostilities and tensions distinguishing Indo-Pak relations that have resulted in several conflicts, overt and covert in the past, which casts a pall over the region. These enmities are deeply inter-twined with their domestic politics and have now acquired a serious nuclear dimension.

Secondly, the preponderance of India in the South Asian polity is unique; its Indo-centricity erects a psychological barrier that accentuates the insecurities of its small neighbours since marked differences in politico-military weight between states is hardly conducive to building confidence between them.

Thirdly, the civil society is replete with socio-economic and ethno-political strife manifested by caste, class and sectarian conflicts, communal violence and armed struggles against central authority. Inter- and intra-state insecurities are linked and spill across national borders; they have often been fomented by the regional countries against their neighbours.

Fourthly, the newer security threats and threat perceptions in South Asia "largely arise from non-military causes like cross-border movements of population; ethno-political, socio-economic, and communal-religious politics; terrorism, with its seminal linkages to money- laundering operations, and drugs/arms smuggling; environmental degradation, spawning its related problems of deforestation and desertification; internal migration; chaotic urbanisation, and so on".[5] But regional elites are focused on traditional/military sources of insecurity.

## Nature of CBMs in South Asia

### Military CBMs

Between India and Pakistan, at the military level, several CBMs have been initiated with varying scopes and limitations. Here are some of these military CBMs.

### Communication measures: Military Hotlines

Following the 1971 war between India and Pakistan, a secured communication link, or 'hotline,' between the Pakistani and Indian Directors General of Military Operations (DGMOs) was established. In December 1990, India and Pakistan agreed to re-establish the DGMO hotline and to use it on a weekly basis, if only to exchange routine information. At the February 1999 Lahore Summit, India and Pakistan agreed to review all existing communication links with a view to upgrade and approve the DGMO and other hotlines.

### Hotline between Prime Ministers

The first hotline was installed in 1989 by Prime Ministers Benazir Bhutto and Rajiv Gandhi of Pakistan and India respectively. In November 1990, Indian Prime Minster

Chandra Shekhar and Pakistani Prime Minister Nawaz Sharif re-established the hotline to facilitate direct communication. In May 1997, Indian Prime Minister I.K. Gujral and Pakistan's Prime Minister Nawaz Sharif pledged to reinstate the hotline.

## Declarations on Non-Use of Force, Bilateral Resolution of Differences

The 1966 Tashkent Declaration facilitated by the Soviet Union, formally concluded the 1965 Indo-Pak war. It stipulated that relations between India and Pakistan shall be based on the principle of non-interference in the internal affairs of the other. The 1972 Simla Accord followed the 1971 Indo-Pak war which obliges both countries to renounce the use of force as a means of settling outstanding disputes between the two countries. In addition, both sides agreed to resolve their disputes in bilateral forum only.

## Notification Measures: Military Exercises

An Agreement of Prior Notification of Military Exercises was completed in April 1991. Notification is required for exercises comprising two or more divisions in specified locations. Near the Line of Control, notification is required for any exercises involving division level or above. Troop maneuvers directed toward the international border are proscribed. Exercises at the corps level must be held forty-five kilometers away from the border. At the division level, exercises must be held twenty-five kilometers away from the border. No military activity is permitted within five kilometers of the border.

## Non-intrusion of Air Space

An Agreement on the Prevention of the Violation of the Air Space was signed in April 1991, and entered into force in August 1992. It stipulates that combat fixed-wing aircraft are not to fly within ten kilometers of foreign airspace. Unarmed transport and logistics aircraft are permitted up to 1,000 meters from the border; flights within this range for supply or rescue missions are permitted if advance notice is given.

### Transparency Measures

Pakistan invited US observers to watch major military exercises (Zarb-e-Momin) in 1989 while India in 1990 in order to diffuse tension arising from a major 1990 military and, invited US observers to monitor troop and equipment deployment as an assurance of non-hostile intent.

### Constraint Measures: Non- Attack of Nuclear Facilities

An Agreement on the Non-Attack of Nuclear Facilities was signed by Indian Prime Minister Rajiv Gandhi and Pakistani Prime Minister Benazir Bhutto in December 1988. It was ratified by both countries and implemented in January 1992. The agreement requires an annual exchange of lists detailing the location of all nuclear-related facilities in each country. The measure further pledges both sides not to attack listed facilities.

### Bilateral Accord on Chemical Weapons

A Joint Declaration on the Prohibition of Chemical Weapons was concluded in August 1992. Both countries agreed not to develop, produce, acquire, or use chemical weapons.

### Non-Harassment of Diplomatic Personnel

In November 1990 the Indian and Pakistani Foreign Secretaries worked out a code of conduct to protect diplomatic personnel, guaranteeing them freedom from harassment.

### Additional Highlights of the February 1999 Lahore Summit

Both India and Pakistan agreed to provide each other with advance notification in respect of their ballistic missile flight tests. India and Pakistan also agreed to maintain the respective unilateral moratorium on conducting further nuclear test explosions unless either side, in excess of it national sovereignty decided that extraordinary events had jeopardized its supreme national interests. Furthermore, the Memorandum of Understanding (MoU) sought a review of the existing communication links between Directors General Military Operations (DGMOs) with a view to upgrading and improving these links, and to provide for fail-safe and secure communications.

## Other suggestions on military CBMs:

On October 18, 2001, Pakistan's Ambassador to the UN, Mr. Munir Akram, while addressing the UN General Assembly's debate on international peace and security[6], said that to promote nuclear restraint and prevent the use of nuclear weapons, Pakistan and India could agree to:

1. formalise their respective unilateral nuclear test moratorium, perhaps through a bilateral treaty;
2. not operationally weaponise nuclear capable missile systems;
3. not operationally deploy nuclear-capable ballistic missiles, and to keep them on de-alert;
4. formalize the previous understanding to provide prior and adequate notification of flight tests of missiles;
5. observe a moratorium on the acquisition, deployment or development of anti-ballistic systems;
6. implement further confidence-building and transparency measures to reduce the risk of the use of nuclear weapons by miscalculation or accident; and
7. open discussions on the nuclear security doctrines of the two countries with a view to forestalling an all out nuclear arms race and an agreement on non-use of force, including the non-use of nuclear weapons."

## Non-Military CBMs

As in the case of military CBMs, non-military CBMs are also

germane in diffusing tension between the two adversaries, India and Pakistan.

Non-military CBMs cover areas such as the following:[7]

- Collaboration in science and technology
- Dialogue on art and culture
- Free movement of People and ideas (easing of visa restrictions for the nationals of adversarial countries)
- Exchange of information, views and analyses, i.e., newspapers, books, magazines
- Commerce and trade
- Strengthening democracy
- Goodwill Measures.

Although termed as short term by analysts and observers, both India and Pakistan since their independence in 1947, have embarked on number of peace making steps as goodwill measures.[8] These measures adopted by the two countries exist in the form of:

- Transfer of official assets (1948)
- Prevention of an even larger exodus of refugees (1948)
- Protection of rights of minorities (1950)
- Maintenance of places of worship (1953,1955)
- Resolution of some lingering territories claim (1958,1959, 1960, and 1963)
- Indus Water Treaty (1960)
- Tashkent Agreement (1966)
- Agreement relating to the Rann of Kutch dispute (1968)
- Some provisions in the Simla Agreement (1972)
- Joint Commission agreement signed in March 1983 to cooperate in areas other than military and political matters.

Some of the more contemporary CBMs initiated and undertaken by India and Pakistan in the non-military arena are the following.[9]

1. Various military goodwill measures (1993):
   (*i*) Participation of senior military and civilian officials in various seminars in each other's country (1993),
   (*ii*) Inviting Guest Speakers at each other's national defence colleges,
   (*iii*) Participation and visits of various sports teams particularly Cricket and Hockey (which received a set back when BJP, the ruling government in New Delhi decided to disallow sporting contact but it has now been allowed in 2003),
2. Visits of Parliamentarians;
3. Visits of businessmen;
4. In May 1984 and followed by another meeting of Indo-Pakistan Joint Commission held in July 1989, decisions were made to promote tourism, easing visa difficulties;
5. Opening of the regular bus service between Indian-administered Srinagar and Pakistan-administered Muzaffarabad in April 2005 and between Poonch and Rawalakote in June 2006;
6. Resumption of Amritsar (India)-Lahore (Pakistan) bus service;
7. Khokrapar-Munabao rail link is at an advance state of completion;
8. Family re-union and meetings planned along the Line of Control in Mendhar, Poonch, Suchetgarh, Uri, Tangdhar;
9. Trade and commerce across Jammu-Sialkot line; and
10. Promotion of Pilgrimage centers and Open Visa systems on both sides.

## The Kashmir Issue

Kashmir has been a bone issue of contention between India and Pakistan ever since both countries achieved independence in 1947 from the British colonial rule. While India considers Jammu and Kashmir to be an integral part of its union, Pakistan advocates in favour of self-determination to be given to the people of Kashmir valley for determining their future as well the state's status. Pakistan also considers Indian accession of Kashmir as a legal ploy devoid of any popular support.

On Kashmir, both India and Pakistan have realised an urgent need in developing a structured dialogue.[10] This may include the following in terms of ushering CBMs:

- Formalising structure of dialogue, in terms of mechanisms and issues involved in the dispute
- Formal recognition by the two sides that there is no military solution to the Kashmir dispute
- In determining the wishes of the Kashmir's population, representatives of all different constituents and faiths of J & K need to be effectively involved in the dialogue process
- Encouraging and initiating intra-Kashmir dialogue on both sides of the LoC on the final status of Kashmir
- Involving people of Kashmir ('Kashmiriyat') in the bilateral dialogue process of Kashmir
- Setting a timeframe for structured dialogue on Kashmir
- The resolution of the Kashmir conflict and restoration and development of mutual trust should be treated as interdependent processes
- Kashmir solution must be based on the principle of mutual respect of India and Pakistan have for each other and dignity and justice for the people of Kashmir

- The pursuit of solution around zero-sum game needs to be avoided
- The process of de-escalation of hostilities needs to be initiated and efforts should be made to de-link Kashmir from point-scoring domestic agendas
- The hostile domestic propaganda around Kashmir in both electronic and print media needs to be stopped
- Unofficial dialogue through Track-II should be encouraged by the two governments to assist official-level talks between India and Pakistan
- The heads of governments of both sides should meet twice a year to assess the progress of the dialogue and sort out the deadlocks around various points.

On the more immediate issue of de-escalation along the Line of Control in Kashmir, some of the CBMs suggested along these lines can also be pursued:[11]

- Relocation of heavy weapons which are considered a major cause of tension-escalation across the LoC
- Exercises along the LoC and working boundary may not exceed one division involving 12,500-15,000 troops, and the number of combat vehicles must not exceed 100 combat vehicles and 50 artillery pieces
- Continuous scheduled and unscheduled visits to forward areas by journalists, representatives of various national and international human rights organizations, diplomats, defence and UN military observers.
- Commitment not to violate airspace across the LoC/ Working Boundary
- Military commanders of India and Pakistan should meet and explore the reduction of troops in both Indian and Pakistan administered Kashmir

- On Siachen and Sir Creek: avoid lateral movement of troops on the glacier, total commitment against using artillery fire and no violation of air space in the region.

## Track-II Diplomacy and CBMs

Track-II diplomacy is a process of active interaction between individuals in countries in dispute who in their private capacities exchange innovative ideas and various plausible options with or without the prior knowledge of the authorities and governments of their respective countries. However, these types of interactions and exchanges are not officially authorised or mandated from either of the governments. Government officials at the very least, under Track-II diplomacy, have the benefit of valuable feedback and input that could possibly be expanded in Track-I dialogue with some modifications or alterations.

## Definition and Characteristics

Track - II diplomacy is often defined as a process of unofficial dialogue among non-official representatives of the parties locked in a dispute.[12] Influential persons or opinion makers, who have the ability to influence both the government and the public, undertake the Track-II process. Track-II diplomacy may involve a neutral third party either for observation purposes or for the initial push. This is particularly relevant when there is a backlog of suspicion and animosities along with institutionalised intolerance, hatred and distrust. In such situations the participation of government officials is prone to a wide range of misinterpretations and misperceptions, which policy and decision makers can hardly afford. Thus, influential, non-governmental individuals on both sides, who are seen to be relatively balanced in their approach are brought together to discuss the issues. The basic objective of Track - II is to prevent conflict and to facilitate the process of conflict resolution. Being influential persons most of the members of the Track - II concept have either direct access to their governments or are in a position to effectively influence the public opinion in their respective countries. The governments are informed either directly or by suggestions floated through the media.

A scrutiny of the groups engaged in Track - II diplomacy reveals two dominant characteristics; (a) all members of these groups are often fully cognizant of the need to resolve the disputes as speedily as possible, (b) and all have the ability to make constructive contributions towards the desired resolution of ongoing conflicts in one form or the other. Many of these individuals are already involved in their individual capacities, to improve conflicting regional situations either through their writings (both general and research) or through teaching, seminars, conferences, travel etc.

A Track - II group is often formed in two ways. First, it might be the product of a macro level initiative of an individual or an institution like a university or research institute or a newspaper group etc. Second, it might be formed by the encouragement and efforts of interested outsiders. However, it needs to be clarified that groups formed because of the efforts of outsiders invariably emphasise a scrupulous avoidance of external interference. It is indeed up to the participants to jointly agree to have an outsider as their chairperson who is known for his expertise and knowledge of the area and whose balanced and impartial treatment of the issues has already earned him the respect of many insiders.

## Objectives

The major objectives of the Track - II diplomacy are threefold; (a) to make attempts to resolve ongoing disputes; (b) to discourage and prevent the emergence of new disputes; and (c) to make efforts with a view to bringing the two estranged countries and societies closer by introducing innovative and workable confidence building measures (CBMs). Indeed, it is the most difficult objective to attain, especially if the dispute has lasted for more than a decade.

## Nuclear Risk Reduction Measures

Another of the CBMs that have been discussed in scholarly writings pertain to initiating nuclear risk reduction measures between India and Pakistan after the two countries went for overt nuclearisation in the summer of 1998. Broadly stated, nuclear risk reduction measures in South Asia context may envisage the following:[13]

- To serve as a central clearinghouse for data exchanges and notifications of existing agreements and to formalize the provision of information in a transparent manner
- To help institutionalise and foster proper impleme-ntation of unilateral, bilateral or multilateral measures for nuclear risk reduction, arms control, and/or force reduction in the region;
- To build trust and confidence by providing data that could assist monitoring and compliance - as well as to nullify misperceptions.

Even a preliminary investigative study and analysis of basic nuclear risk reduction measures (NRRM) in the four key areas of potential risks such as miscalculation, unauthorised use, accidents and panic behaviour as proposed by members of an influential peace group, MIND (Movement in India for Nuclear Disarmament), are yet to be initiated by either India or Pakistan at the present time. According to Praful Bidwai and Achin Vanaik, "the role of NRRM should not be exaggerated. NRRMs can make South Asia less unsafe in nuclear terms. But they can not make it nuclear safe. NRRMs or kindred confidence-building measures have another limitation. They become most effective when located in a cooperative context. But that is no excuse for not beginning a process to negotiate NRRMs for the safety and security of South Asian peoples."[14]

## Nuclear Risk Reduction Centers

In line with nuclear risk reduction measures, scholars have also voiced support of having nuclear risk reduction centers in both India and Pakistan. Michael Kreppon has argued in favour of 'ten commandments' of nuclear risk reduction that had evolved to help keep the Cold War from becoming white hot.[15] These commandments were:

- Don't change the territorial status quo in sensitive areas by use of force;
- Avoid nuclear brinkmanship;
- Avoid dangerous military practices;
- Put in place special reassurances measures for ballistic missiles and other nuclear forces;
- Implement properly treaty obligations, risk reductions, and confidence-building measures;
- Agree on Verification arrangements, including intrusive monitoring;
- Establish reliable lines of communication, between political leaders and between military leaders;
- Establish redundant and reliable command and control arrangements a well as intelligence-gathering capabilities to know what the other side is up to, especially in a crisis;
- Keep working hard on these arrangements; improve them, don't take anything for granted; and
- Hope for plain dumb luck or divine intervention.

## Paused Deployment Posture

Another major step which can take India and Pakistan towards nuclear risk reduction and confidence building would be a bilateral agreement what can be termed as a posture of 'paused deployment'.[16] By a Paused Deployment Posture (PDP), it may mean deliberate, mutually verifiable built-in-delay of about a day in the arming of delivery vehicles with nuclear weapons, agreed upon by both countries. Sometimes, called 'de-alert', delay could be by a full day or more or just few hours and by precluding instant deployment, it will greatly diminish the probability of hasty, emotionally driven or accidental use of nuclear arms and hence provide much needed breathing space to respective decision makers on both sides for finding ways and means at diffusing an impending crisis.

## Paradoxes in pursuing the CBM Modality

Proceeding further, three unresolved paradoxes can be identified in South Asian region concerning the applicability and viability of CBMs. These steps have relevance for other conflict-prone regions in other parts of the world as well.

First, CBMs admittedly "provide the atmospherics for improving inter-state relations, and providing the instrumentality to proceed further with an arms control and disarmament process"[17] They can establish trust between adversarial states; but the paradox remains that trust is required before CBMs can be negotiated. The need for some limited confidence between adversarial states is therefore essential before CBMs can be negotiated.

Second, CBMs are difficult to establish, but easy to disrupt and abandon. Continued adherence to them requires adversarial states to perceive the balance of advantage to lie in not abrogating them, particularly during periods of deep crises. Experience reveals, on the contrary, that the hotline established between the Directors General of Military Operations became non-functional during the Indo-Pak war of 1971 due to telephones being either left unattended or manned by junior officers with no real authority. In addition, during the Brasstacks crisis (1987), "...information shared through the hotline was deemed unreliable because of mutual suspicions; hence, information supplied on Pakistani request was only minimally complied with".[18] Obviously, hotlines can only be relevant in crises if trust is evident on both sides. They are known to work satisfactorily in times of peace. Hence the paradox that states may abide by CBMs in normal times, but ignore them in emergency situations.

Third, public declarations can serve as useful CBMs to alleviate tensions and promote stability; they "can take the form of joint summit statements, negotiated agreements of a declaratory nature—such as non-attack pledges—and/or unilateral statements".[19] The historical record shows that national leaders in India and Pakistan routinely make conciliatory statements, but they are meant either for domestic consumption or to impress international audiences or lower the other's guard. The paradox then emerges: "Rather than to promote security and confidence building, such declarations have often exacerbated existing regional tensions."[20]

## The Sum of All Parts

In spite of the seemingly difficult terrain in generating and implementing confidence-building measures in South Asia, all are not doom and gloom as this chapter suggests. It is thus plausible to make the following conclusions based on existing regional and sub-regional arrangements in South Asia.

1. India and Pakistan, as the two new nuclear weapon states in the nuclear club, have embarked upon nuclear risk reduction measures through a series of bilateral agreements.

2. In South Asia, both India and Pakistan have initiated a series of meaningful Track-II dialogues and discussions at the people to people basis outside of the regular

governmental to governmental channels. Idea of having a nuclear risk reduction center in both the countries have received favorable reactions both inside and outside of South Asia including the skeptics who felt such a proposal to be too ambitious and hence unrealistic and unworkable.

3. In South Asia, through SAARC (South Asian Association for Regional Cooperation) both India and Pakistan have tried to address various bilateral; issues including trade, commerce, and cultural contacts within the regional framework.

4. At the highest level of government, both India and Pakistan have tried to evolve composite dialogue (including on the vexed issue of Kashmir). In particular, between 1999-2008, President Pervez Musharraf of Pakistan and Prime Ministers of India during that phase, Atal Behari Vajpayee and Dr. Manmohan Singh, have met several times one on one and have agreed on the basic modalities of confidence-building measures. The very fact that the current government of India led by Dr.Manmohan Singh from the Congress Party has committed itself to pursue and continue the path of dialogue since 2004 is a welcome sign. It is extremely imperative that even after the heinous terrorist attack in Mumbai on 26 November 2008 and repeated terrorist attacks in Pakistani cities, both sides agree that the peace process must continue unabated.

5. Although the hard liners in India and Pakistan still profess to have nuclear superiority over their respective rivals, yet the pro-engagement wing seems to have the upper hand at the present time.

6. By branding President Pervez Musharraf who was in power, 1999-2008 and other leaders including present President Asif Ali Zardari, Prime minister Raja Pervaiz

Ashraf, and former Prime ministers Nawaz Shariff, Sartaj Aziz, Zafar Jamali, Yousuf Raza Gilani, of Pakistan as irrational minds have only raised the spectre of nuclear threat in South Asia. The key to stability lies in dealing with whoever is in de facto charge in Islamabad.

7. Confidence-building measures such as the establishment of secured Hot Lines between New Delhi and Islamabad provides a mechanism for the reduction of tension and in diffusing any imminent security issue that may snowball in to a potential grave crisis. However, the key lies in building and expanding beyond these CBMs which are/were already agreed upon among the known (India/ Pakistan) adversaries.

Six elements are critical to sustain this process of dialogue:[21]

One, preservation of agreements and CBMs (military and non-military) instituted so far between India and Pakistan;

Two, promoting resolution of disputes so that peace process gains momentum into a conflict resolution mode;

Three, a problem-solving proactive approach applied by both sides;

Four, principle of reciprocity and goodwill guiding the dialogue process;

Five, political contacts sufficiently at high level to the highest level are needed to discuss issues critically and keep the engagement process moving;

Six, evolving a convergent vision for a future of peace and cooperation in the entire South Asian region;

In this regard, a high-level Track II meeting in 2009 between India and Pakistan has suggested several concrete ways to take forward the bilateral relationship.[22]

1. Peace between and stability in India-Pakistan relations is vital for the well being of South Asia. After nearly 63 years of hostility between India and Pakistan, it is critical that all stakeholders work for sustainable peace between the two countries. Civil societies in India and Pakistan, by and large, support the goal of peace and reconciliation; peace constituencies in both countries must, therefore, be further strengthened by providing them greater space, depth and support. It is essential that the trust deficit and the burden of history not be allowed to impact on the task of moving relations forward.

2. Trust can be best built through multiple uninterruptible dialogues, positive incremental steps, Confidence and Trust-building Measures, and most critically through acts of bold statesmanship and farsightedness by the leaders of the two countries.

3. A grand reconciliation can only be ensured, in the long-term, through engagement at every level: civil society meetings, official dialogues, proactive engagement of political leaders, cooperation between business and corporate leaders, visits of artists, sportsmen, media, talks between the armed forces, Track - II dialogues, etc.

4. Temporary and occasional setback in inter-governmental relations should not be allowed to impinge on people-to-people cooperation. Attempts should be made to facilitate a visa-free regime for important stakeholders: including academics, journalists, businessmen, students, artists and former senior officials.

5. Progress made in previous rounds of talks should be carried forward in the official dialogue so that there is an element of continuity.

6. Terrorism is of deep concern to India and Pakistan. The memory of the 26/11 Mumbai attacks is still alive and continues to inform public opinion in India. Today, terrorism and extremism pose an existential threat to Pakistan. Indian concerns about terrorism and the terrorist threats to India are as much of a serious concern for Pakistan. Terrorism and extremism need to be addressed upfront and comprehensively and permanently defeated.
7. India and Pakistan should seriously consider initiating an institutionalised, regular but discreet dialogue between the intelligence chiefs and units (the heads of R&AW, IB and ISI and IB Pakistan) of both countries.
8. The back channel talks on Jammu and Kashmir must be resumed at an early date keeping in view the fact that all stake-holders, particularly the people of J&K, will have to be consulted at some stage. If Jammu and Kashmir is considered as a piece of real estate there is little hope of a way ahead. Therefore, the overall welfare of the people of Jammu and Kashmir must be considered to be of paramount concern. In this context, all agreed CBMs must be more robustly and honestly implemented.
9. The media are playing a critical role in shaping popular perceptions. They have thus a great responsibility to help strengthen the constituency for peace. A continuing dialogue between journalists, editors and proprietors of media houses is needed in ushering a climate of trust.
10. A sustained dialogue on ensuring strategic stability in South Asia must be an essential part of the bilateral dialogue. There is also need for discussion amongst experts on critical doctrinal issues and the need to work towards creating a Nuclear Safety, Assistance and Collaboration Regime in the region within the framework

of minimum deterrence. In this context, a trilateral nuclear dialogue which includes China must also be pursued.

11. The issue of water is becoming a matter of great concern and there is a need to address misperceptions in this regard. The Indus Water Treaty has withstood the test of time and has a well established dispute-settlement mechanism. Any concern about hydro-resources of the Indus river system should be taken up through the Permanent Indus Water Commission. Within the framework of the treaty, the two countries must also share best practices on water management with each other. Environmental and other experts with domain knowledge, from both countries, must be encouraged to provide concrete recommendations for better and optimal management of hydro resources given the huge challenge that the scarcity of water will pose for the region in the future in terms of human security.

12. A stable, prosperous, sovereign and independent Afghanistan is in the interest of India and Pakistan and both countries must work assiduously for this goal and hold regular talks to allay each other's apprehensions.

13. Track-II dialogues are designed to move beyond officially stated positions, find a way forward, and can provide alternative approaches to the governments of Pakistan and India as well as other important stakeholders. It is vital that Track II dialogues be encouraged by both New Delhi and Islamabad.

What is more important in the context of bringing about peace between India and Pakistan is the perception of risk which appear to be only limited regional perceptions of the shared bilateral risks of nuclear war and avoidance of possible catastrophe. In the short to intermediate term, viable solution(s) must be evolved for solving the various, bilateral intractable issues so as to have saleability and acceptability by all stakeholders. There is also a compelling need to recalibrate other national strategic priorities - national defense, Kashmir, viable civil society, convert 'trust deficit' into 'trust surplus', etc. The issue is complicated further by the profound asymmetry between Pakistan's obsession with India in its security thinking and India's substantial strategic space and its focus on a range of security imperatives of which Pakistan is but one.

**Annex**

**Source: The Henry L. Stimson Center, Washington, DC**

URL : http://www.stimson.org/southasia/?SN = SA20060207948

**South Asia Confidence Building Measures (CBM) Timeline 1988–Present**

| Date | Description |
|---|---|
| December 31, 1988 | Agreement on the Prohibition of Attack Against Nuclear Installations and Facilities signed in Islamabad. |
| April 6, 1991 | Agreement on Advance Notification on Military Exercises, Maneuvers and Troop Movements signed in New Delhi. |
| April 6, 1991 | Agreement on Prevention of Airspace Violations and for Permitting Overflights and Landings by Military Aircraft signed in New Delhi. |
| January 1, 1992 | India and Pakistan exchange lists of their nuclear installations and facilities under the 1988 agreement on Prohibition of Attack Against Nuclear Installations and Facilities. |

| | |
|---|---|
| August 19, 1992 | Joint Declaration on the Complete Prohibition of Chemical Weapons concluded in New Delhi. |
| January 1, 1993 - 1999 | Even during a low point in relations, both countries exchange lists of their nuclear installations and facilities on the first of every year. |
| February 20, 1999 | Bus service between New Delhi and Lahore initiated by Prime Minister Atal Behari Vajpayee. |
| February, 1999 | Memorandum of understanding reached during Indian Prime Minister Atal Behari Vajpayee's historic visit to Pakistan. |
| January 1, 2000 - 2003 | Both countries continue to exchange lists of their nuclear installations and facilities on the first of every year. |
| May 26, 2003 | India announces resumption of Delhi-Lahore bus service and release of 70 Pakistani fishermen and 60 civilian prisoners. |
| September 25, 2003 | Musharraf calls for a ceasefire along the Line of Control (LoC) at the UN General Assembly in New York. |
| November 25, 2003 | India and Pakistan implement a formal ceasefire along the International Border and the Actual Ground Position Line in Jammu and Kashmir at midnight. |
| January 1, 2004 | Air links between the two countries resume. |
| January 1, 2004 | Both countries exchange the list of their nuclear installations and facilities. |
| January 4-6, 2004 | Vajpayee and Musharraf hold direct talks on January 5 at the 12th SAARC summit in Islamabad. |

| | |
|---|---|
| January 15, 2004 | Passenger and freight rail service resumes between Attari and Lahore. |
| February 17-18, 2004 | Pakistani and Indian Foreign Secretaries meet in Murree, Pakistan for May-June preparatory talks. |
| February 20, 2004 | First flag meeting between Indian and Pakistani army units in three years takes place in Chorbat La sector in India. |
| February, 2004 | India and Pakistan agree on a five-point agenda to initiate dialogue process. |
| March 10-April 18, 2004 | Indian cricket tram travels to Pakistan for a historic cricket series, the first at a non-neutral site since 1989. |
| June 15-16, 2004 | Meeting of narcotics officials in Islamabad where both parties agree to share information and adopt a coordinated strategy to prevent drug trafficking and smuggling between the two countries. |
| June 20-21, 2004 | Foreign Ministers of both countries meet at the Asia Cooperation Dialogue (ACD) meeting in China where they reaffirm their intention to open both countries' consulates in Karachi and Bombay. |
| June 26-27, 2004 | Meeting of Foreign Secretaries in New Delhi when they discuss dialogue on Peace and Security and Jammu and Kashmir. |
| June 29-July 2, 2004 | Foreign Ministers of both countries meet at the ASEAN Regional forum in Jakarta where Pakistan is formally accepted as a member of the ARF after India drops its objections. |
| July 20-21, 2004 | Foreign Ministers of both countries meet at the SAARC Council of Ministers meeting in Islamabad. |

| | |
|---|---|
| August 9, 2004 | Both countries carry out an exchange of six prisoners of war at the Wagah border post. |
| August 11-12, 2004 | Meeting of commerce secretaries in Islamabad to discuss dialogue on economic and commercial cooperation. Both sides agree to promote bilateral trade ties and enhance cooperation in various sectors. |
| August 31, 2004 | India and Pakistan exchange 55 prisoners along the Wagah border crossing. |
| September 8, 2004 | Meeting of Foreign Ministers in Delhi where the two sides agree on thirteen points, and indicating willingness for a 'road map' for peace process. |
| September 19, 2004 | India announces it will ease visa rules for visiting Pakistani journalists, doctors and academics. |
| September 24, 2004 | President Musharraf and Indian Prime Minister Dr.Manmohan Singh meet for talks in New York on the occasion of the United Nations General Assembly. |
| October 4-11, 2004 | Pakistani journalists visit Jammu and Kashmir. |
| October 11-14, 2004 | Biannual meeting between Indian Border Security Forces and Pakistani Rangers in Chandigarh at which there is an agreement on nine areas. They also agree that local commanders meet more frequently to resolve local problems. |
| November 9, 2004 | Twenty-five Pakistani prisoners handed over by India at the Wagah border crossing. |
| November 16, 2004 | On the eve of a visit to Jammu and Kashmir, Prime Minister Dr.Manmohan Singh announces to reduce the deployment of troops. |

| | |
|---|---|
| November 21, 2004 | Over 4,000 Indian Sikh pilgrims arrive for a visit to religious sites in Pakistan. |
| November 23, 2004 | Pakistan Prime Minister Shaukat Aziz travels to India for the first time as Chairperson of SARRC. |
| December 14-15, 2004 | Indian and Pakistani delegations hold expert level talks on Nuclear CBMs in Islamabad. Expert level talks on Conventional CBMs held on December 15th. |
| January 1, 2005 | Both countries exchange lists of nuclear installations and facilities. |
| January 6, 2005 | Pakistan releases 266 Indian fishermen arrested in 2004. |
| February 16-17, 2005 | Indian Foreign Minister Natwar Singh visits Islamabad. |
| February 28-April 18, 2005 | Pakistan's cricket team travels to India for the first time in six years. |
| April 7, 2005 April 18, 2005 | First bus service from Srinagar to Muzaffarabad is flagged off by Prime Minister Dr.Manmohan Singh and United Progressive Alliance chairperson Sonia Gandhi. |
| May 10, 2005 | Expert level meeting in Rawalpindi held on the establishment of a communication link between Pakistan Maritime Security Agency and Indian Coast Guard. Both sides resolve outstanding issues in a Memorandum of Understanding. |
| August 5-6, 2005 | Talks on nuclear confidence building measures commence between high level Indian and Pakistani experts. |
| August 8, 2005 | Expert level meeting on conventional confidence building measures. |

| | |
|---|---|
| August 29-30, 2005 | Expert level meeting on terrorism and drug trafficking. |
| September 1, 2005 | Meeting of Foreign Secretaries in Islamabad where they review the implementation of the peace process. |
| September 2, 2005 | India allows Pakistan access to 208 prisoners. |
| October 3, 2005 | Signing of an agreement on advance notification of ballistic missile tests. |
| October 4, 2005 | Agreement reached on the establishment of hot line between the two their maritime security agencies to facilitate early exchange of information regarding apprehended fishermen who inadvertently stray into the other side's territorial waters. |
| October-November, 2005 | Pakistan accepts 25 tons of food, medicine, tents, blankets, plastic sheets from India after the earthquake. |
| January 1, 2006 | India and Pakistan exchange lists of their respective nuclear installations and facilities. |
| January 20, 2006 | Bus service from Lahore to Amristar begins. |
| January 7-February 19, 2006 | India-Pakistan cricket series in Pakistan. |
| February 1, 2006 | Pakistan and India agree to open rail links between Munnabao in Rajasthan and Khokhrapar in Sind on February 18th. |
| February 7, 2006 | India redeploys 5000 troops from Jammu and Kashmir citing 'improvement' in situation. |
| February 18, 2006 | India and Pakistan resume train service after 40 years. |

| | |
|---|---|
| February 22, 2006 | Pakistani journalists travel to India. |
| February 27, 2006 | Fibre optic link between Armitsar and Lahore becomes operational. |
| March 7, 2006 | Pakistan and India agree to expand air service agreement. |
| March 7, 2006 | Indo-Pak night bus service from Ferozepur and Fazilka to Ludhiana-Chandigarh resumes. |
| March 8, 2006 | India and Pakistan agree in principle to expand airline service between the two nations. |
| March 22, 2006 | India and Pakistan agree to jointly fight human trafficking, counterfeit currency trade, and illegal immigration. March 24, 2006 Amritsar-Nankana Sahib bus service is flagged off. |
| May 3, 2006 | India and Pakistan reach an agreement to revive trade in Kashmir. |
| May 24, 2006 | India and Pakistan fail to reach an agreement to withdraw troops from the Siachen Glacier. |
| May 25, 2006 | India announces the establishment of five working groups based on issues central to the Kashmir problem. |
| May 30, 2006 | India and Pakistan formally agree to trade raw products between divided regions of Jammu and Kashmir. |
| June 1, 2006 | India and Pakistan agree to host festivals displaying each other's movies. |
| September 16, | President Musharraf and Prime Minister Singh agree to "put in place an India- |

| | |
|---|---|
| | Pakistan anti-terrorism institutional mechanism to identify and implement counter-terrorism initiatives and investigations." |
| December 15, | India and Pakistan sign a revised shipping protocol that removes restrictions in place since 1975. The protocol allows lifting of third country cargo by Indian and Pakistani vessels from each other's ports and it also lifted the restriction that the cargo destined for the other country could be carried only by an Indian or Pakistani vessel. |
| February 21, 2007 | India and Pakistan sign agreement on "Reducing the Risk from Accidents Relating to Nuclear Weapons." |
| July 6, 2007 | India's University of Mumbai and Pakistan's University of Sindh sign a memorandum of understanding for exchange of faculty, scholars, and students. |
| August 14, 2007 | India released 72 Pakistani nationals, including 48 fishermen and 24 prisoners from Indian jails, and Pakistan released 135 Indian nationals, including 100 fishermen and 35 prisoners, from its jails. |
| August 16, 2007 | India released and repatriated 16 Pakistani militants from eight jails in Jammu and Kashmir. |
| October 1, 2007 | The first overland truck route between India and Pakistan is opened at the Wagah border crossing. |
| October 19, 2007 | Pakistan and India hold the Fifth Round of talks to review nuclear and missile related CBMs as part of the Composite Dialogue process. The second round of the Joint |

| | |
|---|---|
| | Anti-Terrorism Mechanism (JATM) was held the following week. |
| February 5, 2008 | India and Pakistan sign an agreement allow regular contact between India's military-funded Institute of Defence Studies and Analysis (IDSA) and Pakistan's state-run Institute for Strategic Studies (ISS). The purpose is to build channels of communication at the level of scholars. |
| February 26, 2008 | The first meeting of a joint Indo-Pak judicial committee of eight retired senior judges from Pakistan and India was held to look into the condition of prisoners jailed in both countries, seek release of those who's sentences have been served, and to discuss all related matters, including future procedures. |
| March 3, 2008 | Kashmir Singh, an Indian national in prison in Pakistan for 35 years on charges of spying for India and sentenced to death, is released. |
| March 19, 2008 | A Pakistani national arrested in India over two years ago on charges of spying and possessing fake currency was released and handed over to Pakistani authorities at the Wagah land border after being acquitted by a court. |
| April 4, 2008 | "Khuda Kay Liye" or "In the Name of God" becomes the first Pakistani film in four decades to be approved for release in Indian theaters. |
| April 24, 2008 | India joins a signed a framework agreement with Turkmenistan, Afghanistan and Pakistan on a $7.6 billion gas pipeline |

| | |
|---|---|
| | project. The line will be 1,680-km Turkmenistan -Afghanistan- Pakistan - India (TAPI), supply 3.2 billion cubic feet per day (90 MMSCMD) and gas flows are expected from 2015. Pakistan and India have agreed to share equally in the gas volume. |
| May 21, 2008 | The Foreign Ministers of India and Pakistan agree to a series of Kashmir-specific CBMs, including a triple-entry permit to facilitate crossing the Line of Control. The two ministers also agree to provide consular access to prisoners in each others' countries. |
| May 25, 2008 | Pakistan's top rock band, Junoon, was allowed by the Indian government to perform at Srinagar in the biggest musical event in the disputed valley in decades. |
| June 24, 2008 | India and Pakistan, meeting under the aegis of the Joint Anti-Terror Mechanism, agreed to exchange information to prevent terrorism and violent attacks. |
| September 25, 2008 | Pakistani President Asif Ali Zardari and Indian Prime Minister Dr. Manmohan Singh formally announced the opening of several trade routes between the two countries. The Wagah-Atari road link and the Khokrapar-Munnabao rail link will both be opened to trade, as will the cross-LoC Srinagar-Muzaffarabad and Poonch-Rawalakot roads. |
| October 9, 2008 | A delegation of business leaders from Pakistan-administered Kashmir visits the Indian-controlled side to discussed cross-LoC trade. |

| | |
|---|---|
| October 21, 2008 | Trade across the Line of Control commences as the first trucks cross the line that divides Kashmir. Trade is limited to 21 items, and can take place on two days each week. |
| October 22, 2008 | A second trade route across the Line of Control is opened. The route connects the cities of Rawalkot and Poonch. |
| November 25, 2008 | Pakistan frees 101 Indian prisoners, including 99 fishermen, in advance of a meeting in Islamabad between the Home Minister of India and the Federal Interior Secretary of Pakistan. |
| November 25, 2008 | At the fifth round of home secretary-level talks, Pakistan and India agree to enhance cooperation between their civilian investigation and security agencies to deal with several cross-border issues. |
| December 27, 2008 | In the aftermath of the Mumbai attacks by Islamic extremists that result in over 180 fatalities, the Indian and Pakistani Directors General of Military Operations make unscheduled use of their hotline to discuss troop movements along their border. One likely topic of discussion was Indian troop rotations to exercise areas near the Pakistan border and small-scale counter-deployments by Pakistani troops. |
| January 1, 2009 | For the 18th consecutive year, India and Pakistan exchange lists of their respective nuclear facilities (see entry for December 31, 1988). The two countries also exchanged lists of Pakistanis held in Indian prisons and Indians held in Pakistani prisons (see entry for May 31, 2008). |

| | |
|---|---|
| June 15, 2009 | Chinese President Hu Jintao and Indian Prime Minister Manmohan Singh agree to establish a hotline between the Prime Ministers of India and China. |
| July 16, 2009 | The Prime Ministers of India and Pakistan, meeting on the sidelines of a summit of the Non-Aligned Movement in Egypt, issue a joint statement "charting the way forward in India - Pakistan relations." |
| January 1, 2010 | India and Pakistan exchange lists of their respective nuclear facilities |
| February 6, 2011 | Foreign Secretaries Nirupama Rao and Salmon Bashir agree to resume structured dialogue |
| July 1, 2012 | Pakistan and India exchange lists of prisoners in each others' custody |

## References

1. Hoist Johan Jorgen. 1983, "Confidence Building Measures: A Conceptual Framework", *Survival*, Vol. 25, No.1, January/ February, p. 2 & 4. *Indian Express*, New Delhi, December 19, 2003.
2. Hoist, Ibid, No.1
3. Kreppon, Michael, 1998, "Conflict Avoidance, Confidence-Building, and Peacemaking", in Michael Krepon, Khurshid Khoja, Michael Newbill, Jenny S. Drezin, Eds, *A Handbook of Confidence Building Measures for Regional Security*, 3rd Edition, The Henry L. Stimson Center, Handbook No.1, March, p. 4.
4. Dhanpala, Jayanta, 1993, "Conclusion", in Jayanta Dhanapala; *Regional Approaches to Disarmament: Security and Stability*. Cambridge; Cambridge University Press, p. 271.

5. Chari, P.R. 1988. Newer Sources of Insecurity: The Crisis of Governance in India. RCSS Policy Study, Colombo: Regional Center for Strategic Studies, p. 2.
6. Ahmar, Moonis (ed.). 2003, Paradigms of Conflict Resolution in South Asia. Dhaka: Bangladesh, The University Press Limited, pp. 49-50.
7. Chari, *Ibid*, No. 5.
8. Ahmar, *Ibid*, No. 6.
9. Cheema Pervaiz Iqbal, 2004, "Assessing the Role of Confidence-Building Measures in the India, Pakistan Tangle", Islamabad; Pakistan, Islamabad Policy Research Institute (IPRI), Winter , p.22; also, see, The Hindu, Chennai, April 15, 2005; also see *The Hindustan Times,* Delhi, April 18, 2005; also see "Another Indo-Pak Road to Peace", *The Hindustan Times,* Delhi, June 2, 2006, see Annex for full details.
10. Ahmar, *Ibid,* No.6.
11. Cloughley, Brian, 1998. "Nuclear Risk Reduction Measures in Kashmir", *Nuclear Risk Reduction Measures in South Asia.* Washington, D.C. The Henry L. Stimson Center, Report Number 26, p.70; see *The Indian Express,* New Delhi, May 25, 2005; also, see, The Times of India, New Delhi, May 24, 2006.
12. Cloughley, *Ibid,* No.11.
13. Khan Rafi Uz Zaman. 2003. "Nuclear Risk Reduction Centers", Washington, D.C, The Henry L. Stimson Center, October.
14. Bidwai, Praful, 2002, "From the Worlds' Most Dangerous Place", June 3, available at www.antiwar.com/bidwai/particleid = 607.
15. Kreppon Michael and Jerry S. Drezin, 1999, "Introduction", in Michael Kreppon, Jerry S. Drezin, Michael Newbill, eds; *Declaratory Diplomacy: Rhetorical Initiatives and Confidence-Building,* Report No. 27, April, p.11
16. Rajaraman, R., 1999, "Delayed Deployment: Towards Nuclear Risk Reduction", *The Times of India,* October 1.

17. Bajpai, Kanti; P.R.Chari, Pervaiz Iqbal Cheema, Stephen P. Cohen, Sumit Ganguly. 1995. Brasstacks and Beyond: Perception and Management of Crisis in South Asia, New Delhi: Manohar, p.41
18. Bajpai, *Ibid,* No.17.
19. Kreppon and Drezin, *Ibid,* No. 19.
20. Chari, *Ibid,* No. 5.
21. Maleeha Lodhi, 2006, "Nuclear Cloud over South Asia", *The Times of India,* New Delhi, May 1; also see Shaun Gregory, "A Formidable Challenge: Nuclear Command and Control in South Asia", Disarmament Diplomacy, The Acronym Institute, Issue No.54, February 2001, see, "An Empty Threat", *The Times of India,* January 22, 2009
22. "Building Stability in India-Pakistan Relations", *The Hindu,* Chennai, February 15, 2010.

■■■

# 5

# Nuclear and Radiological Terrorism: Thinking the Unthinkable

*Animesh Roul*

With the advent of Nuclear, Biological, Chemical, Radiological weapons the basic understanding of terrorism as a socio-political phenomenon has moved to the realm of real threat of mass destruction and disruption. The news of terrorists searching for nuclear weapons in Russia and Afghanistan coupled the threat emanating from groups such as Al Qaeda and other groups has brought this threat to the forefront.

Observers have broadly categorised non-state terrorists as actors who can resort to a nuclear strike against nation states. For example, Charles Ferguson has clubbed them into four groups: Apocalyptic groups (e.g., Aum Shinrikyo), Politico-Religious Terrorist groups (e.g., Hezbollah, Al Qaeda, Lashkar-e-Taiba) Nationalist and Separatists groups (e.g., LTTE, Baloch Rebel group), and Single issue Terrorist (e.g eco-terrorist).[1]

There are many ways a terrorist or any radical group could perpetrate a nuclear strike using either a nuclear bomb with the aim of causing mass casualties and widespread destruction or disperse radioactive contamination through a radiological dispersion device to simply provoking mass fear with both environmental and economic disruption. They are:

- A similar 9/11 style attack with a nuclear device on board, no matter how unsophisticated;
- Taking control of a nuclear power plant or overpowering nuke materials during transportations, followed by the threat of radioactive release;
- An attack on nuclear radioactivity materials during transportation or shipment;
- Radiological attack on major urban public space (Shopping Mall, Subway, Railway Stations, etc.) to maximise the impacts;
- An attack on a nuclear reactor or a waste storage/disposal site.

There are two imaginable ways for terrorists to get nuclear explosives. They could build a radiological bomb or an improvised nuclear device or they could seek to steal or buy a miniaturised nuclear weapon. Before dealing with the kind of threat our civil society could face in a nuclear catastrophe triggered by terrorists, it would be useful to discuss and understand various types and effects of nuclear weapon and material used in it, on the human environment. A terrorist group or an individual 'lone-wolf' terrorist would not face serious technical barriers in creating a basic or a crude nuclear device. With some degree of technical sophistication it would be easier to build weapons which could maximise the damage on any given environment, both civil and military.

### Preferred Nuclear Weapons or Materials for Terrorist

The basic nuclear weapon is the fission bomb, generally called the 'atomic bomb'. This is the simplest form, a gun type weapon, involves shooting one mass of uranium-235 into another, as used in the Hiroshima bombing. To date the atomic bombs built have used two fissile materials, uranium-235 and plutonium-239. The maximum yield achievable by pure fission weapons is limited to a few tons of kilotons. Experts believe that a terrorist group could build a gun type nuclear weapon if it could obtain some kilograms of enriched Uranium.

The next significant advance in warhead design after the atomic bomb was the hydrogen bomb in which fusion is used to obtain high yields. However, this type of weapon may be beyond the reach of any terrorist groups, but with state support which has already mastered this technique, this can be achieved by global terrorist group like Al Qaeda or Lashkar-e-Taiba. Similarly some other types of nukes for example Reduced Residual Radioactivity weapon (RRR) is considered as an anti-material weapon that destroys infrastructures and super structures, but doesn't kill people on a large scale. Another bomb, considered an anti-electronic weapon, is the Enhanced Electromagnetic Pulse weapon (EMP). It is associated with the intense ionisation of the atmosphere by the radiation from the bomb. Though few details are known about the bomb, it is known that it enhances the electro-magnetic effects, and, as a result, electronic devices (all conducting devices) like radios, TVs, and computers and other communication tools are damaged by it. Again, only a rouge state or a state sponsored terror group could attempt to build and make use of these kinds of advanced nuclear devices to cripple the communication system and rule the airwaves.

Radiological Dispersal Device (RDD), also known as 'dirty bomb', is considered to be a favorite weapon option for terrorist groups.[3] It should be noted that RDDs are not true nuclear weapons as they lack or don't involve any nuclear fusion or fission process. Any method used to deliberately disperse radioactive material to create terror or harm can be considered an RDD. It is made by packaging explosives (like dynamite or Plastic explosives) with radioactive material to be dispersed when the bomb goes off. The radioactivity in an RDD could also be distributed through other methods, such as through spraying or spreading by placing a radioactive source in a crowded area to expose people in large number. While a RDD would be much less deadly than other types of bombs, it is much easier for terrorist group to obtain the needed material and fabricate the device in-house. For example, radioactive cobalt (Isotope 60) is commonly in use at many food irradiation plants in many different countries. According to an Iraqi report obtained by the Wisconsin Project on Nuclear Arms Control, Iraq had once tested an Isotope 60 laced dirty bomb sometime in 1987. Though the radiation levels were too low in that experiment to cause any significant damage, Isotope 60 continues to remain a threat. There are nine isotopes of interest for RDD: Americium-241, Californium-252, Cesium-137, Cobalt-60, Iridium-192, Plutonium-238, Polonium-210, Radium-226, and Strontium-90. While the radium-226 and a small amount of polonium-210 exist in nature, the rest are man-made.

No terrorist group to date has detonated a dirty bomb. Since it is not likely to produce mass casualties, a dirty bomb attack would likely be directed against a highly symbolic target, such as one representing the economy or government, and designed to cause the maximum amount of disruption at the target site. The bomb would not destroy the target sites, but would deny access to them for as long as it takes to clean up the sites. While the terrorist use of a nuclear bomb remains hypothetical due to serious technical obstacles, international terror groups could conceivably mount a future terrorist event involving a full-fledged nuclear weapon. However, the use of a RDD by non state actors seems like an eventuality as many past cases suggest their access to the technology and material. Because of this threat, countries like the U.S. have invested a great deal of money in radiation detection equipment, and have strategically located that equipment along the border at ports of entry and near critical sites to thwart any such event.

### What would happen in A Nuclear Terror Event?

The nuclear terrorism phenomenon is neither a single entity nor a narrow category, it is actually encompasses a broad spectrum of threats from low level threat of radiation to a higher level threat of terrorist strikes involving nuclear bombs or blowing up nuclear reactors. Until now, we don't have enough evidence to conclude that terrorists groups are not capable or intended to perpetrate a nuclear attack against any nation state. Again, the theory of nuclear deterrence does not work against non state actors or terrorist groups, as they operate in multi geographical locations and don't have fear of retaliation against citizens under their suzerainty. Therefore, with the potential of this holocaust in mind, it is quite imperative to assess the possible effects of nuclear weapons on physical as well as human environment.

The effects produced by a nuclear weapon whether it is exploded by a terrorist group or a state actor, the effects of the blast will almost guarantee some effect on the physical environment. Assuming that a terrorist group or a state sponsored terrorist group possesses a nuclear device, supposedly a basic but sophisticated nuclear weapon or a crude radiological device, the effects of such nuclear incident can be divided into five major categories. Most of the basic nuclear explosions produce varied types of effects but in varying degrees depending on the type of bomb used and to some extent, the size of the bomb or (bombs in the case of multiple attacks), the height at which it is detonated, and the atmospheric conditions also effect the magnitude. The most worrisome effects is the Radiological effect. In a nuclear device detonation several, types of energetic ionising radiation are produced. The initial radiation consists of neutrons and gamma rays, most of which are emitted simultaneously with the explosion and within one minute after the detonation. The intensity of the radiation depends on factors like density and humidity of the air and the explosive yield of the bomb. More than half of all individuals subjected to the radiation doses would develop diarrhea, malaise, and tensions of the mucous membranes. Though there is uncertainty about the acute effects of radiation, under war conditions it is likely that the majority of persons exposed to radiation would die in due course, depending on the level of exposure to radiation. The example of radiological effects can be examined through the Goiânia accident, (Brazil) which shows that some forms of intentional radiological attack could kill hundreds of people and sicken hundreds or thousands more. The Goiânia accident was an incident of radioactive contamination that killed 4, injured 28, and produced 249 cases of detectable radiation poisoning in September 1987.[4]

The other example of radiation effect out of a nuclear accident that took place on April 26, 1986 at the Chernobyl nuclear power plant near Pripyat, Ukraine. Since then, the radiation has caused some 100,000 people to flee their homes in Ukraine and Belarus. The accident has triggered a rise in cancer, neurological disorders and genetic mutations every year since. It is estimated that the disaster released as much as 300 times more radioactive fallout in comparison to the atomic bomb detonated at Hiroshima. In 2008, a report prepared by the Chernobyl Forum indicated 56 direct deaths (47 accident workers, and nine children with thyroid cancer), and estimated that as many as 9,000 people among the approximately 6.6 million most highly exposed, may die from some form of cancer. The other noteworthy accidents were in the Three Mile Island in the US in March 1979 when the reactor suffered a partial core meltdown and a fire at the British nuclear reactor in Windscale in October 1957.

## Nuclear Accidents / Sabotage

Nuclear reactors worldwide present a variety of risks: theft of radioactive material, internal sabotage, and external attack. Terrorist can make use of material from nuclear power plants-- even spent fuel to make a RDD. Or a terrorist group could try to crash an airplane into a nuclear power plant or carry out a suicide attack to cause widespread radiation. An emergency situation could occur during any nuclear accident whether in the reactor or during the transportation of nuclear materials. This could be triggered by a technical failure, human error, or a terrorist act. In the past, the Jihadi terrorist groups have expressed their desire to carry out suicide attacks against nuclear facilities which would bring the enemies of Islam to their knees. In the last many years, speculations are made in Pakistan that Taliban and Al Qaeda operatives could attempt to target various nuclear facilities, which has raised serious questions about the physical security of Pakistan's nuclear infrastructures, especially in the face of terror attacks, including attacks on the nuclear missile storage facility at Sargodha or an attack on Pakistan's nuclear airbase at Kamra by a suicide bomber, all in the year 2007. Again in the middle of 2008 another suicide attack carried out in the military cantonment at Wah (Attock district) which house the nuclear weapons assembly site.[5]

Sabotage on a nuclear plant would have an equally devastating effect. Nuclear plants have been the subject of some terrorist interest: threats or attempts to blow up or penetrate nuclear reactors have been reported in Argentina, Russia, Lithuania, Western Europe, South Africa, and South Korea. In May 2008, two contractors were arrested (and later released for lack of evidence) for plotting sabotage in the nuclear power plant in Oskarshamn (southern Sweden) using explosives. The explosive material detected was believed to be Triacetone Triperoxide (TATP), which is relatively easy to make and has surfaced in a number of recent terrorism investigations, including bombings in the Middle East and the London bombings in July 2005. Given these threats, the possibility of a nuclear-terrorist event is significant.

The scientific and technical information on the assembly of nuclear device, some of which is now available on the Internet, has increased the risk that a terrorist organisation in possession of sufficient fissile material could develop its own nuclear weapon. The complete production of a nuclear weapon strongly depends on the terrorist group's access to fissile material and scientific expertise. Terrorists may, however, seek to link up with a variety of facilitators to develop their own nuclear capability. These facilitators include black market proliferators or transnational criminal networks that may seek to profit from the sale of nuclear material, a weaponised device, or technical knowledge gathered from nuclear experts involved in a national nuclear program. Investigations into Pakistan's notorious A Q Khan networks (dubbed as Nuke Wall-mart) has unraveled the mysteries behind the North Korean, Iranian and Libyan nuclear programs. The international community is yet to fathom the actual spread of this network and its actual reach into the terrorist groups.

Besides Al Qaeda, who according to many reports tried to gain nuclear weapons from black markets, Sri Lanka's Liberation Tigers for Tamil Elam (LTTE) has tried to buy nuclear weapons and know-how from Western countries. The LTTE's plan was to use this technology against the Sri Lankan Armed forces. It is to be noted that the LTTE was successful in purchasing anti-aircraft missiles from arms dealers in the USA and aircraft components from South Africa and other countries in the past.

Nuclear material smuggling is another threat that could exacerbate nuclear terrorism. Large quantities of Soviet fissile material, stored at more than 50 nuclear facilities that are not directly controlled by authorities, pose a significant threat. These complexes lack physical security and any credible accounting systems. It's easier for the disgruntled states like North Korea, Myanmar, Iran (already developed) and terror groups like the Al Qaeda to acquire sufficient materials and expertise from these unsecured nuclear facilities largely under mafia rings with successful nuclear smuggling track records.

The global nuclear watchdog, International Atomic Energy Agency (IAEA);s Illicit Trafficking Database has documented a total of 884 incidents involving illicit trafficking in nuclear and other radioactive materials, of which 540 incidents were confirmed by States, between January 1993 and December 2003 The majority of the confirmed incident involved criminal content, e.g. theft, illegal possession, smuggling, or intent to illegally sell the material.[6] The bulk of this flow involved radioactive materials involving low-grade uranium (cesium-137), which is useless in making fission weapons but effective when used in a RDD. Again, if terrorists groups seek to acquire radiological materials for use in a RDD, they would find it easy to get Radionuclides (there are at least nine isotopes that could attract terrorist's attention for RDDs) that are used in a variety of industrial, medical, and scientific research applications. Most radiological materials lack sufficient strength to present a public health risk, but public panic and the economic disruption caused by a radiological dispersal device would be significant. Radiological materials are used widely across the medical industry including medical isotopes and sources used in some X-ray machines; and in the oil industry where they are used in well-logging devices and other measuring instruments. Its widespread use makes radiological material significantly easier to procure than fissile nuclear material. Three noteworthy instances are given below; all came to light in the year 2008. In the the months of May and September at least ten people were arrested in India's Northeastern state of Meghalaya for allegedly trying to smuggle uranium ores worth millions of Indian rupees. In early that year, one Russian and a Ukrainian were convicted in Novoshakhtinsk, Rostov oblast, for conspiring to smuggle radioactive substances into Russia and sell them. The investigation revealed that the Ukrainian has smuggled into Russia 21.209 grams of metal uranium-238, crossing the border on foot to avoid inspections and detection. In another instance same year, a citizen of Uzbekistan was charged with smuggling a consignment of the dual use material tantalum from Russia to Iran. The suspect, Anar Godzhayev, is owner of AGS Impeks, an enterprise incorporated in 2006 in Astrakhan, Russia, which engaged in exporting goods to Iran.

## Portable Nuclear Device or Suitcase Nukes

Cold War era Super powers, the United States and the erstwhile Soviet Union, are believed to have developed and possessed nuclear suitcases or backpack nukes, a miniaturised version of nuclear weapon system, which is otherwise known for its portability and easy deliverability. The bomb would be small enough to fit into a suitcase or a portable box as the delivery system with full-scale nuclear explosion effects and significant radiological fallout. These characteristics of Portable Nuclear Device (PND) make these weapons a terrorist favorite. The details available are still sketchy and there are no confirmations from these countries that they have these weapons or if they are commercially available. However, the smallest nuclear warhead or Special Atomic Demolition Munitions (SADM), known as 'W54', were manufactured by the United States in the 1960s and were used in the Davy Crockett 120 mm recoilless rifle launched warheads, especially developed to counter Soviet forces. The 'W54' miniaturised nuclear warhead was designed at the Los Alamos National Laboratory and built by the Atomic Energy Commission.

There is information that Soviet era scientists had also produced nearly seven hundred miniaturised nuclear devices such as backpack bombs for use against NATO targets. These devices are too small to cause a catastrophic event. The basic mechanism is a kiloton of fissionable plutonium and uranium that are separated within the box or suitcase and connected to a remote triggering mechanism.

For obvious reasons these devices represent an urgent threat if they were to fall into the hands of terrorists. The news that Al Qaeda's bin Laden paid $30 million and tons of narcotics to purchase nuclear suitcases from his Russian sources sometime in 1996 became the trigger for alarmists to think that nuclear terrorism would be a reality sooner or later.

Many experts observed that such a threat gets undue attention as terrorists might not get access to this sophisticated suitcase nuke so easily. Even if they get the components of a suitcase nuke from their underground sources, assembling a nuclear suitcase device would be more difficult for terrorist groups. In contrast, counter proliferation experts believe that the threat remains as there are many readymade, cold war era lost nuke suitcases whose whereabouts are still unclear. According to experts the real threat emanates from terrorist groups who can assemble a device from stolen or nuclear material available on the black-market. One of the comments on loose nukes came from former Russian National Security Advisor Alexander Lebed in 1997. He claimed that more than a hundred weapons are not under the control of the Russian armed forces. Another Russian Intelligence official Stanislav Lunev also had similar claims identifying these devices as RA-115s which weigh from fifty to sixty pounds. However, these claims were refuted by Senior Russian leaders as 'legends'.

Past investigative research into the threat of Cold War era suitcase nukes shows that there is little probability of a threat from these lost suitcase nukes and even if they fell into terrorist hands their effectiveness should be very low or maybe even non-existent primarily due to lack of maintenance over these years.

## Nuclear Terrorism: South Asia and Beyond

A revolution in terrorist activities has occurred due to the proliferation of Nuclear, Biological Chemical and Radiological (NBCR) weapons or lethal materials and the advent of a new breed of terrorists called "fidayeen." They are identified with Islamic world view and consider it their religious duty to counter infidels and nonbelievers; to kill the non believers is the only way for them to reach heaven. This has changed the threat emanating from various Islamic terrorist organisations in the last couple of decades. With the advent of suicide bombers, combined the dangers of WMD, nuclear and radiological terrorism have become imminent with the improving capabilities of terrorists to develop or acquire these lethal weapons.

Among the Non State Actors, Chechen Separatists and Osama bin Laden's Al Qaeda network are heading the suspect list. Of course, anybody can avail or build a crude device with enough money and covert connections to the nuclear black market. The most vital element, technological know-how, is available on the internet and other open sources for terrorists to make a radiological device or a crude nuclear bomb. Another concern is the thousands of rogue or 'loose' and jobless Russian scientists who have gone missing after the disintegration of the Soviet Union. In 2001, two Pakistani scientists Sultan Bashiruddin Mahmood and Chaudhary Abdul Majid, left Pakistan's nuclear program and reportedly confessed to have shared WMD secrets with Osama bin Laden during their meetings in Kabul, Afghanistan.[8] As of now these confessions provide the most convincing evidence about Al Qaeda network's WMD. The mortar attack by Baloch rebels on a Pakistani nuclear establishment at the Baghalchur Uranium Mine (BC-1), near Dera Ghazi Khan in May 2006, reinstated the long perceived threat to nuclear installations by non-state actors. Fortunately the mortar attack sparked a conflagration in the forests surrounding the establishment, but the fire was extinguished before it could spread to the establishment. However, nobody knows the consequence if the conflagration had spread to the nuclear establishment itself.

Considering these possible catastrophic scenarios, the vital question now gaining ground among the security establishments around the world is how to face the situation and how to manage the consequential effect of a terrorist act involving nuclear or radiological weapon or device. The spectacle of the tragic events of a terrorist strike in the United States reinforced governments around the world to devise strategies to face a similar kind of apocalyptic scenarios.

There are number of factors why a terrorist group would pursue a nuclear weapon program or to acquire the capabilities. The most plausible would be to achieve an effective political bargaining tool and ultimate recognition. This bargaining tool would put them on par with the largest nation's of the world and allow the group to dictate their demands like a superpower. The other factor would be the religious fanaticism. Once Al Qaeda's Bin laden has once said that it would be a sin for Muslims not to seek possession of the weapons that would prevent the infidels from inflicting harm on Muslims.

Though experts may disagree on the threat of fission/ fusion nuclear weapons, all remain unanimous on the threat of terrorist detonation of a dirty bomb (radiological dispersal device-RDD). This consensus has re-focused governmental attention on efforts to mitigate the effect. Even an RDD attack could cause damage and could spread public panic and widespread chaos. Like all the effects discussed above, an RDD attack also depends on many variables like meteorological conditions, type and amount of radiological material, duration of exposure, and method of dispersal to cause extensive damage. While the resultant radioactive fallout is unpredictable and the danger is extended in time as well as in space, radioactive materials can contaminate vast areas with lethal levels of radioactivity depending on the winds, but it is unlikely that it could kill immediately depending upon the material used in the attack.

The darkest fear is that a terrorist group might attack a large metropolis using nuclear bombs. Even in a worst case scenario, terrorists could use the radiological device against civilian or military targets as another form of nuclear terrorism. Although until now no terrorist outfit has used such device, there have been a couple of incidents involving RDDs. The success of using a RDD may be more of a psychological success than a real physical threat. To the public at large, the terror inflicted from a RDD attack would be more harmful than the physical attacks themselves.

Some terrorist organisations like al Qaeda and religious cults like Aum Shinrikyo of Japan have openly stated their desire to acquire and use nuclear weapons. Aum cult chief

Soko Asahara had vision of a nuclear Armageddon. Aum's associate Hayakawa had reportedly made frequent visits to Russia to acquire military hardware that includes nuclear weapon components. During police raids on Aum Shrnrikyo facilities after the Tokyo Subway Sarin gas attacks in 1995, Japanese police have reportedly confiscated technical information on Uranium enrichment process and a list of enquries about the cost of obtaining a nuclear warhead. During a court hearing on March 21, 1997, Dr. Ikuo Hayashi, another member of the Aum Shinrikyo cult, reportedly told the court that once the cult chief Soko Asahara asked him, "What do you think would happen if an atomic bomb was dropped on Washington?"[9] Hayashi who was dubbed as "Dr Death" by the Japanese media was sentenced to life imprisonment in connection with Sarin gas attack, among other cult members.

During mid 1990s, Chechnya separatist leaders, including Samil Basayev, Aslambek Abdukhadyev and Salman Raduyev, blackmailed the Russian government by threatening to use radiological weapons as well as to attack and destroy Russian nuclear facilities. They made a series of threats to detonate radioactive containers in Russian cities, to target nuclear facilities in Russia, and even to explode a nuclear device. Basayev frequently threatened to attack Moscow with nuclear weapons, but Russian officials dismissed the threat claiming that the material was caesium-137 used in X-Ray equipment and that it was only capable of minimal destruction.

In 1995, Chechen rebels placed a RDD in a Moscow park containing Cesium-137. The park was a popular recreational place for Russians and tourists. However, before anything dangerous could happen, the situation was defused following the the rebel group had alerted Russian Television Network about the buried radioactive material.

Alarmists as well as counter terrorist experts believe that Osama bin Laden's Al-Qaeda network has been diligently trying to acquire radioactive materials from the nuclear wastelands of Soviet Russia and 'loose nukes' from Pakistan.[10] With Russia's nuclear security in severe decline due to financial troubles and disorganisation, there have been global concerns about unsecured and unguarded radioactive materials in Russia. Experts like Paul Williams believe that bin Laden's search for nuclear weapons began in 1988 when he hired a team of five nuclear scientists from Turkmenistan. The team's project was the development of a nuclear reactor that could be used "to transform a very small amount of material that could be placed in a package smaller than a backpack." According to Williams, bin Laden had hired hundreds of atomic scientists from the former Soviet Union for $2,000 a month to work in a highly sophisticated and well-fortified secret laboratory in Kandahar, Afghanistan. In mid 1990s, allegations surfaced that Osama bin Laden paid two million USD in an attempt to procure a tactical nuclear device from Kazakhstan, and had also made efforts to purchase enriched uranium. Some reports which came to light during that time claimed that bin Laden may have already acquired tactical nuclear devices from nuclear black market. In 1993, associates of bin Laden reportedly tried to acquire weapons grade uranium by colluding with Salah Abdel alMobruk, a Sudanese military officer and former government minister. Most recently, a French physicist, Adlène Hicheur, who is of Algerian origin involved with the European atomic research centre CERN was charged with terrorism offences after investigations reveal ed that he offered to work with the Al-Qaeda in the Islamic Maghreb (AQIM) which has been active in the northern African regions, especially in Algeria, Morocco and Tunsia.

Since September 11, 2001, terrorist arrests and prosecutions overseas have revealed that individuals associated with

Al-Qaeda planned to acquire materials for a RDD. Al Qaeda operatives reportedly tried to acquire and develop nuclear device through Pakistani expertise in 2001. Abu Zubaydah, an Al Qaeda member, told his interrogators that such a device existed. In Kabul, in April 2002, International nuclear watchdog (IAEA) experts secured several powerful unguarded radiation sources, mainly cobalt, once used in medical and research applications. In May 2002, one arrested Al-Qaeda terrorist, Jose Padilla (also known as Abdullah al-Muhajir), confessed for plotting to build and use a dirty bomb in the United States, though he never used it. The federal investigating agency revealed that Padilla had undergone training in Lahore, Pakistan, where he allegedly studied the mechanics of dirty-bomb construction, including how to wire explosive devices and how to optimise bombs for radiological dispersion. Padilla, who arrived in the U.S. carrying a suitcase packed with $10,000 in cash was on a reconnaissance mission for a future dirty-bomb attack. He is presently serving a 17 years imprisonment sentence for terror conspiracy charges.[13]

In the aftermath of September 11, scenarios that have particularly worried homeland security officials include the detonation of a "dirty bomb"—an ordinary explosive laced with radioactive material—and the sabotage of a nuclear power plant with the intent to release radiation into the environment. Dhiren Barot, another Al Qaeda sympathiser from North London had planned to kill civilians in the UK and US using a radioactive device and conspired to target underground car parks in and around vital installation of the UK and the US. In August 2004, British authorities arrested Barot along with several associates on various charges, including conspiring to commit public nuisance by the use of radioactive materials. In 2006, Barot was found guilty and sentenced to life. British authorities disclosed that Barot developed a document known as the "Final Presentation." The document outlined his research on the production of 'dirty bombs,' which he characterised as designed to "cause injury, fear, terror and chaos" rather than to kill.[14]

British police arrested another Qaeda suspect Salahuddin Amin and six others on terrorism-related charges in 2004. Amin was accused of making inquiries about buying a "radioisotope bomb" from the Russian mafia in Belgium while he was in Pakistan. His involvement in the alleged plot was said to have stemmed from an association with a man named Abu Munthir whom he met in a Luton mosque. While neither Barot nor Amin had the opportunity to carry their plans forward to an operational stage, these arrests demonstrate the continued interest of terrorists in acquiring and using radioactive material.

Much evidence has been accumulated about Al Qaeda's inclinations to adopt a full fledged nuclear strategy. In a recent discussion on a Jihadi forum at www.muslm.net (August 25, 2009), terrorists have reportedly discussed the future strategy of possible nuclear deployment against the western world, the primary target the US. The title of the topic says it all: "Al-Qaeda's nuclear bombings - Where would the battle start?" In many such forums, it is speculated that Al Qaeda should attack the US with nuclear weapons which would end its tyrannical rule over the world. And they believe that such an attack is only a matter of time and propose a large scale evacuation of Muslims from the western world to avoid mass Muslim fatalities during a nuclear event.[16]

At a global level, any form of nuclear terrorism could have a devastating effect when it leads to war or armed conflict between two countries or among a group of nuclear powers. The impact of a nuclear-terrorist act would be far greater when it would be misconstrued as an attack by the enemy country. However, while there is a clear consensus about an increased threat of nuclear and radiological terrorism in the post 9/11 period, there are also others who have tagged this threat as 'overrated nightmare' since using and acquiring nuclear capability may well be beyond the purview of a terrorist group. Again, the evident efforts by jihadist terrorists to acquire nuclear and radiological weapons continue to be among the key challenges.

## References

1. Charles D. Ferguson, et.al., The Four Faces of Nuclear Terrorism, Routledge, 2005.
2. Some of the observations are noted by Rajesh M Basrur in "Nuclear Terrorism and Nuclear Posture in India and Pakistan", Paper presented at the 13th International Security Conference, Sandia National Laboratories, Albuquerque, NM, April 23-25, 2003.
3. "Radiological Terrorism Fact Sheet: Radiological Weapons - "Dirty Bombs", CSB&EI, September 2002.
4. International Atomic Energy Agency (Vienna), The Radiological Accident In Goiania, 1988 <http://www-pub.iaea.org/mtcd/publications/pdf/pub815_web.pdf>
5. Shaun Gregory, "The Terrorist Threat to Pakistan's Nuclear Weapons," CTC Sentinel, Vol. 2 (7), July 2009.
6. IAEA Illicit Trafficking Database (ITDB),URL < http://www.iaea.org/newscenter/features/radsources/pdf/itdb_31122003.pdf>
7. James Martin Center For Nonproliferation Studies, "Suitcase Nukes: A Reassessment", September 23, 2002.
8. "Rogue scientists gave bin Laden nuclear secrets," The Telegraph, December 13, 2001.
9. Nadine Gurr and Benjamin Cole, The new face of terrorism: threats from weapons of mass destruction I.B. Tauris, 2000, p. 294.
10. For a timeline see, Rolf Mowatt-Larssen, "Al Qaeda's Pursuit Of Weapons Of Mass Destruction," Foreign Policy, January 25, 2010.
11. See, Paul L. Williams, ''Al Qaeda: Brotherhood of Terror,'' Alpha Books, 2002. pp.169-70.
12. Peter D. Zimmerman & Jeffrey G Lewis, "The Bomb in the Backyard", Foreign Policy, Washington: Nov/Dec 2006.
13. J.M. Berger, "Backgrounder: Jose Padilla," April 2004. http://intelwire.egoplex.com/padilla011104.html

14. "The Final Presentation" is available at the NEFA Foundation webportal. <http://nefafoundation.org/file/Barot/Final Presentation.pdf>
15. "Suspect tried to buy dirty bomb from Russians" *The Independent*, March 23, 2006; Also described in James W. Jones, John R. Haygood, *The Terrorist Effect - Weapons of Mass Disruption: The Danger of Nuclear Terrorism*, iUniverse, Bloomington, 2011, p. 32.
16. Abdul Hameed Bakier, Jihadis Speculate on al-Qaeda's Nuclear Strategy, Terrorism Monitor, Volume VII, Issue 28, September 17, 2009.

# 6

# Nuclear Stability in South Asia and the Challenge of Strategic Technologies

*Yogesh Joshi*

During the "India-Pakistan Expert Level Talks on Nuclear CBM's" held in December 2011, India relayed its concerns over Pakistan's amorphous nuclear posture and its growing nuclear arsenals.[1] India requested Pakistan to clear the air around its nuclear doctrine: what are the thresholds beyond which Pakistan would respond with nuclear weapons; what role Pakistan ascribes to tactical and strategic nuclear weapons and whether Pakistan considers nuclear first strike as a viable option? Though Pakistan rejected to oblige to the Indian request, these questions are important for the deterrence stability from an Indian point of view.[2] Pakistan's official silence on such issues is source of instability in the deterrent equation between the two countries. Since nuclear signalling is an important attribute for a stable deterrence and doctrines a medium through which nuclear signalling is in fact effectuated, Pakistan has been found guilty of sending confused signals across the border.

Nuclear signalling, however, is not only a function of stated doctrines but also of existing and developing capabilities especially in terms of emerging strategic technologies. When seen in this light, India may be equally culpable of creating nuclear instability in the subcontinent.

During the talks on nuclear CBM's, there was no reference to India's pursuance of some high profile strategic technologies. India's Fast Breeder Reactor Programme (FBR), the Ballistic Missile Defence (BMD) system and the Nuclear Submarine project have a potential to dilute Pakistan's nuclear deterrence substantially. The pursuance of such strategic technologies also challenge the substance of India's declared nuclear doctrine as its strategic capabilities stand in contradiction to its stated posture.[3]

In the first four months of the current year, India has again test fired a ballistic missile interceptor and also leased a nuclear submarine – the Akula Class sub renamed Indian Navy Ship (INS) *Chakra* – from Russia for a period of 10 years. Not only that, India's indigenous nuclear submarine - INS *Arihant* – has started undergoing sea trials and will be ready for induction in a couple of years. The work on FBR is continuing and is slated to finish by the year end. At the same time, some stark revelations have appeared in the media about Pakistan's nuclear programme especially the colossal amount of money – approximately $2.5 Billion a year – being spent on nuclear weapons by Pakistan. It not only adds to the report of the Bulletin of Atomic Scientists on increasing Pakistani arsenals but it also underlines how much the government in Pakistan is committed to nuclear weapons even when the country is going through its worst financial crisis. In all it suggests that the South Asian nuclear scene is moving in a dangerous direction with potential of spiralling an arms race in the subcontinent. It is therefore important to understand the dynamics behind India's pursuance of strategic technologies and the security dilemma it is creating in South Asia.

This essay strives to investigate the effect of pursuance of strategic technologies by India and its impact on the South Asian Balance of Power. The first section of this essay would reflect on the regime of strategic restraint which many in the academic world claim guides India's views on use of force and its strategic necessities. The argument, in general, is that India, in its relations with its neighbours, especially Pakistan, is guided by the logic of strategic restraint when it comes to the use of force. However, as will be argued in this section, the concept of strategic restraint does not capture the essence of instability created in India-Pak conflict dyads by India's burgeoning force projection capabilities. The second section deals with India's nuclear doctrine. Here the focus is the essential contradictions between the political component of India's nuclear doctrine and its operationalisation aspects. The third section deals with the problem of increasing Indian capabilities in the realm of strategic technologies. The argument here is that irrespective of how a nation thinks about his strategic culture and war-fighting doctrines, it is its capabilities which induces imbalances in the balances of power and hence, prove to be the precursors of arms races. Given the huge leap India seems poised to take when it comes to strategic military technologies; it also fundamentally induces conflict into the Indo-Pakistan military dyad. The last section sums up the essential argument of this essay: India, not Pakistan, may be the reason behind the instability in India-Pakistan nuclear equation.

## The Idea of Strategic Restraint

The idea of strategic restraint corresponds to the self-limiting use of force even under situations which are otherwise advantageous for precipitation of military action and its initiator. Many have argued that such a notion of a limited use of force guides India's military practices and its external relations. For Cohen and Das Gupta, strategic restraint is the "most remarkable attribute of India as an independent nation" and "reticence in the use of force its most dominant political condition.[4]

If strategic restraint is accepted as the fundamental principal of military thought in India, what are the causal mechanisms through which it has assimilated into the anatomy of the Indian state? Many find this notion steeped in Nehruvian dictums. As Srinath Raghavan has comprehensively argued in his brilliant narrative on Nehru's strategic practices, India, under Nehru, always resorted to the use of force as a last instrument in its paraphernalia of state power . This was evident in how Nehru dealt with a number of conflicts which surfaced just after India's independence starting with the Kashmir Operations in 1948. The most revealing aspect of India's strategic restraint was the referral to the UN of the Kashmir problem when finally India was well positioned to take the fight to the enemy. Nehru's treatment of the crisis in Bengal, Junagarh as well as Hyderabad further corroborated the practice of strategic restraint. Even in the post-Nehruvian period, strategic restraint has guided India's policy choices. India did not use the advantage of Pakistan's abysmal defeat in 1971 war to impose its will on Kashmir over its arch enemy. In fact, some have argued that India lost a wonderful opportunity at reaching a final settlement with Pakistan on the Kashmir and other outstanding issues with the conclusion of the Shimla agreement.[6]

Another source of strategic restraint has been located in India's cultural attributes. The most relevant study in this regard is George Tanham's work on India's strategic culture.[7] According to Tanham, India's indecisiveness regarding use of force emanates from a culturally systematized lack of strategic thinking where the mysticism and otherworldliness of Hinduism has percolated in the state psyche to the effect that adhocism rules the roost when it comes to defining and attaining India's strategic interests.

Another argument which is made to explain the presence of strategic restraint, though not so strongly, is the idea that a massive democracy such as India with its labyrinth of contending bureaucracies has an inherent disadvantage in cohesively formulating strategic policies. In other words, its strategic practices are vulnerable to bureaucratic politics. This is most evident in a number of studies conducted by both Foreign and Indian scholars on civil- military relations in India.[8]

A number of scholars contend that the concept of strategic restraint has helped India's cause more often than it has been to its disadvantage. As Sunil Das Gupta and Stephen Cohen argue, strategic restraint has been particularly positive for India for two reasons.[9] First, it has helped India to avoid unnecessary conflict in the region which is already one of the most conflict-prone regions of the world. Second, and the more important of the two observations, is the fact that India's inherent restraint on use of force has made the world to welcome India's rise on the global scene. For Das Gupta and Cohen, countries lining up for selling modern military hardware to India is a case in point. Instead of China, where all the money is, most countries are more comfortable in exporting military technologies and weapons to India. In some sense, strategic restraint provides India a soft power which allows it to be more acceptable in the global community.

However, it is important to understand that strategic restraint, irrespective of the arguments mentioned earlier, emanated largely from the lack of military resources on India's part. Though most of the writings on India's strategic culture accept this fact, they tend not to emphasise this aspect adequately. This inadequacy in emphasis on the role of India's limited capabilities engenders wrong impressions of India's strategic motivations and practices. First, it conjures a picture where India is projected as a benign regional power with no ambitions of aggrandisement as well as projection of power over its neighbours. India might favour a status quo as far as territorial boundaries in the region are concerned, but it has also, from the very beginning, attempted to be the unquestionable leader in South Asia, the most aggressive formulation of which was the Indira doctrine. India has also interfered extensively in the internal matters of its smaller neighbours especially when it comes to their internal governance. In so far, a power relationship is always dependent upon how the weak perceive the powerful;[10] the idea of India being a benign power fails miserably in context of South Asia since India has often been seen as a potential threat by its smaller neighbours.

Second, irrespective of India's quest for leadership, its neighbours in South Asia have never accepted India as a regional leader.[11] Rather they often perceive India as a potential hegemon. The difference between leadership and hegemony is the idea of followership.[12] A leader has automatic followers; a hegemon forces others to follow her. If strategic restraint would really be a component of India's soft power, why the smaller states in South Asia not enamoured by it?

And lastly, it also gives credence to the spurious idea that even when India's military capabilities may rise exponentially, the idea of strategic restraint would continue to be the edifice guiding India's use of military power. Rather than axiomatically accepting the logic of strategic restraint, this should be a question of empirical testing. The most important evidence, however, which has been forwarded in defence of this argument is India's rather restrained behaviour in a number of recent crisis situations in South Asia. The most commonly cited examples of strategic restraint on India's part are the Kargil war, India's self-restraint after the attack on India's parliament and the Mumbai carnage of 2008. However, all these crisis situations actually took place under the shadow of the nuclear umbrella in the region. It is very hard to eliminate the logic of nuclear deterrence from being a factor in India's supposed restraint in using force to settle its grievances with Pakistan.

It is, therefore, important to acknowledge the fact that strategic restraint is not an immutable genetic code which constitutes Indian state's DNA. It is open to change and therefore, the idea of strategic restraint should also be open to serious analysis. It is also important to understand that state capabilities play a major role in how a particular state responds to crisis situations.[13] Capabilities are also important for another reason: they induce fear among rivals and hence, initiate conflicts and arms races.[14]

## Shifting Sands of India's Nuclear Posture

The Indian request during the Indo-Pakistan Nuclear CBM's assumed two important things. First is the assumption that having a declared nuclear doctrine makes deterrence equation stable. In that case, India has fulfilled its obligation and Pakistan has not. Second, it also conveyed an insinuation so far as India considers its nuclear doctrine to be morally justified. This superiority complex engenders from two principles that guide India's nuclear doctrine: 'Credible Minimum Deterrence' and 'No First Use' Policy.

At a closer scrutiny perhaps both these assumptions come a cropper. Declaration of nuclear intentions or doctrine does not necessarily lead to a stable deterrence equation. In fact, the stability of nuclear deterrence has no objective reference to be measured against; it is a subjective evaluation of how a nation perceives external threats and plans to tackle the same effectively.

Whereas, officially speaking, India seeks deterrence only against Weapons of Mass Destruction, Pakistan employs nuclear deterrence to achieve dissuasion of hostilities along the whole spectrum of conflict: from limited conventional war to full scale conventional and nuclear war.[15] In such a case, ambiguity concerning the possibility of nuclear use by Pakistan – India's principle complaint – buttresses

Pakistan's deterrence. Given India's preponderance in conventional weapons and its modernisation of the defence forces, it is natural for Pakistan to hide more and more under the nuclear umbrella. It is also important to remember that even India, for considerable period in its history till it openly went nuclear in 1998, achieved existential deterrence by maintaining ambiguity and uncertainty around its nuclear capability.[16]

In 1998, India declared its draft nuclear doctrine which was finalised after the CCS review in 2003.[17] CMD and NFU became the cardinal principles of India's proposed nuclear posture. In the last one decade or so, Indian nuclear doctrine has been analysed threadbare and many have concurred to the opinion that both CMD and NFU makes India's nuclear posture one of strategic restraint.[18] This perception has been further reinforced by the de-alerted and de-mated status of India's nuclear arsenal. In simple words, therefore, India is supposed to be one exhibiting an exemplary behaviour in a world where nuclear brinksmanship rules.[19]

However, such a conclusion is highly premature. Declarations aside, not much can be said about the substance of both the CMD and the NFU. At the political level, they definitely indicate India's deep abhorrence of nuclear weapons as instruments of force projection. They also symbolise India's retaliation only nuclear doctrine. However, there are some very important contradictions which abound India's nuclear doctrine.

First, it is hard in principle to prove the validity of CMD and NFU as policy formulations which really guide India's nuclear strategy rather than just being an empty rhetoric with no possible way to ascertain the validity of such propositions. India also has taken no pains to explain how these declarations will be followed in the policy realm. As far as NFU is concerned, Pakistan has never believed in India's 'retaliation only' nuclear motives as has India disbelief of China's NFU policy. Also, scholars have expressed their reservations in India holding dear to a NFU policy under the clouds of war and nuclear threats especially from China.[20] Clearly, the uncertainty in international relations makes promises such as NFU appear hollow.

Second and the bigger problem lies with the CMD. As Rajesh Basrur has argued, India's CMD consists of two elements.[21] First, it clearly indicates that at the political level India is content with nuclear minimalism: it not only perceives nuclear weapons as political entities and not weapons supposed to be used in fighting actual wars but also that deterrence can be achieved with a small nuclear arsenal. Nuclear minimalism is in turn inspired by the idea that deterrence is essentially contingent upon the risks which an enemy perceives in a nuclear confrontation. And since all nuclear confrontations are inherently high risks events, deterrence in served well even by very low numbers of nuclear weapons.

Second is the operationalisation part of India's nuclear deterrence. The emphasis over here is on the credibility of India's nuclear deterrent and the maximum attention is given to India's readiness in terms of making the others believe in its deterrent potential. The effort therefore is to strengthen India's deterrent potential by refining India's nuclear payloads (for example the debate over fission versus fusion weapons), develop robust delivery vehicles such as Intercontinental Ballistic Missiles and the Nuclear submarines and to protect India's command and control of nuclear weapons in the event of a first strike by deploying theatre ballistic missile defences, to name a few. Clearly the political aspect of nuclear deterrence does not sit comfortably with the operationalisation part of it. Whereas nuclear minimalism as a political doctrine is based on nuclear risks as perceived by the enemy, operationalisation of nuclear deterrence is primarily an exercise to demonstrate will and resolve both to the enemy as well as to the self that if need be, nuclear weapons will be used. Operationalisation of the deterrent does two things. First, it opens up the possibility for development of an open ended deterrence potential by not only giving a compelling reason to increase the number of nuclear weapons but also to develop assorted technologies such as ballistic missile defence and nuclear triads. Second, it allows scientific and military bureaucracies entrusted with operationalisation aspect of the deterrent to follow independent technological paths without directions from the political high-command.

Operationalisation aspect of India's deterrent is best served by the technological evolution argument: India will keep itself abreast with technological progress in order to increase the credibility of its deterrent.[22] The technological curve on which India's strategic scientific enclave has embarked upon should leave no one impressed with the idea of minimum deterrence any more. Technological progress is also undermining India's NFU policy given that capability wise India is slowly moving towards a first strike capability. Also, as far as NFU is concerned, Pakistan has never believed in India's NFU policy just as Indians have never believed the Chinese. With no mechanism to ascertain the NFU, national security imperatives of Pakistan will always be dictated by India's capabilities and not its intent.[23]

## The Burden of Capabilities

Take the case of India's fissile material inventories. According to an estimate by Prof. R. Rajaraman, India has more than 600 kgs of weapon grade plutonium and more than 1300 kgs of reactor grade plutonium.[24] Given that one of the nuclear devices in the 1998 tests was based on reactor grade plutonium and one warhead would use 5-7 kgs of fissile material, India sits on top of a nuclear arsenal comparable to China: something close to a capability of 300-350 nuclear warheads.

In addition, if India pulls off its FBR programme, a single breeder reactor of the kind being currently constructed at Kalpakkam would generate more than 140 Kgs of plutonium with a fissile content of more than 95 percent annually.[25] India has not officially rejected the use of Fast Breeder Reactor Programme for its strategic needs. During the tense negotiations on the Indo-US nuclear deal, the department of Atomic Energy fought tooth and nail to keep the FBR programme outside of the purview of IAEA with the chairman of the DAE Mr. Anil Kakodkar claiming that the FBR's are not only important for India's energy security but also for its strategic needs.[26]

Given that states in international relations react to capabilities and not mere declarations, CMD is a meaningless concept. To assume that Pakistan should be satisfied with India's pronouncements of minimum deterrence and neglect India's nuclear wherewithal is unlike the way international politics is played out in reality. Pakistan's callous attitude to the FMCT emanates from the threat of India's fissile material inventory and it will be extremely hard for the international community to persuade Pakistan to do otherwise.[27]

On the other hand, with the development of a robust Ballistic Missile Defence system in the pipeline, Pakistan has reasons to fear a first strike from India.[28] For India, BMD, by increasing the survivability of its nuclear arsenal in case of a first strike, will increase the credibility of assured retaliation and hence is in complete harmony with its intended nuclear doctrine.

However, for Pakistan, if India develops a working BMD system, it will feel its nuclear deterrence compromised because the later will than have an incentive to initiate a major conventional or nuclear attack with impunity. Given that BMD technology is in its infancy, such scenarios are quite far-fetched. However, since states try to respond to developing threats via their perceptions of future balances of power rather than present realities, the impact of BMD technology can be easily felt on the subcontinent's precarious nuclear balance. To off-set any dilution of its nuclear deterrence, Pakistan has drastically increased production of nuclear weapons and delivery vehicles. It is trying to develop missiles with Multiple Independently Targeted Re-entry (MIRV) technology[29] and transforming its nuclear command and control structure to suit a 'ready to use' nuclear posture.[30]

Technological achievements will also affect the de-alerted and de-mated nature of India's nuclear arsenal. The most important factor in this transition from a posture of recessed deterrence to one of active deterrence is the nuclear submarine project: the actualization of India's nuclear triad.[31] In 2009, India unveiled its first indigenously developed nuclear submarine- Arihant.[32] It is claimed that the submarine will be ready for induction by late 2013. It will carry a dozen K-15 or Sagarika submarine launched ballistic missiles (SLBM) capable of delivering nuclear weapons with a range of 700 Kms.[33] For an effective underwater deterrence, which India considers an imperative for the credibility of assured retaliation, nuclear weapons will have to be both mated with delivery vehicles as well as put in a state of constant alert. It is particularly so because without mating and alerting of weapons onboard the submarine, the idea of achieving effective deterrence by employing a nuclear triad shall remain an empty one.

Transition in deterrence postures notwithstanding, nuclear triad will also unravel a very serious inter-services rivalry between the three wings of India's defence. At present, no service wing of the India's military deals with nuclear warheads. Whereas Army and Navy control delivery vehicles in the form of surface to surface missiles and fighter aircrafts respectively, DAE controls the storage of warheads and is entitled with the mating of warheads with the delivery vehicles. In case Indian Navy gets to surpass these obstacles and comes to command both delivery vehicles and nuclear warheads, which logically it should under the nuclear triad, other services will not remain quite spectators to this grant of exclusive privilege. This will surely entail an increase in nuclear arsenals for satisfying all service wings, not to talk about the consternation which it will engender within the DAE which perceive control of nuclear warheads as essential to its importance in India's strategic scene. This scenario is not quite different from what ensued in the US military after the Second World War.

## Conclusion

It is more than obvious that the path which India has taken in the matter of strategic technologies poses serious challenge to deterrence stability in South Asia and will further aggravate the trust deficit. Under such circumstances, rather than adopting a holier than thou approach, India must understand that NFU and CMD were and are a *realpolitik* ploy. India was able to veil its doctrine in a moral garb after the 1998 nuclear tests because India's capabilities were underdeveloped. But as India leapfrogs into a different plane of strategic capability with maturing of technologies such as FBR, BMD and nuclear triad, states will increasingly observe India's actions and not its moral rhetoric.

In such a scenario, it is not very helpful to blindly believe in the doctrine of strategic restraint as guiding India's strategic thought and practice. It will also not influence its neighbours who will increasingly feel threatened by India's rising capabilities and India's declaratory policies will do little do clam their paranoia. Therefore, if there is a serious intention to build confidence with Pakistan on nuclear matters, India must look inwards to assess the role which its increasing nuclear capabilities play in destabilising the nuclear equation. For real confidence building in the nuclear sphere, India must explain the rationale of the current technological drive in India's nuclear strategy and must also understand the consequences for regional balance of power through the eyes of others specially Pakistan.

## References

1. Declare Nuclear Doctrine: India to Pak, *Indian Express,* 30 December, 2011, http://www.indianexpress.com/news/declare-ndoctrine-india-to-pak/893731/0
2. Pak Rejects India's Proposal to Declare Nuclear Doctrine, Pakistan Defence Forum, http://www.defence.pk/forums/pakistan-strategic-forces/149949-pak-rejects-indian-proposal-declare-nuclear-doctrine.html
3. India's Draft Nuclear Doctrine, http://www.armscontrol.org/act/1999_07-08/ffja99
4. Dasgupta, Sunil and Cohen, Stephen P. (2010), Arming Without Aiming: India's Militray Modernisation, The Brookings Institution Press: Washington DC, p.1; also see Sunil Dasgupta and and Cohen, Stephen P. (2011), "Is India Ending Its Strategic Restraint Doctrine", *Washington Quaterly,* 34(2): 163-177. Another scholarly piece on strategic restraint by Sunil Dasgupta recently appeared in *Current History.* See Dasgupta, Sunil (2012), "The fate of India's Strategic Doctrine", *Current History,* 111(744): 129: 35.
5. Raghavan, Srinath (2010), *War and Peace in Modern India,* Permanent Black: Ranikhet. For Nehruvian idea of international relations and strategy also see Bajpai, Kanti (2010), "India and the World", in Jayal, Niraja Gopal and Mehta, Pratap Bhanu (eds.) *The Oxford Companion to Politics in India,* Oxford University Press: New Delhi. On the idea of hegemony through a Nehruvian lense, see Bajpai, Kanti and Sahni Varun (2008), "Hegemony and Strategic Choice", in Chandra Chari (eds.) *War, Peace and Hegemony in a Globalised World: The balance of power in the twenty-first Century,* New York: Routledge.
6. Fabian, K.P. (2011), *Diplomacy: Indian Style,* HarAnand: New Delhi. Also see Karnad, Bharat (2002), *Nuclear Weapons and Indian Security: Realist Foundations of Strategy,* Macmillan: New Delhi.
7. Tanham, George (1992), *Indian Strategic Thought: An Interpretative Essay,* Rand Corporation: Santa Monica. Available at http://www.rand.org/content/dam/rand/pubs/reports/2007/R4207.pdf
8. *Ibid.*

9. Sunil Dasgupta and Cohen, Stephen P. (2011), "Is India Ending Its Strategic Restraint Doctrine", *Washington Quaterly*, 34(2): 175.
10. Berenskotter, Felix (2007), "Thinking About Power", in M.J. Williams and Felix Berenskoetter (eds.), *Power in World Politics*, London: Routledge. Also see Lukes, Stephen (1986), Power: Readings in Social and Political Theory, London: Basil Blackwell.
11. Sahni, Varun (2011), "Regional Dynamics of Emerging Powers: Power/Control or Leadership/Consent?" in E. Sridharan (ed.), International Relations Theory and South Asia: Security, Political Economy, Domestic Politics, Identities, and Images (New Delhi: Oxford University Press, 2011), pp. 56-107.
12. Destradi, Sandra (2010), Regional Powers and Their strategies: Empire, Hegemony and Leadership, Review of International Studies, 36: 903-936.
13. Mearshimer, John J. (2001), The Tragedy of Great Power Politics, New York: W.W. Norton.
14. Waltz, Kenneth (1979), *The Theory of International Politics*, Random House: New York.
15. Salik, Naeem (2010), *The Genesis of South Asian Nuclear Deterrence: Pakistan's Perspective*, Oxford University Press: New York.
16. Mattoo, Amitabh (1996), India's Nuclear Status Quo, Survival, 38(3): 45.
17. Government of India (1998), "Paper laid on the Table of the House on the Evolution of India's Nuclear Policy". Available at http://indianembassy.org/pic/nuclearpolicy.com. Also see, Government of India (2003), "Press Release of the Cabinet Committee on Security on Operationalisation of India's Nuclear Doctrine" in Gupta, Arvind, Chaturvedi, Mukul and Joshi, Akshay (eds.), Security and Diplomacy: Essential Documents, National Security Council and Manas Publications; New Delhi, 19-20.
18. Basrur, Rajesh (2006), Minimum Deterrence and India's Nuclear Security, Stanford University Press: Stanford, California. Also see, Tellis, Ashley (2006), "The Evolution of US-India Ties: Missile Defence in an Emerging Strategic Relationship", *International Security*, 30(4): 113-151.
19. Basrur, Rajesh (2001), "Nuclear Weapons and India's Strategic Culture", Journal of *Peace Research*, 38(2):181-98.
20. Salik, Naeem (2010), *The Genesis of South Asian Nuclear Deterrence: Pakistan's Perspective*, Oxford University Press: New

York. Also see, Khan, Feroze, Hassan (2012), Minimum Deterrence, "Pakistan's Dilemma", RUSI Journal, 156(5): 31.

21. Basrur, Rajesh (2012), "Low Profile Deterrence: Lessons from Indian Experience", RUSI Journal, 156(5): 24.
22. Tellis, Ashley (2001), *India's Emerging Nuclear Posture: Between Recessed Deterrent and Ready Arsenal,* RAND corporation, p. 399.
23. See Salik, *The Genesis of South Asian Nuclear deterrence*, p. 225.
24. Rajaraman, R. (2010), "India's Nuclear Arms Control Quandary", *Bulletin of Atomic Scientists,* 66(2): 27-36.
25. Ramana, M. V. and Glaser, Alexander (2007), "Weapon Grade Plutonium Production in Indian Prototype Fast Breeder Reactor", *Science and Global Security,* 15: 85-105.
26. On Fast Breeder Programme, Begin a Civil Debate, *Indian Express,* 10 February 2006 http://www.indianexpress.com/oldStory/87591./
27. Colina, Ton Z.and Horner Daniel (2011), "The South Asian Nuclear Balance: An Interview with Pakistani Ambassador to the CD Zamir Akram", *Arms Control Today,* 41. http://www.armscontrol.org/act/2011_12/Interview_With_Pakistani_Ambassador_to_the_CD_Zamir_Akram
28. Yasmin, Ghazala, "Missile Defence in South Asia: Implications for the Region", *The Institute of Strategic Studies Islamabad.* http://www.issi.org.pk/old-site/ss_Detail.php?dataId=399
29. Pakistan Builds Low Yield Nuclear Capability http://www.dawn.com/2011/05/15/pakistan-builds-low-yield-nuclear-capability-concern-grows.html
30. Ansari, Usman (2011), "Pakistan Seeks to Counter Indian ABM defences", *Defence News,* http://www.defensenews.com/story.php?i=6012501
31. Karnad, Bharath (2002), *Nuclear Weapons and Indian Security: Realist Foundations of Strategy,* Macmillan: New Delhi.
32. Panda, Rajaram (2009), "Arihant: Strengthening India's Naval Capabilities", *IPCS Issue Brief.* Available at http://www.ipcs.org/pdf_file/issue/IB115-Rajaram-Arihant.pdf
33. SSBN Arihant Class Submarine, India, Global Defence Technology. Available at http://www.naval-technology.com/projects/arihant-class./

■■■

# 7

# Nuclear Disaster Management

*Tughral Yamin*

## Introduction

The primary objective of this paper is to highlight various aspects of a nuclear disaster involving a nuclear power plant (NPP) and the need to involve the common man in preparing for it. In building up this case the author has examined the subjects of natural and manmade disasters and explained various aspects of the science and art of disaster management (DM). Although civilian nuclear disasters have been covered substantially, the effects of a nuclear weapon strike have also perfunctorily been touched upon.

Although nuclear crises caused by the use of nuclear weapons and a malfunctioning NPP overlap in a number of places, and both need different treatment, the author has deliberately left out the former for the latter.

## DM and Mismanagement

Recorded human history is replete with incidences of floods, plagues, pestilence, epidemics, droughts, fires, earthquakes and wars. Disasters of biblical proportions like the flood that engulfed the people of Prophet Noah, about 7,500 years ago, find mention in religious texts. For centuries the venerable Noah tried in vain to bring his incorrigible nation to the right path. When he reached the end of his tether, the Lord decided to drown the unrepentant from among his flock. Noah was told to construct the Ark and board it with a pair of each living species to escape the ravages of the great flood.[1] This page from history informs us that not only did the Prophet prepare for the forthcoming disaster; he planned for the life after it. Nature still provides significant warnings, which if taken seriously can substantially reduce the quantum of disaster.

Disaster is defined as "A serious disruption of the functioning of a community or a society causing widespread human, material, economic or environmental losses which exceed the ability of the affected community or society to cope using its own resources."[2] The experiences of domestic and international crisis management agencies have led to the recognition of DM as a new genre in management sciences.[3] This subject covers aspects like understanding disasters, the risks involved and the likely preparations to reduce expected losses. DM involves capacity building to mitigate the effects of a disaster. This includes preventive means to stop manmade disasters like terrorist attacks and preparatory measures in areas prone to natural calamities like earthquakes and hurricanes. The effectiveness of DM depends on the ability of the authorities to analyse potential threats and prepare contingency plans. These actions encompass the standard DM theory.[4] Risk analysis, assumes fundamental importance in reducing losses by instituting preventive and emergency measures. Risk is a combination of hazards and vulnerabilities. A hazard signifies the threat and the vulnerability and the weaknesses in the system. The degree of risk increases if anyone or both these factors are higher in proportion to the acceptable norm. The *International Strategy for Disaster Reduction* (ISDR) explains risk in the following manner:

The probability of harmful consequences, or expected losses (deaths, injuries, property, livelihoods, economic activity disrupted or environment damaged) resulting from interactions between natural or human-induced hazards and vulnerable conditions. Conventionally ***risk*** is expressed by the notation ***risk*** = Hazards x Vulnerability. Some disciplines also include the concept of exposure to refer particularly to the physical aspects of vulnerability. Beyond expressing a possibility of physical harm, it is crucial to recognise that risks are inherent or can be created or exist within social systems. It is important to consider the social contexts in which risks occur and that people therefore do not necessarily share the same perceptions of risk and their underlying causes.[5]

The quality of disaster response can be improved if DM plans and procedures are prepared on the basis of the available meteorological data and empirical evidence. An effective DM response depends on adequate preparations. This includes a slew of actions like deploying reliable warning systems, building the capacity of the rescue and relief organisations and enhancing the level of preparedness at the official and public level to handle different kinds of catastrophes. A nuclear DM response would include additional items like short term and long term decontamination measures.

## The Problems of a Standard DM Response

Each upheaval has its own peculiar dynamics and there is no one-size-fits-all solution. A number of institutionalised responses at the national and international levels have been developed to handle disasters. None of these have so far proved to be comprehensive. In spite of a number of studies and efforts to fine tune this discipline, disaster management has invariably been held hostage to personal and institutional follies and foibles. The political and bureaucratic leadership have often been found wanting in handling and managing emergencies and their personal reputations have been washed away with the flotsam and jetsam of the receding disaster. It has been rare that a head of state or his team of crisis managers has come out of a disaster unscathed. One notable exception has been that of the Chilean President Sebastian Pinera. Last year Pinera personally spearheaded the campaign to rescue the trapped coalminers and personally received each one of the 33 men, as they were hoisted to safety from the collapsed mine after 68 days.[6] In comparison the official response was muted, when more than 40 Pakistani miners lost their lives on March 20, 2011 in the Sorrange (also spelled Sorenj) coalmines near Quetta.[7] Official apathy is not unique to developing countries. It happens in the most technologically advanced nations as well. Bush administration's response to Hurricane Katrina, which struck the predominantly Black area of New Orleans in 2005, was slow and haphazard. A US congressional report declared failure at all levels i.e. "individual, corporate, philanthropic and governmental" to meet the Katrina challenge.[8] The first responders sent by the City and State administration failed to bring the situation under control and the Federal Emergency Management Agency (FEMA) did not measure up to the task given to it. In his autobiography President Bush admitted his failure in not physically visiting the disaster hit areas.[9]

DM in less developed countries is doubly difficult. The government machinery is not only hobbled by inertia at all administrative tiers, it is also hamstrung by resource scarcity. Patchy and ragged responses to human tragedies have often caused deep rooted grievances and resulted in fatal political fallouts. One natural disaster that actually hastened the dismemberment of Pakistan was cyclone Bhola that struck East Pakistan on 12 November 1970. An estimated 500,000 people lost their lives, 2000 square kilometres of land was devastated, islands disappeared and losses worth billions of dollars were reported. A country already wracked and weakened by an insurgency funded and sponsored by neighbouring India desperately needed a healing touch. This godsend opportunity was callously wasted, when President Yahya Khan on his return journey from Beijing failed to touch down in Dhaka. He merely overflew the devastated area to make a detached assessment of the losses.[10] Bhola proved to be the last nail in the coffin of a united Pakistan. The inept handling of the crisis added to the public anger against the federal government located in West Pakistan. Nearly a year and a bloody civil war later East Pakistan chose to go its own way. More recently, an independent media did not leave any stone unturned to highlight the deficiencies in the official response to the 2010 floods, which ravaged almost all parts of Pakistan. The government survived because the common man never got an opportunity to build up on his grievances, as the country reeled from one disaster to another.

## Nuclear DM

As compared to a natural disaster, a nuclear emergency caused by war or an industry related incident is far more complex to handle. A nuclear disaster has far graver implications since it involves long term radiation effects. A nuclear and radiation accident is defined by the IAEA as "an event that has led to significant consequences to people, the environment or the facility. Examples include lethal effects to individuals, large radioactivity release to the environment, or reactor core melt."[11] The likelihood and potential impact of the release of nuclear radiation in the environment has been the subject of discussion ever since the first nuclear weapon was used and the first nuclear reactor was installed. Nuclear disasters are a matter of acute public concern owing to the long term environmental and biological damages that they can cause. Nuclear DM involves a number of technical measures and special equipment to reduce the risk of radioactivity. The response involves a host of agencies like the ministries of defence, energy, interior, foreign affairs, health, food, environment etc and requires intricate coordination.

Whereas, in case of a nuclear strike on a city can cause widespread damage to the civilians and is difficult to control, the damage from an industrial accident can be localised and restricted, with proper planning. An accident at a nuclear power plant requires an onsite as well as offsite response. The first responders from law enforcement agencies, rescue and relief services and medical facilities are trained to react to within the precincts of the nuclear establishment as well as in the contiguous areas. In case the meltdown does take place and the adjoining areas are threatened, an evacuation plan has to be organised. In case the nuclear fallout spreads, neighbouring countries have to be informed. A huge decontamination exercise has to be launched to sanitise men, material and foodstuff. Areas irretrievably damaged have to be closed to human and animal entry until, in years to come, the effects of radiation wear off. For instance the crippled reactor at Chernobyl was entombed with cement dropped by helicopters and later by a steel mesh.[12] This place is off limits; it is estimated it will take nearly 20 million years to heal. At times such drastic measures are not possible, particularly in case the radiation seeps to inaccessible places like the ocean bed. In short, nuclear DM requires technical expertise beyond the scope of a standard DM response.

## A History of Nuclear Disasters

### Hiroshima and Nagasaki

Mankind was first exposed to the horrors of mass destruction caused by nuclear strikes on the Japanese cities of Hiroshima and Nagasaki in August 1945. People and property located at

Ground Zero (GZ) instantly vaporised. The casualty estimates during the first two to four months of the bombings were between 90,000–166,000 people in Hiroshima and 60,000–80,000 in Nagasaki. Roughly half of these deaths had occurred on the first day. Out of the people who died on the day of the explosion, 60 per cent died from flash or flame burns, 30 per cent from falling debris and 10 per cent from other causes. During the following months, large numbers died from the effect of burns, radiation sickness and other injuries, compounded by illness. Out of the total immediate and short term causes of death, 15–20 per cent died from radiation sickness, 20–30 per cent from flash burns, and 50–60 per cent from other injuries, compounded by illness. In both cities, most of the dead were civilians.[13]

Since 1945, there has been no further employment of atomic weapons but accidents have taken place in the military and civilian applications of nuclear technology, severely endangering and in certain cases destroying life and property, and causing immense environmental damage. Emergencies at nuclear power plants (NPPs) have attracted wide media attention. NPPs are vulnerable because they hold huge amounts of explosive inventory on their premises, comprising nuclear cores and spent fuel e.g. the six reactor cores at the Fukushima Daiichi held 487 tonnes of uranium. Of this 95 tonnes included 230 kg of plutonium, from MOX (mixed oxide fuel contains plutonium blended with natural, reprocessed or depleted uranium) assemblies,with a further 1,838 tonnes of spent fuel, including 1,838 tonnes stored in the central pool store.[14] An accident at an NPP can cause extensive leaks of radioactivity. The extent of a nuclear and radiological disaster is measured on the scale of International Nuclear and Radiological Events or INES ranging from 0 to 7. The worst disasters at INES 7 or near about have taken place in Three Mile Island (TMI), USA (1979), Chernobyl, former USSR (1986) and Fukushima, Japan, (2011).[15] The first two of these accidents occurred because of design flaws, human error and poor safety regulations. None was caused by a natural disaster before Fukushima. DM techniques played a role in aggravating or lessening the consequences of the disaster. Major nuclear crises are summed up as follows:

## Three Mile Island (TMI)

A 'serious accident' took place at TMI-2 in Middleton Pennsylvania on March 28, 1979.[16] It began with a fairly common steam power plant failure–the loss of feed water to the generator. A "combination of design, training, regulatory policies, mechanical failures and human error," took it to a point, where "it eventually produced the worst known core damage in large scale nuclear power reactors" till that time.[17] As the steam generators stopped removing heat, the turbine and then the reactor automatically shut down and the pressure in the nuclear portion of the plant began to increase. The pilotoperated relief valve, located at the top of the pressurizer, was opened to let off excess pressure but became stuck and did not close down. As a result, cooling water poured out of the stuck-open valve, causing the core of the reactor to overheat. As the coolant flowed from the core through the pressuriser, the instruments failed to give the level of coolant in the core. Since the level of water in the pressuriser was high, it was assumed that the core was covered with coolant. When the alarms sounded and warning lights flashed, it was not related to the loss-of-coolant accident. Instead a series of actions were taken that made matters worse like reducing the flow of coolant through the core. Since adequate cooling was no longer available, the nuclear fuel overheated leading to a meltdown. About half the core melted during the early stages of the accident. Fortunately, the walls of the containment building were not breached and radiation was not released into the environment. Although caught off guard, the plant managers took immediate steps to regain control of the reactor and ensure adequate cooling to the core. Inspectors were dispatched to the site and response teams were mobilised. Helicopters collected radioactive traces from the atmosphere and a ground team assisted in radiation monitoring. The White House was notified and all non-essential staff was ordered off the plant's premises. By the evening of March 28, the core appeared to have cooled and the reactor seemed stable. On the morning of March 30, there was a significant release of radiation from the plant's auxiliary building, as pressure was relieved from the primary system to avoid curtailing the flow of coolant to the core. In an atmosphere of growing uncertainty, expectant mothers and infants within a 5 mile radius of the plant were evacuated. The presence of a large hydrogen bubble in the dome of the pressure vessel that holds the reactor core, stirred worries that it might burn or even explode, breaching the containment building. The crisis ended on April 1, when it was determined that the bubble could not burn or explode because of the absence of oxygen in the pressure vessel. There was no reported loss to life but it did shake public confidence in nuclear reactors and led to the closure of the TMI Plant. The reactor industry was dealt a deathblow, as no more nuclear reactors were manufactured in the US after 1979.

Post incident inquiries revealed a combination of personnel error, design deficiencies, and component failures.[18] The Presidential Commission blamed everyone but primarily blamed the operators.[19] In Charles Perrow's opinion normal or system's accident in an industry take place because of multiple failures in six areas collectively identified as Design, Equipment, Procedures, Operators, Supplies and Materials and Environment (DEPOSE). These areas are either dependent or *tightly coupled,* or independent or *loosely coupled* but each has a bearing on each other.[20] This theory indicates that precautions have to be taken in all areas to prevent a domino effect overwhelming all response options.

## Chernobyl

One of the worst nuclear incidents took place at Chernobyl in Ukraine (former USSR) in April 1986. Massive release of heat and radiation caused death and high degree of exposure among the operators and the rescue and clean-up staff. It also left major environmental scars. One of the survivors blamed it primarily on human error and to a lesser extent on technology.[21] Others held the flawed reactor design accountable for the accident. The Chernobyl NPP had four RBMK-1000 design reactors – two units had been constructed between 1970 and 1977, while two more were completed in 1983. Another set of two RBMK reactors was under construction at the time of the accident. An artificial lake was constructed to provide cooling water for the reactors. The RBMK-1000 is a 'boiling light water reactor,' in which, the reactor core creates heat, producing a steam-water mixture. When very pure water (reactor coolant) moves upward through the core absorbing heat, the steam-water mixture leaves the top of the core and enters the two stages of moisture separation, where water droplets are removed before the steam is allowed to enter the steam line. The steam line directs the steam to the main turbine causing it to turn the turbine generator, which produces electricity. The unused steam is exhausted to the condenser, where it is condensed into water. The resulting water is pumped out of the condenser with a series of pumps, reheated, and pumped back to the reactor vessel. The reactor's core contains fuel assemblies which are cooled by water, which is force-circulated by electrically powered pumps. Emergency cooling water is supplied by other pumps, which can be powered by onsite diesel generators. Other safety systems, such as the containment cooling system, also need electric power.[22] One of the most important characteristics of an RBMK reactor is that it can possess a 'positive void coefficient,' where an increase in steam bubbles or 'voids' is accompanied by an increase in core reactivity. As steam production in the fuel channels increases, the neutrons that would have been absorbed by the denser water now produce increased fission in the fuel. There are other components that contribute to the overall power coefficient of reactivity, but the void coefficient is the dominant one in RBMK reactors. The void coefficient depends on the composition of the core. A new RBMK core will have a negative void coefficient. At the time of the accident at Chernoby 1-4, the reactor's fuel burn-up, control rod configuration and power level led to a positive void coefficient large enough to overwhelm all other influences on the power coefficient. On 25 April, prior to a routine shutdown, the reactor crew at Chernoby 1-4 began preparing for a test to determine how long turbines would spin and supply power to the main circulating pumps following a loss of main electrical power supply. This test had been carried out the previous year, but the power from the turbine ran down too rapidly, so new voltage regulator designs were to be tested. A series of operator actions, including the disabling of automatic shutdown mechanisms, preceded the attempted test. By the time that the operator moved to shut down the reactor, the reactor was in an extremely unstable condition. A peculiarity of the control rods' design caused a dramatic power surge as they were inserted into the reactor. The interaction of very hot fuel with the cooling water led to fuel fragmentation along with rapid steam production and an increase in pressure resulting in the destruction of the reactor. The overpressure caused the cover plate of the reactor to partially detach, rupturing the fuel channels and jamming all the control rods, which were only halfway down at that time. Intense steam generation then spread throughout the whole core causing a steam explosion and releasing fission products to the atmosphere. About two to three seconds later, a second explosion threw out fragments from the fuel channels and hot graphite.[23]

Chernobyl was a terrible blow to the nuclear industry and is considered among the worst incident involving nuclear reactors. It directly or indirectly affected a number of European countries. Angela Liberatore in her book *In the Management of Uncertainty: Learning from Chernobyl,* undertook a study of how different countries interpreted the incident in the light of their national interests, and why they adopted nuclear risk management procedures to suit their own convenience. This comparative analysis included short-term responses and long-term consequences of Chernobyl in the neighbouring countries of France, Italy and Germany and the European Union's regional approach in managing transnational risks. The policy communication model developed by Liberatore illustrated the interaction among scientists, who choose what was 'relevant' knowledge; politicians, who decided how much they want to know (and what they let the public know); social movements and interest groups, which push to utilise and disseminate knowledge; and the mass media, which accesses and selects information to be broadcast as 'news.' Liberatore's comparative focus upon 'uncertainty management' provides a practical framework for the practical management of transboundary environmental risks.[24] Keeping Liberatore's thesis in mind, it is interesting to note, how countries and organisations reacted in the aftermath of the Fukushima incident (discussed later in this paper). For instance, while the commercial nuclear lobby downplayed its negative fallouts, the German government decided to say goodbye to this form of energy by 2022.[25]

## Tokaimura

In Asia, Japan is one country, which is inherently prone to natural disasters like earthquakes and tsunamis. Its position is further complicated because it fulfils one third of its energy needs through NPPs. It has a total of 18 power plants, housing

55 nuclear reactors. Thirteen of these reactors are located on the coastline. Some of these power plants are located in seismically active zones. The Japanese have experienced incidents at their NPPs and have devised elaborate strategies to handle such emergencies. In September 1999, an accident took place at a nuclear fuel processing service firm at Tokaimura, 125 km northeast of Tokyo in Ibaraki Prefecture, when workers handling uranium provoked the release of high levels of radiation from the plant. It was level 4 on the INES scale, but many rated it at level-5. An earlier nuclear disaster in Japan, rated at level-3, had taken place in 1997 at a nuclear fuel reprocessing plant, also in Tokaimura. The Tokaimura disaster raised questions about the flaws in the nuclear DM system. In June 2000, Japan's Special Measures Law for Nuclear Accidents took effect, which required the government to conduct a comprehensive drill every year. After this incident Japan considered additional measures to reform its nuclear safety policy.[26] Japanese regulators are certainly aware of the danger of earthquakes and they take safety extremely seriously. Like other buildings in Japan, nuclear reactors are also able to withstand earthquakes. The problem arises when the earthquake is bigger than the design capacity. This problem was highlighted by the earthquake that centred near the Kashiwazaki-Kariwa NPP in 2007. The earth movements generated by that quake were larger than the plant's design limit. Fortunately, the safety systems worked as designed in spite of the quake's physical impact. Before the plant reopened, new safety features were added to ensure that it was capable of withstanding bigger earthquakes.

## Fukushima

Fukushima superseded Chernobyl as the worst nuclear accident in recent times. On Friday, March 11, 2011, a force 8.9 earthquake triggered a giant tsunami on the north eastern coast of Japan. This double disaster crippled the Fukushima-

Daiichi power plant. It resulted in "hydrogen explosions, fires, partial melting of irradiated or 'spent' fuel in the reactors, the uncovering and possible burning of irradiated fuel in spent fuel ponds at reactor 4 and perhaps other reactors."[27] As a safety measure, seven out of ten operating reactors shut down automatically after the shocks but the radioactive fission products in the reactor's uranium fuel continued to generate heat. The cooling systems malfunctioned because the external power supply had been disrupted due to the quake and the backup generators located in the basement were inundated by the tsunami waters. There was no way to remove decay heat from the reactors' radioactive fuel, resulting in a meltdown. As an emergency measure seawater was pumped in to cool the reactors. Helicopters and fire tenders were also pressed into service to douse the inferno. Immense quantities of contaminated water eventually flooded the tunnels. Weeks later, 11,500 tons of water contaminated with low levels of radiation flowed into the sea.[28] As the crisis developed a number of hydrogen explosions took place. The explosion in the Unit 2 reactor and the fire in the spent fuel pond in the reactor building for Unit 4 raised the level of the INES scale to its maximum limit of 7, signifying large scale release of radioactive material, with widespread health and environmental effects. Although officials of the Japanese Nuclear Safety Commission stressed that it was only one-tenth of the Chernobyl accident,[29] an official of the Tokyo Electric Power Company (Tepco) admitted that "radiation leak could eventually top that of the Ukranian disaster." The effects of radioactivity could have been greater had the westerly winds blown the radioactive plume out to sea, making a landfall on the US west coast.[30] Nonetheless there were reports of high radioactivity in foodstuff and tap water in the local area.[31] Five villages around the Plant have become un-liveable and the residents have left the area for good.[32] It will take a long time before the exact damage from Fukushima could be determined but for now critics blame vested interests in giving the 40 year old plant a ten year extension prior to the disaster.[33] It has also been pointed out that low paid contract employees comprising 88 per cent of the total nuclear work force and 89 per cent of the 10,303 workers employed at the Fukushima were ill trained and poorly equipped to handle radioactive material.[34]

The Fukushima incident has triggered global panic. The Obama administration has asked for $1.9 billion in fiscal year 2012 for nuclear security programmes,[35] and many countries involved in producing electricity from NPPs ordered safety reviews. It also renewed demands by anti-nuclear lobbyists for a closure of the nuclear industry.[36]

## India's Nuclear DM Capability

India has an ambitious plan to produce electricity through nuclear energy. Currently it is operating 20 NPPs and two boiling water reactors similar to the crippled Japanese reactors. Six units at two of these plants are at tsunami risk. A month after the Fukushima incident, the chairman of the state run Nuclear Power Corporation Sheryans K. Jain, declared that inspectors had found the structures of the Indian NPPs adequate to handle severe natural events like earthquakes and tsunamis.[37] Although India had suffered a monumental industrial disaster, when poisonous chemicals leaked from the Union Carbide plant in Bhopal killing thousands of people in 1984, serious observers are of the opinion that Indian NDMA is ill prepared to handle nuclear and radiological incidents. The organisation is said to lack resources and trained manpower, to save people living close to NPPs in case of an explosion or meltdown. Maj. Gen. (retd) J.K. Bansal, head of the nuclear disaster management group of the Indian NDMA, has countered such criticism by contending that his organisation was fully prepared to handle any situation and that there was no cause for worry. He elaborated that well trained and well equipped disaster response teams, located at 12 points in the country, could quickly reach any plant and control the situation as per nuclear disaster guidelines - prepared by core group of atomic energy, defence research, security and health personnel, assembled at a nuclear disaster management workshop in May 2006. The guidelines cover scenarios ranging from accidents at nuclear power plants to 'dirty bomb' attacks in cities. Critics were, however, quick to point out that NDMA workers checking travellers returning from Japan were not donning hazmat suits and were operating in their usual khaki uniforms with last-minute addition of gloves and face masks.[38] Indian nuclear security managers were also found wanting in an earlier incident, when highly radioactive cobalt 60 disappeared from Delhi University's chemistry department in 2010 and found its way into a scrap shop in Delhi's Mayapuri area. Before officials from the NDMA and the Bhabha Atomic Research Centre (BARC) could unravel the mystery and remove the toxic material from the junk market, 10 people had been contaminated and one had died.[39] It has been surmised that if monitors could not prevent cobalt 60 to reach scrap dealers, they could hardly address larger issues like managing food and water supply in a radioactive environment. It has also been pointed out that during a recent drill at the Kalpakkam NPP, walkie-talkies were not in working order and the transport system was in a mess.[40] India's first brush with nuclear disaster took place in March 1993, when a fire caused a blackout at the Narora NPP.[41] Researchers at the American University have calculated at least 124 'hazardous incidents' at Indian NPPs between 1993 and 1995.[42] In September 1986, operators had discovered the presence of radioactive iodine at more than 700 times normal levels at the Tarapur Atomic Power Station (TAPS). An estimated 3000 workers were exposed to 'very high' and "hazardous" radiation levels before the leak was discovered and TAPS was shut down for year-long repairs.[43] In 2004, tidal waves of the Asian tsunami had entered the Kalpakkum power plant located off the coast of Chennai. Official press releases downplayed the incident by claiming that no damage had been done.[44] India has eight nuclear reactors in the southern state of Tamil Nadu and plans to set up another 3 plants by 2015. This puts 20 million Sri Lankans located right next door at extreme nuclear risk. After the Fukushima incident the Sri Lankan government decided to sign a memorandum of understanding (MOU) with the Indian government as a cautionary step against possible nuclear accidents. The Sri Lankan worries are exacerbated by the fact that it was also hit by tsunami on 26 December 2004, when a massive tidal wave hit the coastal belt of the island nation killing thousands of people.[45] India's poor nuclear safety record is indeed worrisome for its neighbours. A well known atomic scientist, P. Balram, actually advised the Indian government to temporarily shut down all NPPs for a thorough safety review. He warned that a nuclear disaster could affect neighbouring countries. His advice has obviously fallen on deaf ears.[46] There have also been public protests against NPPs. Plans to construct the world's biggest NPP – the Jaitpur Nuclear Power Project – on the western coast in the Konkan region, 400 km from Mumbai, by the French company Areva, has been opposed by local fishermen and farmers. Local residents worry that nuclear effluence would contaminate fish, prawns and squid and damage the famous Alphonso mango crop. Violent protests and police retaliation left at least one person dead from among the mainly Muslim fishing community.[47] Nuclear problems in the neighbouring country should also be cause of concern for Pakistan.

## Pakistan's Nuclear DM Capacity

There has been limited debate in the local media on nuclear safety in Pakistan after the Fukushima incident. One opinion piece co-authored by disarmament advocates within the Indian and Pakistani scientific communities cautioned the South Asian nuclear establishments in generic terms about the susceptibility of their atomic reactors to natural disasters, human errors, design failures and poor safety standards.[48] Another op-ed article by a local nuclear physicist, well known for his anti-nuclear sentiments decried the country's capacity to handle a Fukushima type of disaster. It highlighted the Karachi Nuclear Power Plant (KANNUP)'s vulnerability to "sabotage, terrorist attack, equipment failure, earthquake, or a tsunami" and warned that the direction of the sea breeze could put the population of Karachi at risk of widespread radioactive fallout.[49] One reader disagreed with this assessment and called it scaremongering. He reasoned that KANUPP was safely located on a rock 12 metres above the sea surrounding it, and was, therefore, well above the three-metre-high tsunami waves that hit Karachi coast in 1945. He also argued that Pakistani reactors were "designed to withstand earthquakes of a very high magnitude, as much as 9 on the Richter scale."[50] Another article by a well known economist suggested that Pakistan should go for safer reactor designs.[51] One letter to the editor warned against importing radioactivity contaminated Japanese cars and car kits, and exposing the domestic airline crews to resident radioactivity in Japan.[52] A radio report highlighted the apprehensions of the local labour and fishermen from hazards posed by the NPPs. The Karachi based Pakistan Institute of Labour Education and Research (PILER) and the Pakistan Fisher Folks Forum in a joint letter addressed to the PAEC demanded that all NPPs in Pakistan be shut down and the nuclear fuel located at these sites shifted from the vicinity of human habitation and water sources. They also lamented the fact that the PAEC website has not provided any safety instructions, after the Japanese nuclear disaster.[53]

To be fair Pakistan's small nuclear industry, operating under state controls and IAEA safeguards, has done reasonably well and its safety record for 38 years of nuclear operations has been quite satisfactory. Although former Chairman PAEC, Dr I.H. Usmani, had unveiled plans to establish at least three NPPs in 1961, at Karachi, Lyallpur (now Faisalabad) and in East Pakistan in 1961,[54] Pakistan could only establish two NPPs. These produce only 462 MW, which accounts for merely 2.15 per cent of the country's total electricity production. KANUPP's small (137 MW) Canadian pressurised heavy water reactor (PHWR) became operational in 1972 but faced immediate problems like non-availability of fuel and spare parts as a consequence of the Indian nuclear explosion in 1974. Resultantly it was forced to operate below its capacity. After the first thirty years of operation, the plant life was assessed to be actually 11 years and it was given an extension of another 30 years in 2002.[55] Two questions have been raised about the safety of KANUPP: One is its susceptibility to a tsunami generated by an earthquake in the Arabian Sea and two, its location near a major city. Although KANUPP was located away from the populated areas, due to rampant urbanisation, more than 8 million people now live in its vicinity.56 The Geological Survey of Pakistan (GSP) places Karachi in Zone-3 on its hazard map. The sub-surface geology indicates the junction of three tectonic plates i.e. the Indian, Arabian and Eurasian, about 40 km away from Karachi.[57] The real threat of tsunami to the Pakistani coastal cities is an earthquake in the Makran Subduction Zone (MSZ).[58] Out of the 50 earthquakes of magnitude 8 and above that struck the Pakistani coastline during the past 75 years, only four (1919, 1943, 1945, and 1956) were accompanied by tsunamis. The 1945 tsunami did damage the Manora lighthouse and killed more than 4,000 people but its main area of impact was Ormara. According to a meteorologist an earthquake of the magnitude of 8.5 on the Richter scale in the MSZ can unleash tsunami waves of 5 metres height in Ormara, 3.5 metres in Gwadar, 4.3 metres in Pasni and only 0.75 metres in Karachi within 21 to 33 minutes.[59] In such an eventuality those who will bear the brunt of the tsunami would be the coastline communities.[60] Environmentalists contend that growing mangroves in the coastal regions can lessen the effects of a tsunami.[61] The possibility of an earthquake or a combination of an earthquake and tsunami hitting Karachi and damaging KANUPP is not as strong as Fukushima, which was located between two fault lines. However, one lesson that can be learnt from the disaster is to move the population centres away from the close vicinity of NPPs. The Japanese authorities are seriously considering plans to change the trend of concentrating the administrative and business functions in heavily populated areas like Tokyo.[62]

CHASNUPP Unit 1 and 2 are located near Mianwali, far away from high density urban centres. CHASNUPP-1, which started up in May 2000 under international safeguards, operates a 325 MWe (300 MWe net) Chinese pressurised water reactor (PWR). Construction of Chashma-2 started in December 2005 and grid connection is expected this year. Pakistan faces an acute energy shortfall to the tune of 5000 MW. Under its Energy Security Plan, the Government of Pakistan plans to increase electricity production to 8,800 MW by 2030 from all sources including nuclear energy. For this reason site evaluation for new NPP projects is under progress.[63] In order to ensure that Pakistan is not found wanting in its nuclear safety processes, after the Fukushima incident, Pakistan Atomic Energy Commission (PAEC), the utility company running the state owned NPPs, conducted a safety review.[64] After the review, the PAEC declared its NPPs safe against the impact of natural disasters. The Commission stressed that safety had been reviewed by experts from the International Atomic Energy Agency (IAEA) and the World

Association of Nuclear Operators (WANO),[65] and there were no operational problems at any of its nuclear plants.

There is a clear division of labour regarding onsite and offsite management of nuclear emergencies.[66] As per the Pakistan Nuclear Regulatory Authority (PNRA) ordinance, the safety and security of all civil nuclear installations including the NPPs falls under its purview.[67] In order to prevent an accident and the pilferage of radioactive materials it regularly audits the country's medical, agricultural and power generation facilities. It has undertaken various initiatives to improve nuclear safety. It works closely with the IAEA and implements the latest techniques in its operations. Pakistan is a signatory to the Convention on Nuclear Safety (CNS) since 1994. The Convention was ratified in 1997. This obligates Pakistan to maintain appropriate safety standards at all its NPPs. The "Regulations on Management of Nuclear Accident or Radiological Emergency," (PAK/914) was promulgated in 2008. This was followed by KANUPP's offsite nuclear emergency response plan (KOFREP). In 2008 and 2009, C-1 and K-1 carried out exercises to test their onsite emergency responses, which were evaluated by PNRA. The KOFREP was practised in June 2010, involving the Provincial Disaster Management Agency (PDMA), city government, district health authorities, local police etc. The National Radiation Emergency Coordination Centre (NRECC) also regularly participates in international emergency exercises such as Convex conducted by the IAEA.[68]

Once the nuclear disaster extends beyond the limits of the NPPs, it technically becomes the responsibility of the NDMA. Paragraph 1 of the NDMA's National Disaster Response Plan (NDRP) circa March 2010 covers nuclear and radiological incidents. It also includes wars as the cause of a disaster. One can infer that it includes nuclear wars as well.[69] Another document, the National Disaster Risk Management categorises Chemical, Nuclear & Radiological (CNR) accidents as 'human induced.' This gives an impression that a natural catastrophe triggering a nuclear disaster has not been included in the risk calculus.[70] Typically the response to an accident at a power plant could unfold as follows: Soon after the incidence of a nuclear emergency, the operators from PAEC would raise the alarm triggering a response from the PNRA. Trained staff would activate well rehearsed emergency measures to prevent a meltdown and radiological leaks. Reports from government agencies, media and the PDMA would prompt the NDMA to activate a national response in areas likely to be affected by radiological contamination. Distress calls would be made to all principal decision makers and stakeholders. This would include the political and administrative machinery, including the secretariats of the PM, the President, and the strategic ministries. Requests would be made for requisitioning the services of the defence forces, civil defence, police, rescue and relief organisations, foreign governments, international organisations, NGOs, medical teams, food supply managers etc to launch an elaborate rescue and relief operation. First responders including fire fighting units and rescue teams would be rushed to recover the victims from under the rubble and put out the fires. The district administration would be alerted to begin evacuation of the local populace from radioactive hotspots. Transport would be commandeered and police deployed to manage the exodus, from around GZ. Radiation levels would be determined and necessary advisories issued regarding taking appropriate protective measures. The services of the state and private media and loudspeakers of mosques would be used to inform the public about relocation plans. Decontamination measures to disinfect the people and material would be executed. The response trajectory would obviously depend upon the preparedness levels of the government, the federal and provincial DM agencies, the first responders and the public at large. If the common man has not been trained for an emergency, the overall response would be marred by panic and chaos. At the moment the citizenry is not trained to respond to disasters in general and nuclear disasters in particular. The individual reaction to a disaster is instinctive. In case of an earthquake, people rush outdoors. In case of floods, there is a tendency to move to higher ground but there is absolutely no awareness of what to do in case of a nuclear accident or attack. Radioactivity adds a whole new dimension to a disaster. In a nuclear emergency, the shelters or safe zones must be free of radioactive contamination before people occupy these. Food and water will not be issued before it has been declared safe for human consumption. To avoid disorder and to minimise fear and uncertainty, public must be trained to react in an organised manner. The common man should be made part of the disaster management and not merely remain a bewildered spectator, to events as they unfold. There is growing realisation that no public awareness programme has materialised so far.[71] This can be done, systematically by preparing those at high risk i.e. those located near nuclear installations or likely nuclear targets. The public should be encouraged to know the following aspects of the nuclear disaster plan:

- Individual and collective safety measures for nuclear emergencies caused by wars, sabotage or natural calamities like earthquakes or tsunamis;
- Alarm systems and alarm levels;
- Announcement of radioactivity levels;
- Rescue & Evacuation plans;
- Location of Nuclear shelters;
- Availability of hazmat suits;
- Food and water supply in radioactive zones;
- Decontamination plans.

Important information from this list should be placed on the NDMA website and other public service domains. Officials at the NDMA point out that the NBC Policy and Nuclear Emergency Response Plan (NERP) is under formulation in coordination with the PNRA, PAEC and SPD and would be shared when complete.[72] While the agencies concerned fashion out a holistic plan, it is suggested that public awareness should be enhanced by:

- Running a public awareness campaign about nuclear safety precautions on the media;
- Organising nuclear safety days at schools and work places;
- Organising seminars in public and private organisations;
- Holding periodic tabletop exercises and physical drills involving the public as well as all the rescue and relief agencies;
- Running short courses for public representatives and local leaders for handling nuclear emergencies within their own constituencies.

## Conclusion

DM is not a knee jerk reaction to a problem. It requires serious thinking and planning and is a deliberate process. Nuclear DM requires technical knowhow, equipment and preparation. The first step in DM planning of any kind involves identifying the exact nature of hazard, which can cause injury, damage or loss of life and property, disrupt social and economic activity and environmental degradation.[73] The next step is making a detailed disaster risk assessment of the vulnerability of the life, property and livelihood of people located in potentially hazardous zones. This involves "a review of both the technical features of hazards such as their location, intensity, frequency and probability; and also the analysis of the physical, social, economic and environmental dimensions of vulnerability and exposure, while taking particular account of the coping capabilities pertinent to the risk scenarios."[74] The risk scenarios are akin to what are known in the military as the enemy hypotheses. Based on these scenarios, a number of response contingencies are developed. These plans are then disseminated to the rescue and relief agencies and shared with the people likely to be at the centre of this storm.

Public awareness and public information can play an important role in actually reducing the effects of a disaster. The former involves "the processes of informing the general population, increasing levels of consciousness about risks and how people can act to reduce their exposure to hazards. This is particularly important for public officials in fulfilling their responsibilities to save lives and property in the event of a disaster." Public awareness activities can create a culture of risk reduction. This can be engendered through public information, dissemination, education, radio or television broadcasts, use of printed media, as well as, the establishment of information centres and networks and community and participatory actions.[75] The latter involves public dissemination of available "information, facts and knowledge provided or learned as a result of research or study."[76] Nuclear disaster is perhaps the most difficult crisis to handle. It must be based on the available best practices. It needs not only to enhance safety at the NPPs but also prepare the people for the worst case scenarios. The involvement of the common man in the nuclear DM response can prove critical to its success.

## References

1. "Chapter: Hood, Verses 31-49," *The Holy Quran*.
2. "Disaster, Terminology: Basic terms of Disaster Risk Reduction," *International Strategy for Disaster Reduction* (ISDR), http://www.unisdr.org/eng/library/lib-terminologyeng% 20home.htm (accessed March 27, 2011).

3. Mansoor Raza, "Accountability in Disaster," *Dawn*, April 13, 2011.
4. "Disaster Management Theories," *Kobenhavnas Universitet*, www.ku.dk/disaster_management (accessed March 30, 2011).
5. "Risk, Terminology: Basic terms of Disaster Risk Reduction," *International Strategy for Disaster Reduction* (ISDR),http://www.unisdr.org/eng/library/lib-terminology-eng%20home.htm (accessed March 27, 2011).
6. Alexei Barrionuevo and Simon Romero, "Trapped 68 Days, First Chilean Miners Taste Freedom," *New York Times,* October 12, 2010,www.nytimes.com/2010/10/13/world/americas/13chile.html (accessed March 23, 2010).
7. "19 Die in Sorenj Mine Blast, 42 Miners Trapped Inside," *News*, March 21, 2011.
8. "Homeland Security Report: Katrina Response a Failure of Leadership," *CNN Politics,* February 14, 2006, http://articles.cnn.com/2006-02-13/politics/katrina.congress_1_katrina-response-national-emergency-management-associationhomeland-security?_s = PM:POLITICS (accessed March 23, 2011).
9. George W. Bush, *Decision Points* (US: Random House Group, 2010), 310-331.
10. Kamal Matinuddin, *Tragedy of Errors: East Pakistan crisis, 1968-1971* (Lahore: Wajidalis Pvt. Ltd., 1994), 147-48.
11. "Ines – The International Nuclear and Radiological Event Scale User's Manual, 2008 Edition," *LAEA*, Vienna,www-pub.iaea.org/MTCD/publications/PDF/INES-2009_web.pdf (accessed June 14, 2011).
12. K. Samwell, Chernobyl Re-entombed in Steel, Techgage, September 20, 2007, techgage.com/news/chernobyl_re-entombed_in_steel (accessed June 14, 2011).
13. Special Report, 6 August, 1947, "Atomic Bombing of Hiroshima and Nagasaki," *Geo436,* http://www.geo436.com/special-report-6-august-1947-atomic-bombingsof-hiroshima-and-nagasaki/ (accessed March 22, 2011).
14. Paul Dorfman, "Who to Trust on Nuclear," *Dawn,* April 16, 2011.
15. David Teeghman, "Top 5 Worst Nuclear Disasters," *Discovery News,*news.discovery.com (accessed March 23, 2011).

16. John G. Kemeny, *Report of the President's Commission on the Accident at Three Mile Island–The Need for Change: The Legacy of TMI* (Washington DC: Permagon Press, 1979), 2.
17. L. M. Toth, A. P. Malinauskas, G. R. Eidam, & H. M. Burton (eds.), *The Three Mile Island: Diagnosis and Prognosis* (Washington: American Chemical Society, 1986), 2.
18. "Backgrounder on the Three Mile Island Accident," *US NRC*,http://www.nrc.gov/reading-rm/doc-collections/fact-sheets/3mile-isle.html (accessed March 17, 2011).
19. Charles Perrow, *Normal Accidents: Living with High-Risk Technologies* (New Jersey:Princeton University Press, 1999), 7.
20. *Ibid.*, 8.
21. Bernice Han, "Chernobyl Survivor Still Backs Nuclear Energy," *Dawn*, April 18, 2011.
22. "Boiling Water Reactors," *Independent Statistics and Analysis*,www.eia.doe.gov/cneaf/nuclear/page/nuc_reactors/bwr.html (accessed on March 23, 2011).
23. Zhores A. Medvedev, *The Legacy of Chernobyl* (Oxford: Basil Blackwell Ltd.,1990), 26-36.
24. Angela Liberatore, *The Management of Uncertainty: Learning from Chernobyl* (The Netherlands; Gordon & Breach Publishers, 1999).
25. Annika Breidthart, "German Government Wants Nuclear Exit by 2022 at Latest," *Reuters*, May 31, 2011, http://www.reuters.com/article/2011/05/31/us-germanynuclear-idUSTRE74Q2P120110531 (accessed June 14, 2011).
26. "Tokaimura Nuclear Disaster," *Book Rags*, http://www.bookrags.com/research/tokaimura-nuclear-disaster-ema-05/(accessed March 17, 2011).
27. David Albright, Paul Brannan, and Christina Walrond, "Fukushima Crisis: A Chronology: Preliminary Assessment of Accident Sequences and PotentialAtmospheric Radiation Releases," *Institute for Science & International Security* (ISIS), March 31, 2011, isis-online.org/isis-reports/detail/fukushima-crisis-a-chronology/(accessed April 1, 2011).
28. Hiroko Tabuchi and Ken Belson, "Japan Releases Low-Level Radio-Active Water into Ocean," *New York Times*, April 4, 2011, www.nytimes.com/2011/04/05/world/asia/05japan.html (accessed April 5, 2011).

29. "Japan N-emergency at Maximum Level," *Dawn*, April 13, 2011.
30. Ian Sample, "Radiation from Fukushima Spreads, But the Threat to the Rest of the World is Low," *Guardian*, April 12, 2011, www.guardian.co.uk/profile/iansample (accessed April 14, 2011).
31. "Fukushima Nuclear Accident Update Log," *International Atomic Energy* Agency, www.iaea.org/newscenter/news /tsunamiup date01.html (accessed March 22, 2011).
32. Ian Sample, "Radiation from Fukushima Spreads."
33. Hiroko Tabuchi, Norimitsu Onishi and Ken Belson, "Japan Extended Reactor's Life, Despite Warning," *New York Times*, March 21, 2011, www.nytimes.com/2011/03/22/world/asia /22nuclear. html (accessed March 23, 2011).
34. Hiroko Tabuchi, "Japanese Workers Braved Radiations for a Temp Job," *New York Times*, April 9, 2011, www.nytimes.com/2011/04/ 10/world/asia/10workers.html (accessed April 11, 2011).
35. Toby Dalton, "Nuclear Security after Fukushima," *Carnegie Endowment for Peace*, April 13, 2011, carnegieendowment.org/ publications/index.cfm?fa = view&id = 43591(accessed April 15, 2011).
36. "Thousands March Against Nuclear Power in Japan," *Dawn*, April 25, 2011.
37. "India Increases Safety Measures at N-plants," *Dawn*, April 15, 2011.
38. Shobhan Saxena, "How not to Prepare for a Nuclear Crisis," *Economic Times*, March 20, 2011, m.economictimes.com/PDAET/ articleshow/7746907.cms (accessed March 21, 2011).
39. J. M. C. Keati, "Greenpeace Finds Radioactive Hotspots at India's Mayapuri Scrap Yard," *Green Peace Blog*, May 14, 2010, http:// www.greenpeace.org/international/en/news/Blogs/nuclearreaction/ greenpeace-finds-radioactive-hotspots-at-indi/blog/11781 (accessed March 25, 2011).
40. Shobhan Saxena, "How Not to Prepare for a Nuclear Crisis."
41. Ravindra K. Dhir & M. Roderick Jones, *Concrete in the Service of mankind: Concrete Repair, Rehabilitation and protection* (London: Chapman & Hall, 1996), 45.
42. "Nuclear Power Plant Accidents in India," May 30, 2011, http:// www.scribd.com/doc/39458960/Nuclear-Power-Plant-Accidents-in-India (accessed June 14, 2011).

43. Benjamin K. Sovacool, "A Critical Evaluation of Nuclear Power and Renewable Electricity in Asia," *Journal of Contemporary* Asia vol. 40, no. 3 (August 2010): 380.
44. Press releases of the Indian Nuclear Power Corporation (NPC) on the impact of the tsunami that struck Kalpakkam on December, 26, 2004, www.dae.gov.in/press/tsunpcil.htm (accessed March 15, 2011).
45. J.A. Fernando, "Sri Lanka to be Cautious on Indian Nuclear Incidents, Plans to Sign MoU with India," *Asian Tribune,* April 13, 2011, http://asiantribune.com/news/2011/04/12/sri-lanka-be-cautious-indian-nuclearaccidents-plans-sign-mou-india (accessed April 15, 2011).
46. "Indian Atomic Programme Should be Closed," *BBC Urdu Service,* April 1, 2011,http://www.bbc.co.uk/urdu/india/2011/04/110401_nuclear_projects_sz.shtml (accessed April 2, 2011).
47. Phil Hazelwood, "Protests Mount Against Nuclear Power Plant in India," *Dawn*, April 25, 2011.
48. A.H. Nayyar, M.V. Rammana & Zia Mian, "Fukushima Lessons," *Dawn,* January 27, 2011.
49. Pevez Hoodbhoy, "Pakistan Can't Handle Fukushima," *Express Tribune,* March 22, 2011, http://tribune.com.pk/story/136020/pakistan-cant-handle-fukushima/ (accessed March 23, 2011).
50. Zahir Kazmi, "Fact and Fiction, Letter to the Editor;" *Express Tribune,* March 23, 2011, http://tribune.com.pk/story/136738/fact-and-fiction/ (accessed March 25, 2011).
51. Shahid Javed Burki, "Will Japan's Tsunami Wave Hit Pakistani Shores?" *Dawn Economic & Business Review,* April 4-10, 2011.
52. Dr Khuram Shaukat Yusofzai, "Radioactivity Hazard in Pakistan," Letter to the Editor, *Dawn*, April 19, 2011.
53. "Shutdown Atomic Power Plant: Demand," BBC *Urdu Service,* April 1, 2011,http://www.bbc.co.uk/urdu/pakistan/2011/04/110401_labour_nuclear_a.shtml (accessed April 2, 2011).
54. "Plans for Nuclear Power Stations," *Dawn*, April 26, 2011.
55. Rifat Ali, "Ageing Management of Principal Component for K-1 Life Extension," (paper presented at International Seminar on Nuclear Safety and Security Challenges of the 21st Century on 21-23 April 2011, at National Centre of Physics, Islamabad, Pakistan).

56. "Tens of Millions Living in Nuclear 'Danger Zone': Study," *Dawn*, April 23, 2011.
57. Dr Syed Iqbal Mohsin, "Preparing for Earthquakes," *Dawn*, March 17, 2011.
58. Subduction is the process in which one plate is pushed downward beneath another plate into the underlying mantle when plates move towards each other. The denser plate slides under the less dense plate. Faulting occurs in the process, in which rocks break and move along the fractures. The subducted plate usually moves in jerks, resulting in earthquakes. The area where the subduction occurs is the subduction zone. A long, narrow, deep depression forms in this area. It is called an oceanic trench, (accessed April 5, 2011), library.thinkquest.org/17457/platetectonics/5.php
59. Humera Hafeez, 'The Potential of Tsunami Generation along Karachi and the Makran Coast of Pakistan," *Pakistan Journal of Meteorology,* Vol. 4, issue 7 (July 2007): 25-40.
60. Bhagwandas, "Coastal Communities Exposed to Tsunamis," *Dawn,* March 21, 2011.
61. Naseer Memon, "Dealing with Disaster," *Dawn*, April 19, 2011.
62. "In the wake of Disaster," *Japan Times,* April 12, 2011, reproduced in "Other Voices: Far Eastern Press," *Dawn*, April 14, 2011.
63. "Convention on Nuclear Safety: Report by the Government of Pakistan for the Fifth Review Meeting 2011," (Islamabad: PNRA, 2010), 2.
64. PAEC official website, www.paec.gov.pk/ (accessed March 21, 2011).
65. "Nuclear Power Plants Safe, Says Pakistan," *Dawn*, March 15, 2011, http://www.dawn.com/2011/03/15/nuclear-power-plants-safe-says-pakistan.html (accessed March 17, 2011).
66. Discussion with the spokesperson of the PNRA Bushra Nasim, on the sidelines of the International Seminar on Nuclear Safety and Security Challenges of the 21st Century, 21-23 April 2011, National Centre of Physics, Islamabad, Pakistan.
67. The mission of the PNRA is: "To ensure safe operation of nuclear facilities and to protect radiation workers, general public and the environment from the harmful effects of radiation by formulating and implementing effective regulations and building a relationship of trust with the licensees and maintain transparency

in its actions and decisions," www.pnra.org/ (accessed March 17, 2011).

68. "Convention on Nuclear Safety: Report by the Government of Pakistan for the Fifth Review Meeting 2011," (Islamabad: PNRA, 2010), 7.

69. "National Disaster Response Plan (NDRP)," March 2010, www.ndma.gov.pk /Documents/NDRP/NDRP.pdf (accessed March 21, 2011).

70. "Disaster Risks in Pakistan - NDMA Pakistan," www.ndma.gov.pk/ Documents/NDRP/NDRP.pdf (accessed March 21, 2011).

71. Faizan Mansoor, "Public Awareness and Involvement in the Licensing Process for Safe and Secure Use of Nuclear Energy," (paper presented at International Seminar on Nuclear Safety and Security Challenges of the 21st Century on 21-23 April 2011, at National Centre of Physics, Islamabad, Pakistan).

72. Email from Brigadier Sajid Naeem, from NDMA, to the author on March 22, 2011.

73. "Hazard, Terminology: Basic Terms of Disaster Risk Reduction," *International Strategy for Disaster Reduction* (ISDR), http:// www.unisdr.org/eng/library/libterminology-eng%20home.htm (accessed March 27, 2011).

74. "Disaster Risk Assessment, Terminology: Basic Terms of Disaster Risk Reduction," *International Strategy for Disaster Reduction* (ISDR), http://www.unisdr.org/eng/library/lib-terminology-eng%20home.htm (accessed March 27, 2011).

75. "Public Awareness, Terminology: Basic Terms of Disaster Risk Reduction," *International Strategy for Disaster Reduction* (ISDR), http://www.unisdr.org/eng/library/lib-terminology-eng%20 home.htm (accessed March 27, 2011).

76. "Public Information, Terminology: Basic Terms of Disaster Risk Reduction," *International Strategy for Disaster Reduction* (ISDR), http://www.unisdr.org/eng/library/lib-terminology-eng %20home.htm (accessed March 27, 2011).

# 8

# Cold Start in Strategic Calculus

*Sannia Abdullah*

The origin of the hostility between Pakistan and India lies in the historical legacy of the British Empire. The partition of 1947 left some territorial issues that have not been resolved to this day. Unfortunately the struggle to resolve those conflicts has shifted from the political arena to the battlefield making the region highly volatile and unstable.

The development and use of atomic bomb operationalised the concept of Deterrence as part of the US Nuclear Strategy during the Cold War era. Nuclear weapons deterred any hot war between the Superpowers and also mitigated the crisis situations. After the success of nuclear deterrence in Cold War days many analysts and theoreticians tend to believe that the concept of deterrence will continue to remain dominant as part of military strategy between rival nuclear weapon states.

'Nuclear South Asia' represents a different case than US-Soviet rivalry due to several differences between the two cases. The years preceding the post 1998 period witnessed one Low Intensity Conflict (LIC) of Kargil and the crisis involving the role of international community in preventing the outbreak of war. South Asia under the umbrella of nuclear deterrence still has suspicions regarding the stability of the region. The 'Stability-Instability Paradox' is critical in defining the relations between two nuclear neighbours.

In this context, it has to be remembered that India and Pakistan occasionally resort to the compellence pattern under the umbrella of nuclear deterrence. The study will be an endeavour to throw light on the theoretical construct of compellence, applying it on the India-Pakistan situation. The paper will also examine whether limited war is possible under the nuclear overhang and how serious is the Cold Start threat vis-à-vis Pakistan.

## Theoretical Framework – Compellence Theory

The idea of compellence is as old as military history itself. Compellence as a strategy has been discussed by Clausewitz, Byman, Freeman, George, Jakobsen, Mueller, Pape and Schelling. The US has used compellence in counter-insurgency operations of Iraq and Vietnam War.[1]

In case of South Asia, the strategies of compellence and nuclear deterrence have remained operative from time to time. In order to better understand compellence, it would be helpful to first define and differentiate the term from other similar terminologies that are often used interchangeably.

Compellence is defined as: "behavior established to compel an adversary to carry out an action that do not want or stop doing something."[2] On the other hand, deterrence is the ability to persuade the behaviour of an adversary to stop from doing what it intends to do. Schelling defined compellence as "the threat that compels rather than deters often requires that the punishment be administered until the other acts, rather than if the other acts".[3] According to Schelling the use of compellence strategies is observed in conventional wars as in nuclear war this concept would be ludicrous. He distinguishes deterrence from compellence: "There is typically a difference between a threat intended to make an adversary do something and a threat intended to keep him from starting something. The distinction is in the timing in who has to make the first move, and whose initiative is put to the test."[4]

In deterrence the target audience is known and the threat is communicated in order to make deterrence work unlike comepellence in which the actual demonstration of use of force is expressed to prevent further action that usually involves military exercises, testing missiles and several multiple missions of war games etc.[5]

The practice of compellence theory has not yielded positive results as such keeping in view the case studies of the Serbian conflict, Iraq war 2002-03, and Vietnam.[6] The underlying fact is that compellence has brought states to exercise restraint although the temptation to begin war was a zero-sum calculus. The chart below illustrates the path from the coercer to threaten an adversary to fulfill its demands by either use of force or through bargaining, thereby making compellence functional; whereas non-use of force or using force without fulfillment of the objective or denial by the target to attain its aims, leads to the malfunctioning of compellence.

Pakistan never had any hegemonic designs to display either inside or outside the region. Moreover it only pursued policies to secure its defence visà-vis India. It was India that set the stage for nuclear ambition which Pakistan was

Figure 2: Gradations of Success and Failure of Compellence

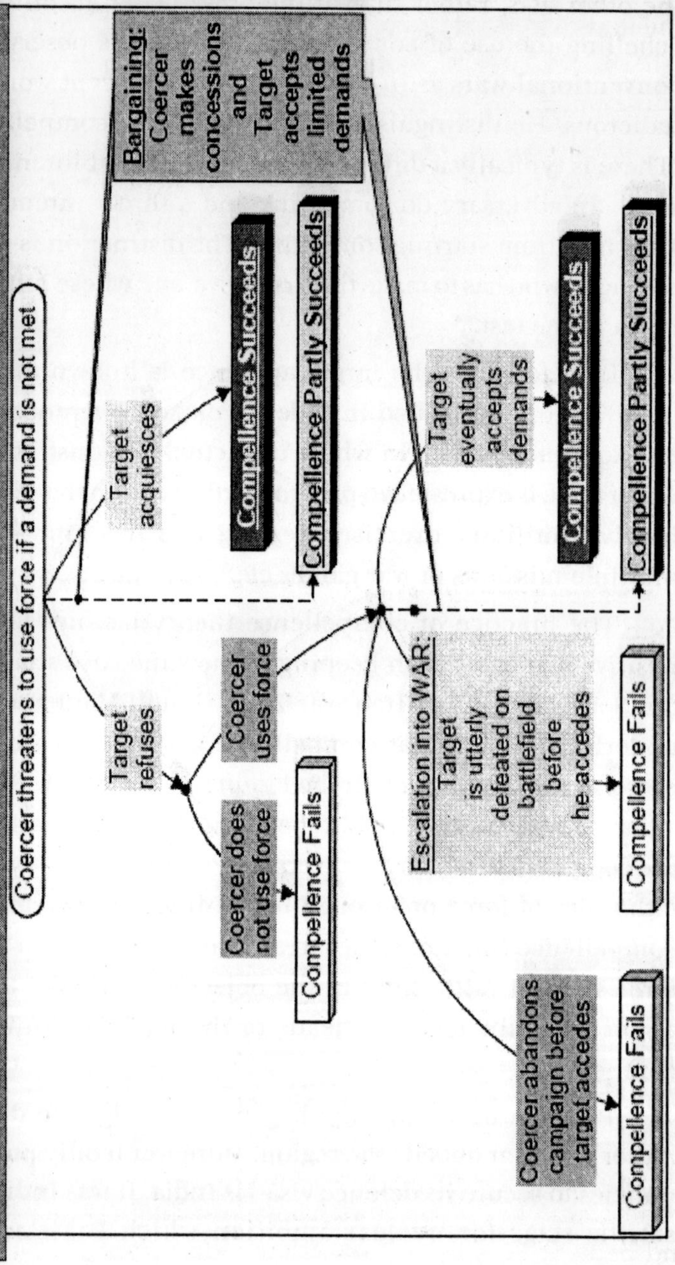

reluctant to follow until all its options[7] were exhausted. The realist paradigm and strategic realities[8] compelled Pakistan to develop its nuclear capability.

India opting for a nuclear status assumed that its regional power status would influence all regional (south Asian) countries including Pakistan. However, the acquisition of nuclear weapons by Pakistan changed India's stance to that of a global player. India stretched its influence outward by improving diplomatic ties with the great powers and enhanced its military posture by exaggerating the security fears vis-à-vis Pakistan and China. The Indian defence expenditure is rising in order to maintain the 'credible minimum deterrence'.

According to the Indian "Budget Estimates (BE) proposed for the year 2010-11, the total expenditure of Central government will be Rs. 11,08,749 crore, which is an increase of 8.6 per cent over total expenditure in BE of 2009-10."[9] Instead of enhancing peace, stability and security, a great chunk of GDP being spent on developing BMD systems and increasing stockpiles may have the opposite effect of bringing more instability and insecurity.[10]

How real is China's threat to India? The question is important as the inter-state rivalry revolves around the security triangle of India-Pakistan and China. India holds responsible the 1962 Sino-India war as break-through for its nuclear decision. Although some theoreticians argue that China's withdrawal from the captured land within two months symbolises China's foreign policy intentions. History reveals that ambivalence has a key role in determining China's international relations with countries around the world. China has never shown a hostile attitude towards India and believes in peaceful coexistence to promote regional peace and harmony.[11] Believing in the cliché that when capabilities are there, intentions can change over-night; India cannot rule out the Chinese threat. Indian Prime Minister Manmohan Singh explicitly declared China as a threat to India; he further added that "China would like to have a foothold in South Asia, and we have to reflect on this reality."[12]

From the Chinese perspective the 'China Threat' is a propaganda waged by few lobbyists in India who intend to gain benefits from other countries by intensifying the magnitude of the abnormal diplomatic relations. They also believe that "to a large extent, the 'China threat' theory is more like a weapon used in public opinion and psychological wars as an attempt to contain China's international diplomacy."[13]

## India-Pakistan Bilateral Relations and History of Crises

The US has remained a key balancer in Pakistan-India relations but always with the intent to mitigate crises but never to address the need to sustain the dialogue process between them.[14] The virtual effect of this intervention has subsequently led to hiccups of crises and a negative peace that never produced a significant outcome from these incidents. The frequency of these events had gained momentum when both states were pursuing their nuclear programme clandestinely.

### 1986-87 Operation Brasstacks

During Operation Brasstacks, India mobilized its 150,000-400,000 troops in its province of Rajasthan, 100 miles away from the international border during November 1986-March 1987. It was a huge military exercise, bigger than NATO's since WWII.[15] It was a well-planned operation to test the Indian army's electronic warfare equipment and demonstration of its computerised/mechanised units.[16]

Pakistan's fear was that India was planning to invade its province of Sindh in order to dismember the country. Pakistan reciprocated by mobilising its forces along the Indian Punjab province. The crisis reached a climax when Dr A.Q. Khan in his interview with an Indian journalist disclosed that Pakistan had developed the capability to develop a nuclear bomb.[17] The hotline channel decreased the intensity of tensions later paving the way for Gen. Zia ul Haq's cricket diplomacy. The Operation Brasstacks was followed by CBMs between the two countries. The most important CBM signed on December 31, 1988 by the two foreign ministers was "Agreement on the Prohibition of Attack against Nuclear Installations and Facilities."

## Kashmir Uprising 1990

The denial of the rights of Kashmiri people and occupation of the state by India led to the first India-Pakistan war of 1947-1948. Subsequently Indian atrocities in Occupied Kashmir resulted in the surge of freedom movement by the Kashmiris in the late eighties when the Indian forces tried to crush the freedom struggle. Being disappointed by the international community and the UN (despite its resolutions) to resolve the protracted conflict, Pakistan then resorted to the compellence strategy by supporting the freedom movement in Kashmir. India accuses these active militant groups of having links with 'Pakistan's intelligence agency.' During Gen. Musharraf's time many of those organisations were banned.[18] On the contrary there was no let up in gross violations of human rights by Indian armed forces19 in the Valley which they tried to hide by banning the entry of neutral observers and media persons in the troubled state. But Indian oppression could not subdue the struggle which continued to simmer.

After the 9/11 events, India was able to exploit the environment, that had become extremely sensitive to violence and the difference between a freedom struggle and terrorism had become rather tenuous, to put the Kashmir issue on the backburner reiterating that the major issue between India and Pakistan was to tackle terrorism and Pakistan cease to support 'state-sponsored terrorism'. Eventually the compellence strategy worked.

### 1999 Kargil

A few Indian analysts hold that it was the Kargil action by Pakistan that prompted India to think of limited war options that could be exercised without escalating the engagement to a nuclear level. Indian Defence Minister George Fernandes declared that "Kargil war has shown that the nuclearization of India and Pakistan has not made conventional war obsolete; rather it simply imposed another dimension on the way warfare could be conducted."[20] The 1999 Kargil conflict deterred India from enlarging the conflict to an all-out war.

According to Mr. K. Subramanyam, Pakistan used compellence vis-àvis India in the Kargil war of 1999.[21] It could be surmised that Pakistan miscalculated the Indian response to Kargil in pursuing compellence in preference to the stability-instability paradox; as being the weaker contestant Pakistan expected to combine the advantages of its strategic position and surprise attack to achieve victory in Kargil.

### 2001-02 Nuclear Stand-off

Five terrorists attacked the Indian Parliament on December 31, 2001 that resulted in the death of nine Indians, although all five of them were killed in the raid by the armed forces. By late night Indian investigations had come up with findings alleging involvement of Pakistani agencies in launching the attack through the Lashkar-e-Taiba and Jaish-e-Mohammad network that was active in Occupied Kashmir. It was probably a hunch of the Indian military to connect the attack to Pakistan. India retaliated by deploying the bulk of its forces on Pakistan's borders in an offensive posture in eye ball to eye ball confrontation with Pakistan that lasted for almost a year.

India raised the level of the media hype on the Parliament attack. But the event could not get the kind of attention in the West that India wanted as US was then busy making plans for its Afghan invasion.[22]

Colonel David Smith, the US Army attaché in Islamabad believed that the Indian Parliament attack was even used by Blackwill, US ambassador in New Delhi, to converge US-India concerns on the issue of terrorism when he stated that jihadi organisations operative in Kashmir were a looming threat to international security due to their linkage with Al Qaeda network. According to Col. Smith:

> *There was a clear perception both in Islamabad and in some quarters in Washington that Blackwill was using the crisis as a vehicle to attain his own goals for US-Indian relations, and that little consideration was being given to the potential adverse impact on the war on terrorism.*[23]

Pakistan remained instrumental in supporting 'Mujahideens' but it does not support all the terrorists' activities taking place across the border. Brig. Feroz Hassan Khan (retd.), former Director Arms Control and Disarmament Affairs (ACDA), also reiterated that "India regularly cooks up such incidents for international effect." India uses international pressure as a tool in its compellence strategies against Pakistan.

## Mumbai Crisis 2008

In 2005, US and India entered into Strategic Cooperation by signing the Indo-US Nuclear Deal. The deal is discriminatory in nature as it has opened avenues for India to gain strategic advantage over Pakistan as it recognises the de facto status of

India (non-NPT state). Subsequently India has been given special waiver by the Nuclear Suppliers Group (NSG) that led India to conclude an agreement to receive nuclear fuel supply. On the one hand, Pakistan is being pressurized for signing the Fissile Material Cut-off Treaty (FMCT), while on the other US-India ties are steering new trends for the international community to dilute the essence of the non-proliferation regime.[24]

On November 26, 2008 terrorists' attacks took place in Mumbai involving shooting and bombing at different locations across the city. The Mumbai attacks caused a media hype in India that tended to equate the Mumbai blasts of 26/11 with the US 9/11 and raised a hue and cry about Pakistan's involvement in the attacks. The investigation said that during the attack telephonic calls were intercepted through satellite that traced their linkage with Lashkar-e-Taiba (LeT) operating from Pakistan.[25] Subsequently India started threatening Pakistan that if it did not prevent such threats emanating from its soil, India would use other means to prevent such acts of terrorism. The relations worsened when India's External Affairs Minister, Pranab Mukherjee, warned Pakistan on December 19, 2008, by stating: "All our pleas have been ignored till date. Pakistan's inaction will force us to consider all options." Indian Air Force threatened Pakistan with surgical strikes by flying Indian Hawks on India-Pakistan international border.[26]

The Mumbai incident resulted in the deadlock of the composite dialogue that was already moving at a snail's pace. India upon resuming the dialogue process conditioned terrorism as a core issue demanding full assurance from Pakistan that it would not allow its soil to be used by terrorists against India. Pakistan - which is witnessing events like 9/11 or 26/11 almost daily - obviously cannot assure anything of this kind. The Indian objective was achieved since many of the suspected organisations operating inside Pakistan were declared 'banned' and their offices sealed.

## India's 'Pakistan-Specific' Cold Start Doctrine

The new Indian Army Chief, Gen. V.K. Singh, renounced the existence of the Cold Start Doctrine (CSD) as part of Indian defence strategy by stating that Indian Army never articulated such a doctrine.[27] This U-turn in the Indian position is difficult to understand unless it means the CSD has been found to be flawed on practical grounds. Gen. V.K. Singh emphasised that the doctrine was a fabrication of the think tanks, as he said: "There is nothing called "Cold Start."...In the recent years, we have been improving our systems with respect to mobilisation but our basic military posture is defensive."[28]

However, this reversal in Indian army's position runs counter to earlier statements about the doctrine. The former Army Chief, Gen. Kapoor, had not only mentioned it but explained its main features on April 28, 2004, some two months after the commencement of the composite dialogue between India and Pakistan. Gen. Kapoor pointed out five major pillars on which the Cold Start Doctrine rested: One, for the Indian army to wage conventional war it must be prepared to face a 'two-front war' creating balance in its army command at both western as well north-eastern border. Second, the Indian army should take into account both military and non-military aspects in strategically fighting the war including measures to deal with WMDs from sub-conventional warfare, cyber warfare, electronic and information warfare. Third, the Indian Army should have enough military strength to take war into the enemy's territory and protect India's geo-political interests in the region by protecting the littoral states in the Indian Ocean. Fourth, enhanced interdependence among the three branches of services, i.e., Air, Naval and Army in order to devise comprehensive war strategy. Fifth, technological advancement is the critical factor for India incorporating electronic warfare in planning and executing future wars.[29]

The CSD aims at making land incursion into Pakistan's territory through forward mobilisation of eight integrated battle groups (IBG's) with the support of Navy and Air force in facilitating Indian army to conduct tactical manoeuvres within 72-96 hours. The political objective of this war strategy is to bring war into the enemy's territory under the nuclear overhang before the international community intervenes to enforce a cease-fire. The military objective is to destroy Pakistan's Army Reserve (North) and Army Reserve (South) during which 3-5 of the Indian strike divisions will penetrate by crossing the international border by keeping simultaneity with the holding corps, thereby creating confusion for Pakistan army to make mistakes by dividing their cohesive strength.[30] The CSD prevents Pakistan's conventional response without crossing the nuclear threshold. Brig. (Retd) Gurmeet Kanwal believes:

> *The only sensible option for India would be to call Pakistan's nuclear bluff and plan to launch strike corps offensive operations to achieve strategic gains in as early a time frame as is militarily possible. This approach will need to be combined with a declaratory policy that a nuclear strike against Indian soldiers, even if they are deep inside Pakistani territory, will constitute the use of nuclear weapons against India and will invite massive counter-value and counter-force punitive retaliation against Pakistan.*[31]

The Indian army consists of three strike corps: I Corps, II Corps and XXI Corps located in Mathura, Ambala and Bhopal respectively. The Cold Start recognises that each of these large strike corps would be divided into eight smaller division-sized 'integrated battle groups' (IBG's) supported by mechanized infantry, artillery and armour to launch offence.[32]

The current strength of the Indian Army is more than 1,200,000 consisting of 38 divisions, subdivided into 5 tactical commands: the Northern Command (stationed at Udhampur is responsible for Indian Occupied Kashmir), Western Command (situated at Chandimandi covers Punjab), Southern Command (headquartered at Poona surrounds Gujrat and Maharashtra), Eastern Command (posted at Calcutta takes account of counter-insurgency operations in Assam and defence of border with Bangladesh) and the Central Command (in Luckhnow; consisting of Indian army's strike elements to take offensive against Pakistan).[33] In recent years a new tactical command named South-Western command has been created and has been formally operative since 18th April 2005 (with its Headquarters at Jaipur). This command will operate in conjunction with the Udhampur-based Northern Command and Chandimandir-based Western Command.[34]

The military objective[35] based on Cold Start is to make 'shallow territorial gains of 50-80 km' through speedy mobilisation of IBG's within 72-96 hours. The idea of 'bite-and hold' strategy is to 'extract concessions from Islamabad'.[36] Brig. Feroz Hassan Khan (retd.), former Director ACDA, reiterated that the aim of CSD of targeting a thin line of Pakistani territory is of strategic value (to Pakistan) as most of the major cities lie within that limited range. The map below demonstrates the target points and cities at stake in case of Cold Start incursion by the Indian Army.[37]

It is in the interest of India that Pakistan defines its red lines so that Pakistan's readiness to use nuclear weapons any time could be publicised against the belief that nuclear weapons were meant for no-use but to deter. Assumptions apart, it seems difficult to presume that a limited war between nuclear weapon states with conventional asymmetry along with the designs to capture a few miles of territory across the border could be contained within limits and conflict escalation could be avoided. The doctrine gives no significant strategic war fighting approach that could help prevent escalation from Pakistan side.

## Cold Start Doctrine is a Mode of Network Centric Warfare

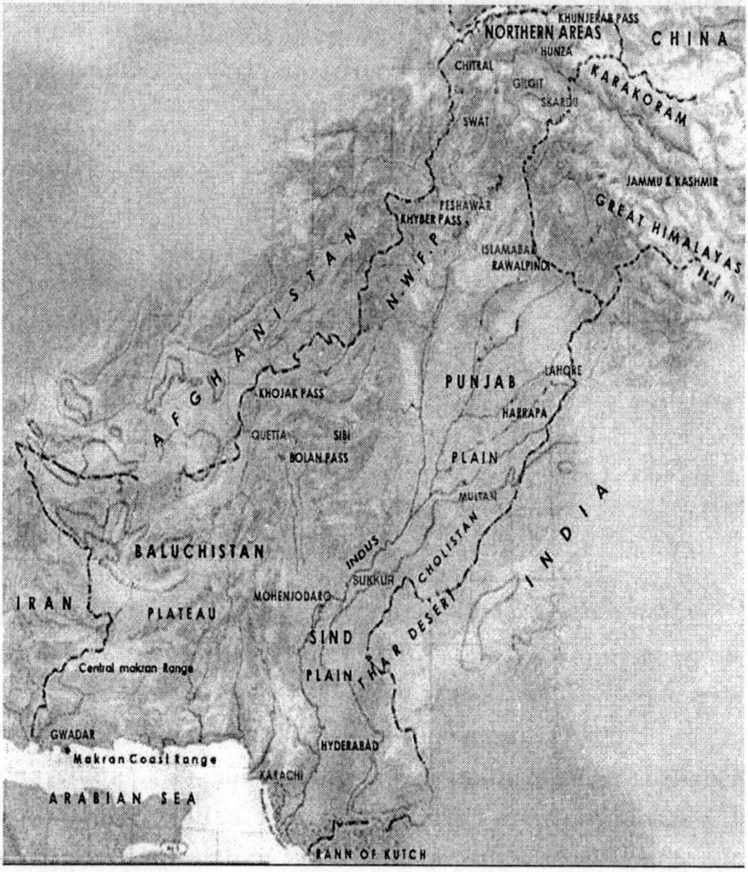

The Cold Start carries the blend of different war strategies of modern times. Some academicians regard it as the replica of Israeli war strategy being practised in Lebanon based on a blitzkrieg offensive operation[38] whereas others regard it carrying the chunk of the US war strategy against Iraq. CSD is a "combination of Information or Network Centric Warfare with Shock-and-Awe Strategy tactics."[39] 'Network Centric Warfare' aims to exploit situational awareness in order to make swift operations by increasing the speed of command to get into the enemy's 'OODA loop'[40] i.e., Observation, Orientation, Decision and Action.

*Source:*

Berndt Brehmer, "The Dynamic OODA Loop: Amalgamating Boyd's OODA Loop and the Cybernetic Approach to Command and Control," 10th International Command and Control Research and Technology Symposium, http://www.dodccrp.org/events/10th_ICCRTS/CD/papers/365.pdf

The Network Centric Warfare (NCW) aims at designing the conduct of war by complementing the military/battlefield strategy based on a resultoriented strategy that will paralyse the enemy's response options. NCW makes use of technology as a force multiplier;[41] for instance the technologies like sensors and information processing[42] etc., work hand in hand in assisting the work of the military forces in making use of information in an automatic correlation form in the battlefield as per changing war dynamics.

According to Admiral Cebrowski, the military assault takes place in a phased manner starting from planning a mission and then mobilising the forces in a coordinated manner to launch the offense. This entire process takes time and affects the ability to act because of fatigue. During the 2001-02 stand-off the Indian army got fatigued while bringing its troops close to the international border. The use of network centric approach before launching an offense will give the

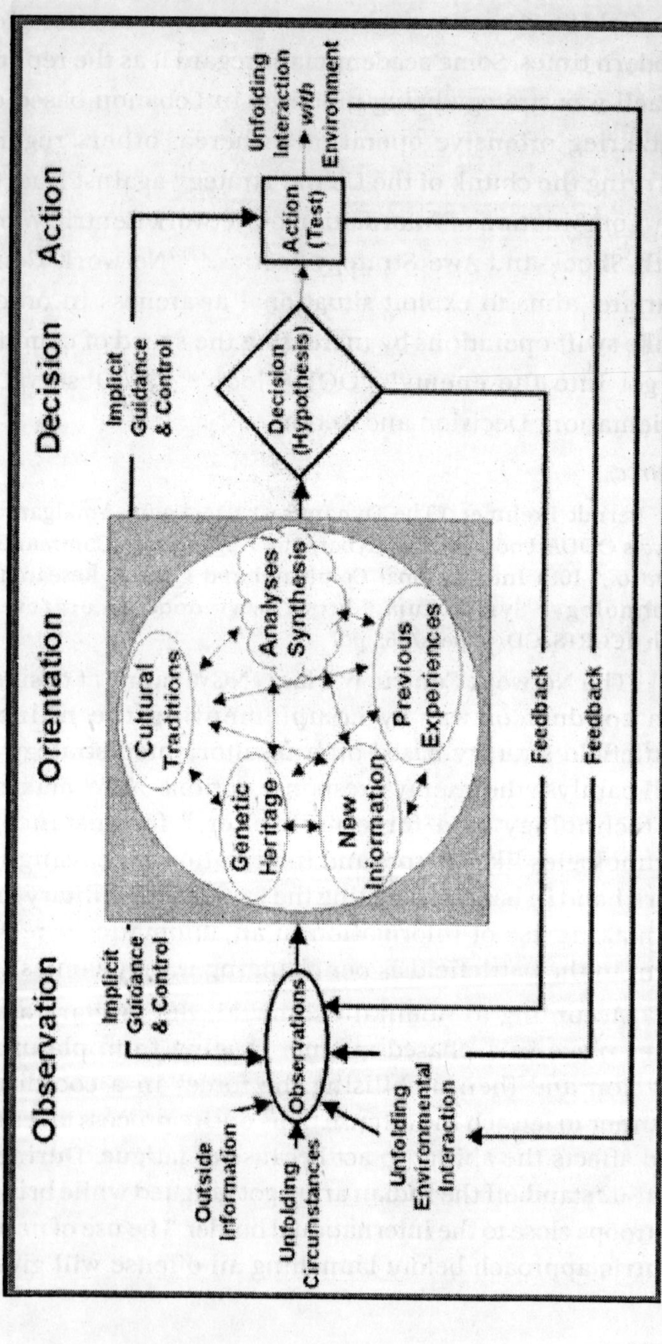
Observation
Orientation
Decision
Action
Outside Information
Unfolding Circumstances
Unfolding Environmental Interaction
Implicit Guidance & Control
Observations
Cultural Traditions
Genetic Heritage
New Information
Analyses / Synthesis
Previous Experiences
Feedback
Feedback
Implicit Guidance & Control
Decision (Hypothesis)
Action (Test)
Unfolding Interaction with Environment

Indian troops enough time to wait and see the adversary's response and then accordingly manoeuvre in accordance with John Boyd's OODA loop. The availability of information about the adversaries' manouvrability at command level will facilitate the coercer to orient and plan their possible move which is termed as 'empowered selfsynchronised' operation instead of preplanned move termed as 'well-planned synchronised' operation.[43] The following figure shows the path of empowered self-synchronisation shown by a thick arrow that facilitates the speed of forces at command level.

The Cold Start Strategy (CSS) believes that by using Network Centric Warfare the adversary command will face chaos and divide under panic, giving enough room to Indian air borne troops and cavalry units to destroy Pakistan army's defense lines and infrastructure and minimising its reaction capacity. Therefore the 8-10 IBG's will be facilitated to undertake a blitzkrieg action which will be coherent due to available information sharing at the troop level and keeping the options open for flexible changes as per the information requirements by commanders in the battlefield. In this way the doctrine will achieve its objectives of surprise and speedy mobility.

## Indian Defence Procurements Supporting NCW Concept

India is allocating huge chunk of its GDP to defence budget and most of the recent defence agreements with Israel and Russia contribute in the employment of new weapon systems that aim at enhancing NCW capabilities.[44] Running short of artillery to materialise the CSS, the Indian Army is paving way to improve its access to conclude defense agreements.[45] Moreover India is also acquiring Airborne Warning and Control System (AWACS) technology to achieve air dominance. These AWACS are of Russian-Israeli origin with effective radar capabilities that aim to detect and intercept enemy fighters and surface-to-air missiles.[46]

The acquisition of AWACS and effective satellites are force multiplier systems which will boost the effectiveness of both offensive and defensive operations executed by Indian Army. The growing Indian military capabilities are hallmark of strengthening the swift mode of operations in lieu of

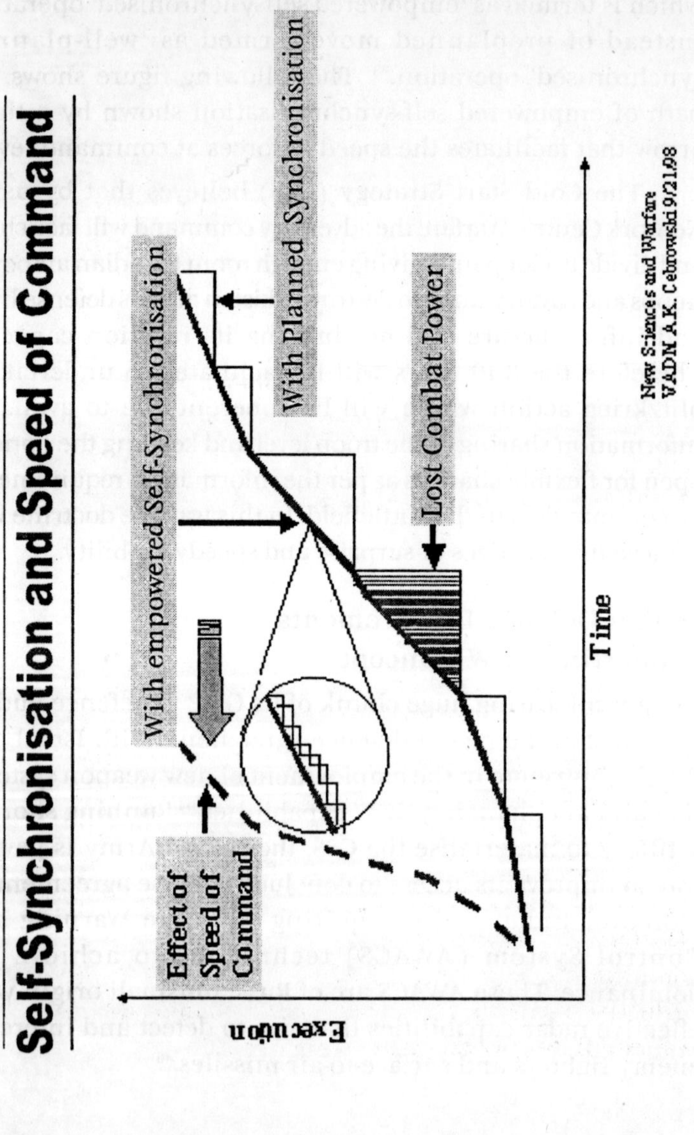

changing war patterns that can be achieved either by the pre-delegation of power at division/brigade level or through synchronisation of command. "The Ilyushin-76 gives India the capability to track hundreds of aircraft and potential threats at sea and on the ground, at considerable distances."[47]

Satellite surveillance facilitating the ground maneuvers was being practised during Indian military exercise Divya Astra (March 2004) that conducted 90 minutes battle where mechanized formations were integrated by air support whereby Long Range Observer System (LOROS) and ELM-2140 Surveillance Radars with range of 14km and 40 km respectively provided "thermal imagers intermeshed with weapon systems. This was the first step towards NCW and the use of devastating firepower to replace casualty intensive...an important prerequisite of CSD."[48]

## 'Myth of Nuclear Deterrence' in South Asia

A total war of nuclear exchange is both theoretically and practically impossible as no nuclear weapon state (NWS) would be so irrational in its decision-making as to push the nuclear button and commit suicide. The concept of limited war is at odds with nuclear deterrence that demands communication of threat of use of nuclear weapons to prevent the adversary from pursuing the same course of action. A limited war if it begins will set the stage for both countries to advance on the escalation ladder from where crossing the nuclear threshold will not be an impossible stage. The deterrence theory needs to broaden its horizon in view of the dynamic war innovations. Nuclear deterrence does not encompass a limited war in its ambit.

Gen. Butler describes "deterrence as a dialogue of the blind with the deaf. He said deterrence failed completely as a guide for setting rational limits on the size and composition of military forces. The appetite of deterrence theory was voracious, its capacity to justify new weapons and large stocks unrestrained."[49]

Bernard Brodie opines that the possession of nuclear weapons is not enough unless it specifies the conditions under which they would be used in order to make deterrence work. According to him, "it would be tactically and factually wrong to assure the enemy in advance...that we would in no case move against him until we had felt some bombs on our cities and airfields."[50] Brodie's version clarifies India's second strike and recessed deterrence. The notion of launching preemptive strike by India has never been ruled out although the main emphasis of its doctrine rests on the second strike capability[51] with punitive, preventive retaliation. Pakistan – with its linear geostrategic location– has categorically articulated through its higher official' statements[52] that it cannot afford to wait for a nuclear war to be imposed upon it. Pakistan's robust Command and Control is responsible enough not to allow any accidental/unauthorised use of nuclear weapons, whereby it keeps the option of first strike open to secure its sovereignty. The strategic outlook extracted from this presumption makes the credibility of deterrence in case of India and Pakistan doubtful when both parties-to-the-conflict are considering the preemptive attacks option from the other side. Therefore it is impossible to predict with absolute assurance about the adversaries' behavior under provocative circumstances.

Easy to strategise, war is hard to calibrate. Nuclear weapons deter both nuclear wars as well as conventional wars because war is a continuum, not a discreet set of actions. Cold Start attempts to compartmentalise war.[53]

## Nuclear Deterrence and CSD

India has postulated CSD as a 'limited war under the nuclear umbrella.' Limited warfare as part of Indian Defence policy vis-à-vis its nuclear neighbours, Pakistan and China, is a challenging task that requires advanced conventional war fighting military capabilities.[54] On paper India articulated the Cold Start Doctrine nicely based on NATO's 'come as you are' war pattern[55] but on ground the Indian force posture stands no comparison to NATO's even after six years of the doctrine announcement.

The limited war theory to be applied in case of South Asia needs to involve the China factor. The conventional wars waged by India either with Pakistan or China at one time can be provocative for a third party's (indirect) involvement in the conflict keeping in view the Sino-Pakistan and Sino-India relations; while on the other hand Indian Defence capability for a simultaneous war with Pakistan and China is yet to figure in the realm of possibility. The divergence of perceptions and immense level of mistrust due to historical baggage have made both countries to draft their nuclear doctrine and respective force postures in contrasting patterns. This notion determines the future course of action vis-à-vis each other.

Terestita C. Schaffer believes that in nuclear environment, the limited conventional war concept propagated by India is not logical. She said it is not possible to quantify the concept of limited war in terms of geography, weapons or political objectives in the Indo-Pakistan equation. A limited war from Indian point of view may not be limited from Pakistani perspective.[56]

The continuous state of turbulence in South Asia along with the development of nuclear weapons have made conventional wars a risky game, since both countries have no history of arms control agreements and the success of CBMs has also remained confined on paper. After the 9/11 attacks, all India has done is projected Pakistan as the hub of terrorism; this perception persists in the West as well. Without realising that the country itself was the worst victim of the terrorism and insurgencies spillover across borders, which is a known fact, India has persistently disregarded the regional dynamics and pressurised Pakistan with the charge of state sponsored acts creating confrontational issues and advanced its strategic motives using compellence. Pakistan COAS, Gen. Ashfaq Pervaiz Kayani expressed this apprehension when he said that "proponents of conventional application of military forces, in a 'nuclear overhang' are chartering an adventurous and dangerous path; the consequences of which could be both unintended and uncontrollable."[57]

## Indian Military Hardware Challenges Confronting CSD

The doctrine is exhaustive in its insistence on maintaining the military fully prepared with all facilities to launch such an offensive operation. Presently India is confronted with a number of issues to practically perform this doctrine.

War preparedness of a high order at all times in terms of strategic reserves of weapons, equipment, ammunition, accessories and petroleum, diesel and aviation fuel is required. Cold Start War Doctrine offensive operations cannot be launched on incomplete inventories.[58]

According to the war plan laid down by CSD, India will convert its defence corps into strike corps. The moment these defence corps will be mobilised in a forward move to launch a penetrative land incursion into Pakistan territory, one brigade of Pakistan army would be able to take the other route to attack India causing heavy damage since India's IBG corps would have got stuck inside Pakistan while the rest of the Indian territory will be having no defence corps providing greater room to Pakistan to inflict damage.

To act under the unified command as postulated by CSD all the three services need to have optimal level of coordination which is important for the success of a blitzkrieg type of action. India is still lagging behind in such manoeuverability and requires a 'revolution in military affairs' to upgrade its air force for better coordination in battlefield in terms of logistics.

## Pakistan's Responses to the Cold Start

Pakistan, on 19 April 2011, conducted the first flight test of its tactical nuclear weapon, the Multi Tube Ballistic Missile Hatf IX (NASR). The NASR has a range of 60 km, capable of carrying nuclear warhead of appropriate yield with high accuracy and "shoot & scoot attributes, which can deter evolving threats." The Director General Strategic Plans Division (SPD), Lt. Gen. Khalid Ahmed Kidwai (retd), announced that "the test was a very important milestone in consolidating Pakistan's strategic deterrence capability at all levels of the threat spectrum."[59] The development of tactical nuclear weapons has lowered the nuclear threshold as believed by many analysts. India wishes to keep the war option open in South Asia between the "strategic space of Low Intensity Conflict (LIC) and Nuclear Threshold."

The NASR missile test was advertised as Pakistan's latest response to India's Cold Start doctrine, which is itself provocative.... Pakistani military planners evidently believe the NASR missile system will close a nuclear deterrence gap that has been opened up by the Indian doctrine.... With little geographic depth but still locally formidable ground and air defenses, Pakistan will not be passive in defense but will rather react with escalatory, punitive manoeuvres of its own."[60]

The NASR is capable of targeting "mechanised forces like armed brigades and divisions envisaged in India's Cold Start Doctrine."[61] The flight test of NASR has proved that Pakistan addresses Indian conventional superiority with its tactical nuclear option.

Earlier Pakistan Army conducted its Azm-e-Nau III as the largest military exercise after Zarb-e-Momin of 1998 in the backdrop of external and internal security threats challenging its security. The exercise began on 10 April 2010 and focused on war tactics of 'Dispersal Techniques' in which 20,000 troops of all services participated aiming to demonstrate Pakistan's enhanced defence capabilities. In the words of Army Chief General Kayani, "We are focused to the defense of Pakistan and fully capable of defending Pakistan today."[62]

The basic contour of this exercise was comprehensive to address the wider range of threats of terrorism and extremism also. Therefore, Pakistan Army tailored its doctrine to respond to a two-front alarm emanating from both eastern and western borders.[63] Pakistan's defence posture is in up-stream particularly its missile capabilities that are fully accomplished to counter any strategic threat. The map below shows that the range of Hatf IV is capable of targeting Indian western Air Force targets just within 3 minutes' launch time.[64]

### Range of Pakistan's Ballistic Missile Arsenal

*Source:* Subhash Kapila, "Pakistan's Ballistic Missile Arsenal: Development and Acquisition Philosophy," South Asia Analysis Group, paper no. 148,http://www. southasiaanalysis.org/%5Cpapers2%5Cpaper148.html

India calls Pakistan's Azm-e-Nau III exercise as 'India-Threat Centric.' The Indian strategists have notified that US military hardware supplies to Pakistan including the F-16s would be used against India, stating that the US F-16 aircraft have nothing to do with terrorism war-fighting strategy.[65] Due to trust deficit between India and Pakistan any military cooperation between Pakistan and the West looks alarming to India. She insists that no matter what the intended purpose ultimately all US supplies given to Pakistan will be used against India and therefore America should not support Pakistan militarily or financially; since US has its own national interests to protect and promote in the region.

Indian apprehensions regarding Azm-e-Nau - III revolved around the geographic location where this exercise was held. Few Indian analysts believe that "operations extended from South Punjab to Sindh...that suggests that it is intended to defeat India's multiple thrusts as part of Cold Start War Doctrine and also an Indian diversionary Corps strike launched against Sialkot."[66] Azm-e-Nau 2010 aims to facilitate

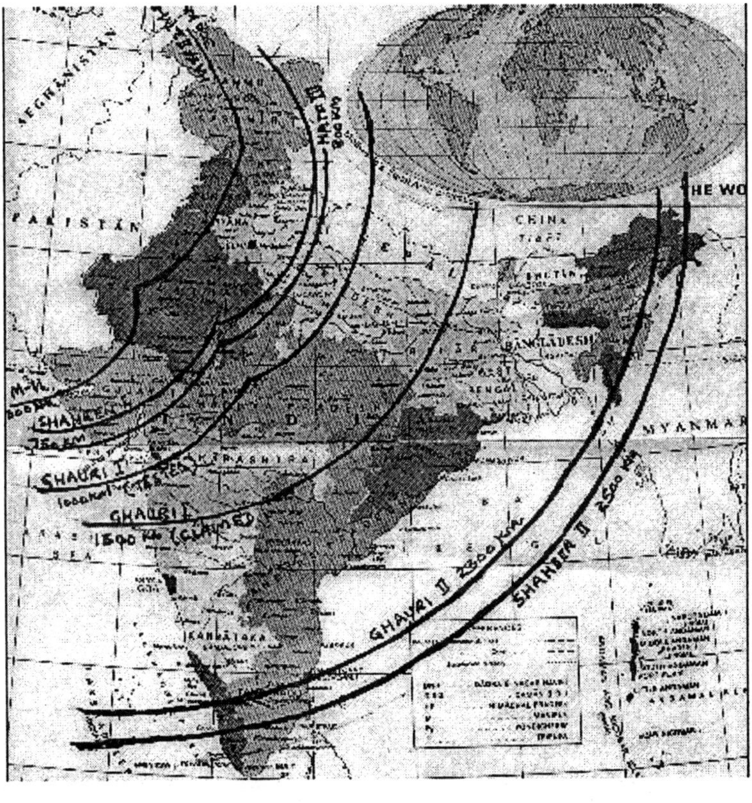


the successful exit of US from Afghanistan so that Pakistan Army will again get the access to strategic depth in

Afghanistan. All these presumptions show the myopia of Indian think tanks that are targeting improvement in US-Pakistan relations by undermining their trust and collaboration in counterinsurgency bilateral cooperative measures.[67]

The war plans as the one being reflected through CSD is likely to thwart regional peace between India and Pakistan. The Cold Start has provided Pakistan reasonable grounds to develop and test tactical nuclear weapons to avert the option of conventional war. It is in the interest of Pakistan to increase the stakes of nuclear war in order to deter India with any conventional preemption strategy.[68]

Apart from war the peace-time contingency plans are always in practice by Pakistan vis-à-vis Indian offensive. Pakistan being well aware of its less strategic depth is opening up other options to secure its defence. The construction of motorways also serves the strategic purpose of runways in order to wider the response options during wartimes. Both the Motorways (M-1 and the M-2) have four emergency runway sections. The Pakistan Air Force (PAF) has used the M-2 motorway as a runway twice during its exercises first in 2000 and later in 2010[69] named 'High Mark-2010'.[70] It is believed that the use of road runways by the PAF during war-time would not only provide alternate link for the communication network in order to meet the need of any contingency but would also provide 'flexibility of operations'. The Motorways are constructed deep inside the territory connecting the north to the south (from Peshawar to Gawadar).[71]

## Future Implications of Cold Start on India-Pakistan Bilateral Relations

Many theoreticians believe that nuclear weapons in South Asia have made the strategic environment more alarming instead of bringing stability in the area. The main reason for this is the divergent doctrinal perspectives of the two countries which hamper the functioning of deterrence. Pakistan is not deterred by India's second strike threat and India, owing to international pressure, does not believe in Pakistan's political will to exercise the use of nuclear weapons. To make nuclear deterrence effective the threat to use nuclear weapons should be credible and well articulated. Since deterrence has psychological connotations, the threat of the use of weapons must be credible enough to deter the adversary's action.

Pakistan pursues 'deterrence by denial' whereas India practices 'deterrence by punishment.' The asymmetry of perspectives on nuclear deterrence undermines its strength leaving the region more volatile and turbulent in the wake of any miscalculation of either side's intentions.

One of the Wikileaks cable reveals that the Cold Start is the brain-child of the BJP government of the time and is not fully endorsed by the present Manmohan Singh government. It is believed that Indian military hawks do adhere to the concept of Cold Start to make it a reality but without the political commitment.[72] If Cold Start is part of its military war games then why did the Indian forces conduct eleven major exercises near the Pakistan border to boost synergy in its defence forces. While conducting the six-day military exercise 'Vihayee Bhav' - one of the Indian officials confirmed the objectives of the exercises by stating that...the battlefield tactics for warfare are being practiced in the exercise which aims at fine-tuning the concept of Cold Start doctrine.[73]

Moreover, India's pursuit of developing a Ballistic Missile Defence (BMD) system in the shape of Prithvi Air Defence (PAD) will raise Pakistan's security calculations in terms of reciprocity to maintain a minimum credible deterrence.

The prevailing trust deficit may erupt into another crisis and would jeopardise South Asian security if a non-state terrorist activity/attack is miscalculated by India. As Chairman Joint Chiefs of Staff Committee (CJCSC), General Tariq Majid said:

> *We have to be mindful of the blatant pursuit of military preponderance in our neighborhood. Growing power imbalance due to continuing build up of massive military machine, including both hi-tech conventional and nuclear forces, adoption of dangerous cold start doctrine and proactive strategy, more assertive posturing especially after very exceptional civil nuclear deal and notions of two front war are all destabilising trends, carrying implications for Pakistan's security. Therefore, retention of essential nuclear capability to maintain credible minimum deterrence against any possible aggression is our compulsion and not a matter of choice.*[74]

## Possible Options to Offset Cold Start Strategy

Pakistan Army needs restructuring/reorganisation in view of the changing perceived threats. In order to improve its reconnaissance capability Pakistan has already purchased four Swedish Saab-2000AEW aircraft whereas four more (ZDK-03 AWACS) are expected to arrive from China.[75]

Pakistan needs to restructure and reorganise its army during the peacetime by adoption of a comprehensive approach to resist and deter any offensive through the use of all available means of modern information technology including psychological or cyber warfare. All this requires incorporating new weapon systems strategised to open war on several fronts to deter any hostile advance of the enemy.

The use of satellite information can be used to detect the manoeuvres being made by the IBG's across the international border. India has acquired Remote Sensing Satellite Imagery[76] that "...will qualitatively enhance the battle-field transparency. Commanders in the field will be able to base their decisions on real-time accurate information. This will greatly assist in shaping the land battle in all its phases.[77]

On the political front the focus should be on improving the economy as a good defence cannot be built on military aid; the economy has to be placed on a sound footing to lend credibility to the defence posture. Resources have to be diverted to develop "combined arms operations" and coordination capabilities need enhancement to offset Cold Start's mechanised operations which demand swift coordinated response.

## Conclusion

The prospect of a nuclear war through escalation is not entirely excluded from the realm of possibility in South Asia. Stephen P. Cohen thinks that nuclear South Asia is a continuous source of concern for the US that regards nuclear war an 'ever-present possibility' that can result either through escalation of conventional war, through misperception or miscalculation due to greater trust deficit or even through preemption.[78]

The absolute functioning of deterrence is in the interest of Pakistan which neither has any hegemonic designs against India nor does it want any conventional outbreak. The nuclear parity is not advantageous to conventionally superior India with 'global' political objectives. In Thomas Schelling's view, "in strategy when both parties abhor collision the advantage goes often to the one who arranges the status quo in his favour and leaves to the other the 'last clear chance' to stop or turn aside." If India continues to pursue such a doctrine it will provide Pakistan all the excuses to develop counter strategies in order to strengthen deterrence.

Pakistan supports peace since indulgence in any war is more costly to Pakistan than India. Therefore Pakistan uses the nuclear card in preventing war believing that a conventional war with India will provide greater room (to

India) to inflict an unacceptable cost on Pakistan and put her in a bad bargaining position. The behaviour of decision making elites (of both India and Pakistan) is motivated by compellence strategy. The technological developments by India including BMD systems and its defence agreements with great powers including Israel and Russia for latest weapons' procurement is compelling Pakistan to look for other options. If this trend continues, deterrence would seem to be moving towards compellence. While the entire strategy under the CSD has been chalked out, the categorical denial by the Indian Army Chief Gen. V.K. Singh regarding the existence of 'Cold Start' has raised questions. One wonders whether India has really abandoned its doctrine or because of the US pressure it is another effort to misguide the West about India's covert designs or it is intended to compel Pakistan to act in an expected move.

The litmus test would be to analyse the on-ground situation and watch the Indian troops' mobility across the border. Any forward move or joint services exercises by Indian Armed Forces should alert Pakistan to readjust its defensive position.

## References

1. Michael T. Plehn, "The Sharpest Swords: Compellance, Clausewitz and Counterinsurgency" (thesis, School of Advanced Airpower Studies (SAAS), Maxwell Air Force Base, Alabama, May 2005).
2. David García Cantalapiedra, "Engagement or Compellence: US Policy Choices in the North Korea Crisis," *UNISCI Discussion Papers,* May 2003, http://redalyc.uaemex.mx/redalyc/pdf/767/76711296002.pdf (accessed August 2, 2011).
3. William S. Huggins, "Deterrence after the Cold War: Conventional Arms and the Prevention of War," *Airpower Journal* (Summer 1993), http://www.airpower.maxwell.af.mil/airchronicles/apj/apj93/sum93/huggins.htm (accessed July 22, 2011).

4. Patrick Bratton, "Signals and Orchestration: India's Use of Compellence in the 2001-02 Crisis," *Strategic Analysis* Vol. 34, issue 4 (July 2010): 594-610.
5. William S. Huggins, "Deterrence after the Cold War."
6. Jan van Angeren, "Opportunities and Limits of Compellence Strategies: The Quest for a Framework for Analysis" (Diss., Leiden University Repository), https://openaccess.leidenuniv.nl/bitstream/1887/4276/3/Proefschrift.pdf (accessed July 28, 2011).
7. Pakistan, year after year in the UN, called for establishing South Asia as Nuclear Weapon Free Zone, also raised voice for zero-missile regime. When all tides went against Pakistan, it went for nuclear detonation of 1998, later it also drafted Strategic Restraint Regime but faced inflexible response from India.
8. Pakistan with relative conventional inferiority, border/territorial disputes with its nuclear neighbours, history of wars with promising future crises demanded Pakistan to bring strategic stability to South Asia.
9. Arvind Kadyan, "India's Defence Budget (2010-2011): Wake up Call for Defence Managers," *Institute for Defence Studies and Analysis*, http://www.idsa.in/idsacomments/IndiasDefenceBudget2010-2011_akadyan_030310 (accessed August 8, 2011).
10. Muhammad B. Alam, "India's Nuclear Doctrine: Context and Constrains," *Heidelberg Papers in South Asian and Comparative Politics*, Working Paper no. 11 (October 2001), http://archiv.ub.uniheidelberg. de/volltextserver/volltexte/2003/4122/pdf/hpsacp11.pdf (accessed August 15, 2010).
11. Herold Leelawardena, "The China Bogey and the Real Threat to India," Lankaweb, June 28, 2010, http://www.lankaweb.com/news/items/2010/06/28/the-china-bogey-and-thereal-threat-to-india/ (accessed September 15, 2011).
12. Mr. Singh connected China's threat to India with historical grievances over Arunachal Pradesh with its rising concerns about "the presence of People's Liberation Army (PLA) personnel in Pakistan-administered Kashmir" believing that "presence of a PLA infantry battalion at the 15,397-ft high Khunjerab pass in Pakistan-administered Kashmir's Gilgit-Baltistan region, there to provide security for Chinese workers building a road and high-speed railway in the area."12 This infrastructure development is likely

to link China's Xinjiang to the Gwadar port in Balochistan. The basic premise that threatens India is the economic prosperity of two countries through joint venture that will facilitate China's access to Persian Gulf from where it gets 60 per cent of its oil supplies. Stephen P. Cohen, "South Asia," *Brookings*, http://www.brookings.edu/~/media/files/rc/articles/2004/11southasia_cohen/20041101.pdf (accessed September 24, 2011).

13. Dang Jianjun, "How to Respond to India's 'China threat' Theory?," *China Org.*, June 3, 2009, http://www.china.org.cn/international/2009-06/03/content_17883584.htm (accessed September 12, 2011).
14. Stephen P. Cohen, "South Asia."
15. "Brass Tacks," *Global security*, April 27, 2005, http://www.globalsecurity.org/military/world/war/brass-tacks.htm (accessed August 2, 2011).
16. Steven R. Weisman, "On India's Border, A Huge Mock War," *New York Times*, March 6, 1987, http://www.nytimes.com/1987/03/06/world/on-india-s-border-ahuge-mock-war.html, (accessed September 18, 2011).
17. "The End of the A.Q.Khan Network: Case Closed?," [chapter four] in *Nuclear Black Markets: Pakistan, A.Q.Khan and the Rise of Proliferation Networks* (London:International Institute of Strategic Studies),http://www.iiss.org/publications/strategic-dossiers/nbm/nuclear-black-marketdossier-a-net-assesment/the-end-of-the-aq-network/#crimes (accessed October 29,2011).
18. Syed Shoaib Hasan, "Why Pakistan is Boosting Kashmir Militants," March 3, 2010,http://news.bbc.co.uk/2/hi/south_asia/4416771.stm (accessed November 21, 2011).
19. Sardar Muhammad Anwar Khan, "Indian Suppression" in 57th session of General Assembly,http://www.ajk.gov.pk/index.php?option=com_content&view=article&id=65&Itemid=23 (accessed November 20, 2011).
20. M.V. Ramana, "The Climate in South Asia," *Lines*, August 2001.
21. Conference on "Asymmetric Warfare in South Asia: Crises of 1999, 2002 and Beyond," held at New Delhi, September 26-27, 2002.
22. Steve Coll, "The Stand-off," *New Yorker*, February 13, 2006,http://www.newyorker.com/archive/2006/02/13/060213fa_fact_coll (accessed August 26, 2011).

23. *Ibid.*

24. Maleeha Lodhi, "FMCT and Strategic Stability," *South Asian News Agency* (SANA), January 26, 2010, http://www.sananews.net/english/2010/01/26/fmct-andstrategic-stability/ (accessed July 26, 2011).

25. Robert F. Worth, "In Wake of Attacks, India-Pakistan Tensions Grow," *New York Times,* December 1, 2008,http://www.nytimes.com/2008/12/02/world/asia/02mumbai.html (accessed September 17, 2011).

26. Zafar Nawaz Jaspal, "Paradox of Deterrence: India-Pakistan Strategic Relations," *Institute of Strategic Studies Islamabad* (ISSI),http://www.issi.org.pk/ss_Detail.php?dataId=507 (accessed August 28, 2011).

27. "No Cold Start Doctrine, India Tells US," Indian Express, September 9, 2010, www.indianexpress.com (accessed July 24, 2011).

28. *Ibid.*

29. "India Army Ready for War against China, Pakistan," *Geo TV,* December 30, 2009,http://www.geo.tv/12-30-2009/55835.htm (accessed September 23, 2011).

30. Gurmeet Kanwal, *Indian Army Vision 2020* (New Delhi: Harper Collins, 2008), 86.

31. *Ibid.,* 81.

32. Walter C. Ladwig III, "A Cold Start for Hot Wars: The Indian Army's New Limited War Doctrine," International Security vol. 32, no.3 (Winter 2007/08): 160-164.

33. Muhammad Bilal Iftikhar Khan, "From Cold Start to AZM-e-NOU III," *Ground Report,* April 10, 2010, http://www.groundreport. com/World/From-Cold-Start-to-AZM-e-NOU-III/2921666 (accessed September 27, 2011).

34. "Northern Command," *Global Security,* http://www.globalsecurity.org/military/world/india/northcom.htm (accessed August 18, 2011).

35. One of the military objectives through Cold Start Doctrine hints at many.

36. Ladwig III, "A Cold Start for Hot Wars."

37. Thanks to Brig. Feroz for sharing this slide.

38. It involves a mechanised move of tanks, infantry, artillery and air power, concentrating with overwhelming magnitude of force at high speed to break through enemy lines. Through constant motion, the blitzkrieg attempts to keep its enemy off-balance, making it difficult to respond effectively at any given point.
39. Shock and awe strategic tactics is also technically known as 'rapid dominance' written by Harlan K. Ullman and James P. Wade in 1996. It is a military doctrine that involves the use of overwhelming power in the battlefield utilizing all sources of intelligence to understand battlefield situation and moves of an adversary and exercise dominant maneuvers in response to them with displays of force to paralyse an adversary's perception of the battlefield through chaos thereby exhausting adversary's will to fight back. Ladwig III, "A Cold Start for Hot Wars," 183.
40. OODA loop stands for Observa tion-Orientation-Decision-Action time cycle or loop. In order to win, some strategies are operated at a faster rhythm than their adversaries so that they get inside the enemy's territory in order to destroy adversary's Observation-Orientation-Decision-Action time cycle or loop. ...Such activity will make the offender army appear ambiguous (unpredictable) thereby generate confusion and fuss simultaneously creating divide among adversary's command. In this situation the adversaries will be unable to stay in compliance with faster transient rhythm of changing moves of adversary they are competing against.
41. Raza Muhammad, "Indian Cold Start Doctrine: A Brief Review," *The Citadel* vol. XXVII, no.1 (2009): 78.
42. The sensors are usually satellite borne that give aerial view for surveillance whereas information technologies provide means for processing and analyzing sensor data.
43. Dr. Edward A. Smith, "Network Centric Warfare: Where's the beef?," *Information Warfare Site* (IWS), http://www.iwar.org.uk/rma/resources/ncw/smith.htm (accessed September 25, 2011).
44. Walter C. Ladwig III, "A Cold Start for Hot Wars: The Indian Army's New Limited War Doctrine," 183.
45. India plans to induct 4000 new 155mm artillery pieces worth contracts of more than US $4 billion. "Murky Competitions for Indian Howitzer Orders May End Soon... Or Not," *Defense Industry Daily*, January 27, 2011, http://www.defenseindustrydaily.com/

murky-competition-for-2b-india-howitzerorder-may-end-soon-0805/ (accessed September 15, 2011).

46. "India Set to Buy Additional Russian-Israeli AWACS Planes," RiaNovosti, November 9, 2011, http://en.rian.ru/mlitary_news/20111109/168530024.html (accessed November 24, 2011).
47. "Indian Air Force Gets Awacs Plane," *BBC News,* May 28, 2009, http://news.bbc.co.uk/2/hi/8072143.stm (accessed November 23, 2011).
48. Raza Muhammad, "Indian Cold Start Doctrine: A Brief Review," 78.
49. V. N. Khanna, *India's Nuclear Doctrine* (New Delhi: Samskiti, 2000), 262.
50. Bernard Brodie, *Strategy in the Missile Age* (Princeton, NJ: Princeton University Press, 1959), 397.
51. V. N. Khanna, *India's Nuclear Doctrine,* 245.
52. Pakistan has not published its nuclear doctrine. The main aspects of the doctrine have been explained at several places by Pakistani higher officials. The guiding principle is minimum credible nuclear deterrence; some officials also refer four policy objectives for Pakistan's nuclear weapons; 1) deter all forms of external aggression; 2) deter through a combination of conventional and strategic forces; 3) deter counterforce strategies by securing strategic assets and threatening nuclear retaliation; 4) stabilize strategic deterrence in South Asia. Paul K. Kerr and Mary Beth Nikitin, "Pakistan's Nuclear Weapons: Proliferation and Security Issues," *Congressional Research Service,* June 12, 2009,http://www.usembassy.it/pdf/other/RL34248.pdf (accessed September 20, 2011).
53. Yogesh Joshi, "The Cold End of Cold Start Doctrine?," *Institute of Peace and Conflict Studies* (IPCS), October 13, 2010, www.ipcs.org (accessed July 27, 2011).
54. Ashley J. Tellis, "Future Fire: Challenges Facing Indian Defense Policy in the New Century," *India Today Conclave,* March 13, 2004,http://www.carnegieendowment.org/files/futurefire.pdf (accessed September 5, 2011).
55. Adnan Gill, "Cold Start or a Cold Myth?," *Asian Tribune,* January 26, 2009, http://www.asiantribune.com/node/15311 (accessed September 19, 2011).

56. Khurshid Khan, "Limited War under the Nuclear Umbrella and its Implications for South Asia," *Stimson*, http://beta.stimson.org/southasia/pdf/khurshidkhan.pdf (accessed August 17, 2011).
57. "Press Release," *Inter Services Public Relations* (ISPR), January 1, 2010, http://www.ispr.gov.pk/front/main.asp?o = t-press_release &id = 1082 (accessed September 27, 2011).
58. Subhash Kapila, "Indian Army Validates its Cold Start War Doctrine," *South AsianAnalysis*, June 7, 2005, http://www.southasiaanalysis.org/papers15/paper1408.html(accessed June 15, 2011).
59. "Press Release," *Inter Services Public Relations* (ISPR), April 19, 2011, http://www.ispr.gov.pk/front/main.asp?o = t-press_release& id = 1721(accessed August 24, 2011).
60. Rodney W Jones, "Pakistan's Answer to Cold Start?", *The Friday Times vol.* XXIII,no. 13 (May 13-19, 2011), http://www. thefriday times.com/13052011/page7.shtml (accessed September 23, 2011).
61. Zafar Nawaz Jaspal, "NASR (Hatf IX) Counteracts India's Cold Start Doctrine," *Weekly Pulse*, April 22, 2011, http://www. weeklypulse.org/details.aspx?contentID = 482&storylist = 2 (accessed April 25, 2011).
62. Raja Muhammad Khan, "Pakistan: Exercises Azm-e-Nau III in the Perspective," *Opinion Maker*, April 22, 2010, http://www.opinion-maker.org/2010/04/pakistanexercises-azm-e-nau-iii-in-the-perspective/ (accessed August 20, 2011).
63. Lubna Umar, "Azm-e-Nau and Renewed Security Trends," *Pakistan Observer*, http://pakobserver.net/detailnews.asp?id = 24748 (accessed September 24, 2011).
64. "Pakistan's Cold Start Strategy Response: India's deployment of Mig-29 on Pakistan Border," http://pkkh.lefora.com/2009/10/05/pakistans-cold-start-strategy-response-indiasdepl/(accessed August 21, 2011).
65. Gurmeet Kanwal, *Indian Army Vision 2020* (New Delhi: Harper Collins, 2008).
66. Subhash Kapila, "Pakistan Army Sends Politico-Military Signals to India through 'Ex Azm-e-Nau'," *South Asian Analysis*, April 21, 2010, http://www.southasiaanalysis.org/%5Cpapers 38%5 Cpaper 3772.html (accessed July 16, 2011).
67. *Ibid.*

68. Walter C. Ladwig III, "A Cold Start for Hot Wars: The Indian Army's New Limited War Doctrine," 72.
69. PAF used the runway to land, refuel and take off its two fighter aircrafts Miraj III and F-7P (during High Mark-2010) apart from Super Mushak trainer and C-130.
70. "PAF Conducts Fighter Operations from Motorway," April 2, 2011, http://www.paf.gov.pk/press_release/uploaded/MOTORWAY-RELEASE02-04-10.pdf (accessed November 23, 2011).
71. "PAF Jets Undertake Landings on Motorway," *Pakistan Tribune,* September 12, 2005 http://paktribune.com/news/PAF-Jets-undertake-landings-on-Motorway-118826.html (accessed November 24, 2011); "F-7 Mirage Makes Trial Landing on Motorway," *Dawn*, November 21, 2002, http://archives.dawn.com/2002/11/22/nat45.htm (accessed November 23, 2011).
72. "WikiLeaks: US on Indian Army's Cold Start Doctrine," *ND TV,* December 2, 2010, http://www.ndtv.com/article/wikileaks-revelations/wikileaks-us-on-indianarmy-s-cold-start-doctrine-69859?cp (accessed September 21, 2011).
73. "Indian Army, Air Force Begin Six-Day Joint Exercise along Western Deserts," May 9, 2011, http://www.india-defence.com/reports-5098 (accessed September 16, 2011).
74. "Press Release," *Inter Services Public Relations* (ISPR), June 17, 2010,http://www.ispr.gov.pk/front/main.asp?o = t-press_release&id = 1333 (accessed September 21, 2011).
75. "India Set to Buy Additional Russian-Israeli AWACS Planes."
76. Remote Sensing Satellite Imagery with Requisite Technological Specifications of 1 Metre/sub-Metre.
77. Satbir Singh, "Shaping the Land Battle through Remote Sensing and Satellite-Imagery," *IDSA,* http://www.idsa-india.org/an-feb00-5.html (accessed November 25, 2011).
78. Stephen P. Cohen, "South Asia."

# 9

# Pakistan's Nuclear Weapons Testing May 1998: External and Internal Pressures

*Zafar Khan*

## Introduction

Pakistan has always considered itself to be an insecure state since its inception in 1947. The country's military build-up in its earlier stages was in response to the demands of state security and territorial integrity. Besides strengthening its conventional forces, Pakistan also formed military alliances with the US to bolster its security in the South Asian region. Pakistan regarded these alliances (SEATO & CENTO 1954-55) as a 'security guarantee' against India. However, the defence treaties failed to provide the kind of security guarantee the country expected from them when confronted with military challenge from India, though they provided substantial economic and military benefits in the 1950s and 1960s. Pakistan's security leadership therefore sought a more dependable defence arrangement that could ensure the country's security. This arrangement presented itself in the shape of the nuclear option.

Although Pakistan had been developing nuclear facilities for peaceful purposes since the 1950s, the idea of acquiring nuclear weapons which had been there and evolving since the 1960s took a policy and practical direction only in the 1970s in the wake of traumatic events like the 1965 war, the country's dismemberment in 1971, and India's nuclear testing in 1974. Pakistan went through various phases of thinking before taking the political decision and actually acquiring a nuclear weapon from the seventies to the time India tested its nuclear devices on May 11 and 13, 1998. That proved the proverbial straw on the camel's back. Pakistan was left with no option but to follow suit and test its nuclear capability on May 28 and May 30, 1998. After testing six nuclear devices, the then Prime Minister of Pakistan, Nawaz Sharif declared, "No matter whether we are recognised as a nuclear weapons state or not, we are a nuclear power."1 The acquisition of nuclear weapons by Pakistan was a major turning point in its long history of nuclear development programme from initially its peaceful uses to military purposes. There were domestic, regional and international factors that proved decisive in the process of Pakistan's nuclear development programme. One of Pakistan's security strategists, Feroze Hassan Khan, now teaching at the US Naval Postgraduate School, Monterey, said, "the West could not dissuade Pakistan to acquire nuclear weapons because they did not understand the actual cause of Pakistan's struggle for acquisition of nuclear weapons."[2]

It is interesting to note that much before Pakistan's nuclear weapons tests in 1998, preparations for such nuclear testing had already been in the making in 1986 when a team of Pakistan Atomic Energy Commission (PAEC) scientists led by Dr. Ishfaq Ahmed explored several sites in Balochistan where a nuclear test could be conducted. Ultimately, a 3,325 feet long tunnel was bored in the Ras Koh Hills of Chagai (the place where Pakistan conducted its nuclear weapons tests in 1998).[3] In fact, Pakistan had already mastered the technique of conducting cold tests before going for the physical test. The first cold test was conducted in the hills of Sargodha in March 1983 under the Wah group headed by

Hafeez Qureshi (the head of Radiation and Isotope Application) and Dr. Zaman Sheikh working under Pakistan Institute of Science and Technology (PINSTECH). Since then, until the 1998 nuclear tests, Pakistan had conducted more than 24 cold tests of its nuclear devices in order to improve the actual testing structure. In addition, one cold test of Pakistan's nuclear weapons device was also carried out independently in 1984 by Kahuta Research Laboratories (KRL).[4]

Both in the 1980s and 1990s Pakistan's leadership gave greater importance to nuclear weapons development rather than developing the economy. But until May 1998 Pakistan had not demonstrated its nuclear weapons capability. Pakistan brought an end to its nuclear ambiguity when India tested its nuclear weapons on May 11 and May 13, 1998. The Indian nuclear tests had altered the strategic and military balance in favour of India. Pakistan and its polity felt a security threat. The people of Pakistan were in the middle of a difficult choice: "explode the bomb, and prepare to eat grass. Or decide against it, and eat the humble pie."[5] There were three possible options for Pakistan. First, to do nothing, that is, to avoid testing and consider India's nuclear weapon tests as not challenging or posing threat to Pakistan's security and its territorial integrity; second, to turn to international community, that is, to seek the major powers' security guarantee and let the major powers provide Pakistan economic and military support if Pakistan decided not to conduct nuclear weapons tests; and third, a nuclear option, that is, to respond to India's nuclear weapons tests and thus achieve and maintain strategic parity despite external and internal pressures against going nuclear. Which options suited Pakistan and why did Pakistan exercise the nuclear option?

This paper aims at finding out why it became imperative for Pakistan to demonstrate its nuclear weapons capability.

The second part examines the internal and external opposition to Pakistan's nuclear tests in 1998. How convincing these arguments were at a time when Pakistan was all prepared for proving its capability. The third section will deal with the public support for Pakistan's nuclear option and its resolve to end the nuclear ambiguity by conducting the nuclear tests. This part also explains the reasons that vindicated the stand of the proponents of Pakistan's nuclear weapons testing. The conclusion will indicate which side was more convincing, the proponents or the dissenters.

## The Significance of Pakistan's Nuclear Weapons Tests

The BJP's declaration to go nuclear if it came to power after the elections gave impetus to Pakistan's nuclear weapons programme. The tests became inevitable for Pakistan. Pakistan's leadership had considered the threat emanating from India's designs of conducting nuclear weapons tests and the implications of such an event in the context of the latter's hegemonic designs in the South Asian region.[6] Apparently, Pakistan was maintaining its status of nuclear ambiguity and was not conducting the nuclear tests unless India did.

Therefore, just before BJP's intention of conducting nuclear weapons test in May 1998, Pakistan tested its Ghauri missile in April 1998. Ghauri is a liquid based missile with a range of 1300 km; however, in the following year in 1999, Ghauri-II was tested which is the improved version of Ghauri-I.[7] This test was significant for Pakistan's nuclear weapons tests for many reasons. First, Pakistan thought that this missile could provide Pakistan a stronger deterring capability because with its range Pakistan could hit major targets in India and the psychological value of its name (after Shahabuddin Ghauri who defeated Pritiviraj Chauhan to establish his rule in the subcontinent) could add to its dread as a weapon. Second, it was not only a response to India's missile Agni tested a decade ago, but also a response to India's Prithvi missile tested in 1997. Third, Ghauri missile test was a reply to the declared intention of BJP of India to test nuclear weapons capability.[8]

According to security analyst Naeem Salik: "Pakistan missile program is aimed at achieving a credible, reliable, and survivable deterrence capability, and it is not aimed at achieving a power projection capability beyond its immediate security arena...the goal is to meet the requirement of *credible minimum deterrence*."[9] Soon after India's nuclear weapons tests, Pakistan deplored India's nuclear weapons tests and accused it of commencing a nuclear arms race unilaterally in the Southern Asian region. Then Pakistan's Foreign Minister, Gohar Ayub, stated on May 11, 1998, "Pakistan strongly condemns this Indian act and the entire world should condemn it. It has sucked Pakistan into an arms race."[10] The aim of this statement was to draw the attention of the international community to the fact that it was not Pakistan which went first to conduct its nuclear weapons capability, rather it was India that acted unilaterally to provoke Pakistan to respond in kind. Two days after India's second round of nuclear testing on May 13, 1998, Pakistan's Defence Committee stated: "Indian government had in recent weeks exhibited a pattern of irresponsible behaviour and taken deliberate steps to further heighten the tension in the region."[11] Pakistan's nuclear weapon tests became more contentious both at home and abroad when rhetoric from its adversary tried to dissuade Pakistan from conducting nuclear weapon tests. For example, the Indian Minister of State for Science and Technology, Murali Manohar Joshi declared that, "India's missiles would be armed and deployed with the country's new nuclear weapons," and Indian Home Minister L. K. Advani explicitly threatened Pakistan with dire consequences if it continued to support Kashmiris for waging a proxy war against India.[12] In response to these statements,

Pakistan had declared its nuclear weapons policy to maintain "minimum credible nuclear deterrence" to counterbalance India's nuclear capability. Pakistan's Prime Minister, Nawaz Sharif stated on May 20, 1998, "Nuclear restraint, stabilisation and minimum credible deterrence constitute the basic elements of Pakistan's nuclear policy."[13] Even though the term "credible minimum deterrence" seems vague to most of the nuclear strategists which, according to them, is yet to be modified and formalised,[14] for Pakistan it seems to mean the country's equal response to every Indian act of nuclear advancement. Pakistan considers this to be necessary as a deterrence assuring security to the state against any threat from nuclear-armed India. The nuclear weapons tests of May 28 and 30, 1998 can be seen in the backdrop of these developments.

## Internal and External Opposition to Pakistan's Nuclear Testing

Though after New Delhi's nuclear test explosion, Islamabad was compelled to do likewise in order to restore the balance of power in the sub-continent, it was exposed to tremendous internal and external pressures. Internally, a minority of pacifists believed that the acquisition of nuclear weapons would be counterproductive since the country's fragile economy could not afford the luxury of a bolted conventional and nuclear arsenal when important sectors of the economy like health, education, agriculture and industry were in a poor shape and would get worse. They argued that rather than going nuclear, Pakistan must seek security guarantees from international community and development aid. The world powers, particularly the West, were on the same page with the local dissenters and even encouraged them in their pursuit of keeping the country de-nuclearized. Interestingly enough, but understandably, the SAARC countries, other than India and Pakistan, opposed the nuclear testing as dangerous to regional security. The external pressure from the international community was to dissuade Pakistan from conducting nuclear tests and in exchange provide Pakistan full economic and military support. This meant leaving India free to test its weapons while forbidding Pakistan to do the same. What kind of pressure was in play to dissuade Pakistan from conducting nuclear weapons tests? How influential these opponents were at the time Pakistan was ready for nuclear testing? Was Pakistan to absorb the internal and external pressures in May 1998? Taking cue from the external powers the anti-nuke lobby at home mounted its offensive against the tests. Let us examine how influential the external pressure was and whether it was able to influence the hawkish polity of Pakistan in 1998.

## The External Pressure

In the wake of India's nuclear tests, Pakistan had to face external pressure from across the world community as Pakistan was getting ready to respond in kind to the Indian nuclear tests. The external pressure was aimed to dissuade Pakistan from conducting a tit-for-tat nuclear test. The US tried to persuade Pakistan to accept the international community's offer of economic and military assistance and show restraint. The US in addition to military assistance offered to lift the economic sanctions on Pakistan. It is interesting to note that the US President Bill Clinton phoned Pakistan's Prime Minister at the time, Nawaz Sharif, several times to change his decision for going ahead with the tests. In addition to this, the US deputy secretary of state, Strobe Talbott, commander of the US Central Command, General Anthony Zinni, and assistant secretary of state for South Asia, Karl Inderfurth, visited Pakistan after four days of India's nuclear weapons' tests and offered Pakistan economic and military support in exchange. The military offer comprised F-16 aircraft too which Pakistan claimed had already paid for in 1980s. The US ambassador to Pakistan, Thomas Simons, stated that these kinds of offers had never been made before to "a non-ally like Pakistan."[15]

China, a traditional ally of Pakistan, had also urged Pakistan to refrain from nuclear testing. The level of support that Pakistan expected from its traditional ally was not provided. Pakistan's Foreign Minister, Shamshad Ahmed's visit to China on May 18-20, 1998 was to seek a security guarantee from China in the event of India's attack on Pakistan. It was hoped that Pakistan would seek some sort of security guarantee and expression of restraint from China after this meeting, but the Chinese officials would call this meeting 'a routine consultation between the two foreign ministers.'[16] It appeared that China publicly avoided any gesture of support for Pakistan's nuclear tests and instead advised Pakistan to show restraint and caution. Admittedly, neither the US nor the Chinese government was willing to provide a security guarantee to Pakistan for not carrying out the test explosions. Also, the Pakistani security management could not feel comfortable with the US security assurances what with its past record of abandoning an ally in the hour of need, both in 1965 and 1971.[17] In 1998, the US had conditioned its offer of an economic assistance package to Pakistan on the latter's renunciation of the nuclear option. It was believed that Pakistan had asked for US $5 billion as an economic and military package if the US was serious in dissuading Pakistan from conducting nuclear weapons tests.[18]

Why did the US not fulfil Pakistan's economic and military demands if it wanted Pakistan to refrain from conducting the tests? Why were the US incentives unconvincing to Pakistan? Despite its apparent seriousness in dissuading Pakistan from taking the nuclear path, there seemed to be some political and logistical problems in materialising these incentives. Many in the west saw the US approach to Pakistan as confusing and unconvincing. For example, Stephen Cohen, an expert on India-Pakistan military affairs before joining the Brookings Institute, has been quoted as saying: "Two things did not happen. The price we offered was not close to what we offered North Korea.[19] And we and Chinese were unwilling to offer the Pakistan's security guarantees that would have made them feel comfortable."[20] Barbra Crossette also quoted Robert Oakley, the former US ambassador to Pakistan, as saying, "For eight years Pakistan has been deprived of everything, and therefore we severely weakened their conventional military capability, which was predicated on the use of American equipment. We certainly weakened their (Pakistan's) confidence in the United States. At the same time, India was getting stronger. So what could the Pakistani's rely upon? Missiles and nuclear capability."[21] Although this paper is not about examining the Indian nuclear tests and the international community's response to them, one of the reasons why external pressure was not effective against Pakistan is because of the discriminatory attitude of the international community towards Pakistan vis-à-vis India. For example, the international community deplored India's nuclear weapons tests in 1998 but its pressure in terms of economic and military sanctions against it remained limited or none. Japan remained reluctant in recalling its private companies from India[22] whilst Russia continued to maintain the Russo-India military deal intact.[23] This sort of discriminatory approach by the international community was not acceptable to Pakistan and it protested against this behaviour. France, Germany and UK at the G-8 summit failed to take a united stand on applying sanctions against India for conducting the nuclear tests while the European Union only expressed its concern that the tests had set a dangerous precedent in the South Asian region and that the EU could put sanctions in the future if India did not join the Non-Proliferation Treaty.[24]

Most of the Pakistanis thought that they would become the first nuclear weapons state in the Muslim world if they indeed went for nuclear tests and Pakistan would get the support of Muslim states. Pervez Hoodbhoy, one of the opponents of Pakistan's nuclear proliferation said, "There is a strong belief that the Bomb would elevate Pakistan's image among Muslim countries. Some cherish the fond hope that if Pakistan explicitly demonstrate its nuclear capability through a test explosion, oil money will pour into the country."[25]

However Pakistan government was stunned by the Muslim states' cold response. In the wake of India's nuclear testing, a stream of representatives and envoys from the Middle East visited Pakistan. Although they regarded India's tests as a security threat to Pakistan, they avoided categorically condemning India's nuclear tests. The Organisation of the Islamic Conference's response in support of Pakistan's nuclear quest was not clear. A strong backing by OIC was not extended to Pakistan. Even Iran, which had been supporting Pakistan in security related matters, refrained from taking a stronger stance against India's nuclear test.[26] Therefore, Pakistan's hopes of withstanding the external pressure through the support of Muslim states especially from Saudi Arabia, United Arab Emirates, and Kuwait, also proved futile. Pakistan found to its dismay that loans from the International Islamic Bank (IIB) would even be difficult to obtain as IIB could not provide loan to any Muslim state without the approval of International Monetary Fund (IMF).[27] Considering all these pressures, the anti-nuke lobby in Pakistan became strident against Islamabad's nuclear tests. The critics seemed to be convinced that the external pressure would not benefit Pakistan at all if it chose the path of nuclearisation. The critics calculated the pros and cons of the May 1998 nuclear testing and tried to convince Pakistan government to adopt the policy of caution and restraint.

## The Internal Pressure

The internal pressure manifested itself in the split in Pakistan's civilian cabinet when it was asked whether to go ahead with the tests or show restraint. One group supported immediate response in kind to India's tests and restore the balance of power structure in South Asia which Delhi had altered. This will be discussed later. First, it needs to be analysed who had opposed Pakistan's nuclear testing from within the polity of Pakistan in 1998 and why were they counselling restraint and caution. In addition, how the external pressure played a role in persuading Pakistan to seek safeguards from the international community.

It is interesting to note that from within Pakistan's polity the opposition, though small, came from Pakistan's cabinet ministers such as Sartaj Aziz, Muhammad Ishaq Dar, Choudhury Nisar, Sheikh Rashid, and General Majid Malik.[28] Amongst them the strongest voice in opposing Pakistan's nuclear tests and favouring the policy of restraint and caution was of Sartaj Aziz because of his apprehension of severe economic implications of these tests. To be sure, Pakistan's economic condition was sluggish in 1998. The Nawaz Sharif government had failed to revive the economy. For example, 4000 industrial units which had been closed because of economic constraints could not be reopened. There was a trade deficit of US $1.36 billion to US$2.62 billion and his government could not provide Rs.305 billion for the fiscal year 1997-98 while running a shortfall of Rs.100 billion. This poor economic condition could become chaotic if Pakistan chose the nuclear path. India's position was different as its economy was stable and much more sound.[29] With a US$32 billion foreign debt, Sirtaj Aziz said, Pakistan could not afford any further deterioration of its economy.

The proponents of caution and restraint argued that there was no need for Pakistan to conduct nuclear tests in response to India's because Pakistan already had this capability and could counter India with its development of Ghauri missile, that is, that Pakistan had achieved a minimum credible nuclear deterrence vis-à-vis India with its delivery system in hand. Therefore, there was no reason for Pakistan to end its nuclear ambiguity by exploding a nuclear device.[30] The critics asserted that Pakistan's tests would not only stop the flow of foreign aid but also discourage foreign investment which would be disastrous for the country's ailing economy.[31]

The critics suggested that Pakistan's nuclear weapons capability did not need demonstration and that restraint would boost Pakistan's image as a responsible state in the international community and would help her gain nuclear guarantee from the US against any possible military threat from India.[32] Other critics such as Qureshi suggested that the international community, especially the US, should bear the cost of Pakistan's economy and military build-up in return for not testing nuclear weapons, that is, Pakistan could demand 200 updated F-16 aircraft, advanced radar, high altitude antiaircraft missiles, anti-ship missiles, air-to-air refuelling tankers, tanks, ships and sub-marines.[33] And Pakistan's two former air force chiefs (Asghar Khan and Nur Khan) including a number of retired army generals were not convinced of Pakistan's so-called strategic and balance of power ideology. They were of the opinion that May 1998 was a God-sent opportunity and that the policy of restraint would result in Pakistan's economic boom.[34]

The arguments of the anti-nuclear lobby that the country's economy could ill afford a nuclear arsenal, though plausible, could not impress the hawks. In fact, the voice of those who wanted a like response from Pakistan grew stronger by the day. The supporters analysed all the options but opted for demonstration of the nuclear capability. How did they support this policy? Were the supporters of Pakistan's nuclear weapons testing more influential than the internal and external critics who were calling for caution and restraint?

How did the proponents of nuclear weapons tests defeat the critics and mould public opinion to their logic? The next section will deal with the factors that answer this question.

## The Proponents of Pakistan's Nuclear Weapon Tests

Before examining the support for Pakistan's nuclear weapons tests in 1998, it is interesting to note that Pakistan's epistemic community emphasised Pakistan's option of nuclear weapons for purposes of deterrence which perhaps played a decisive role in persuading the government to acquire and conduct nuclear weapons.[35] The epistemic community insisted that Pakistan had to unveil its nuclear ambiguity and acquire nuclear weapons. For example, Tariq Jan's edited volume[36] stated that to deter India, the nuclear weapons' option was important for Pakistan. In its view the acquisition of nuclear weapons was necessary both to protect the ideology and territorial integrity of Pakistan. The volume condemned the NPT's nuclear discrimination and urged Pakistan's nuclear leadership to be self-reliant in respect of its acquisition of nuclear weapons.[37] Agha Shahi stated, "In South Asian context, nuclear weapons are instruments of military and political powers that could be turned to advantage in the pursuit of regional hegemony."[38] Whilst Abdul Sattar emphasised, "Not until 1971, when Pakistan's conventional defence capacity proved inadequate to safeguard its territorial integrity, and East Pakistan was militarily separated by India to create Bangladesh, did Pakistan embark upon efforts to acquire nuclear weapons option as a means of deterring the persistent Indian threat."[39] Besides Shahi and Sattar, who were foreign ministers of Pakistan when Pakistan was in a security dilemma whether to acquire nuclear weapons or sign NPT to forgo the nuclear weapons option, others from within Pakistan's epistemic community such as retired army general K. M Arif and former Air Marshal Zulfiqar Ali Khan remained equally influential in urging Pakistan's nuclear leadership to keep the nuclear option open. Arif stated that Pakistan faced a strong Indian conventional might and this could be deterred neither by conventional means nor by the external security guarantee;[40] and Zulfiqar Ali Khan contended that the threat faced by Pakistan from its adversary is not a dream but a 'harsh reality'... Pakistan should have an option for acquiring nuclear weapons in order to offset the might of India's conventional power. The acquisition of nuclear weapons will provide Pakistan a strong deterring force vis-à-vis India, improve its status as a major power in the region even though smaller in size than its adversary, and would ensure Pakistan's security and territorial integrity.[41] Almost every one of these analysts was of the view that Pakistan should not sign the NPT and retain the option for acquiring nuclear weapons that were meant to deter India, and that nuclear weapons would ensure Pakistan's territorial integrity and sovereignty. They linked the acquisition of nuclear weapons to Pakistan's national interest and its security vis-à-vis India.

In addition to these expert views, there was widespread political support from major parties like the Pakistan Peoples Party, the Muslim League, the religious parties and large number of intellectuals who called upon the leadership to go for nuclear tests. The former PAEC Chairman, Munir Ahmed Khan, stated that if Pakistan did not conduct the tests, its nuclear weapons development programme would be 'over-rated and overplayed' and it could be said that "Pakistan might be just bluffing."[42] The Nawaz government took some time to devise an appropriate policy. A cabinet meeting was held to form a committee to evaluate the peace and security situation of the country which had been altered by the Indian nuclear tests. The committee comprised Sartaj Aziz (Finance Minister), Gohar Ayub (Foreign Minister), Mushahid Hussein (Information Minister), Siddique Kanjo (Minister of State for Foreign Affairs), Lieutenant-General (retired) Abdul

Majid Malik (Minister for Kashmir Affairs and Northern Areas) and Raja Zafar-ul- Haq (Minister of Religious Affairs and Minorities). In addition to them, the three chiefs of Pakistan's armed forces were also brought into the core discussion on the issue.[43]

Just before Pakistan's nuclear tests, there also had been a parliamentary discussion over the issue. A strongly worded resolution on May 14, 1998 was passed which condemned the Indian nuclear tests and opposed the international community's pressure for dissuading Pakistan from going nuclear. The Parliamentary resolution was also opposed to those elements within Pakistan that were against Pakistan's nuclear tests and were pleading restraint in order to get the benefits of international economic and military aid.[44] There were, however, voices within the parliament that suggested that Pakistan bargain with the international community for guarantees against India. Others such as Sirtaj Aziz, Sheikh Rashid, General Majid Malik, Choudhury Nisar and Muhammad Ishaq Dar were worried about economic sanctions that the international community might impose if Pakistan conducted the tests (Hussein 1998). At the Foreign Office level it was apparent that Pakistan was ready to join the nuclear weapons club. Gohar Ayub (the then Foreign Minister) stated that testing nuclear weapons was a matter of "when, not if, Pakistan will test."[45] It is interesting to note that his father Ayub Khan, the former military dictator of Pakistan, who went to war with India, did not harbour nuclear ambitions.

The role of Pakistan's public opinion remained equally instrumental in Pakistan's option for the tests. Public opinion was manipulated in such a way that the government could not decide against the nuclear weapons' tests. According to Gallup survey published on May 25, a few days before Pakistan's nuclear tests, 70 per cent of the respondents favoured nuclear testing and 30 per cent suggested restraint to seek military and economic benefits from the international community. According to Kroc Institute's survey, 61 per cent of the people were in favour of the tests and 85 per cent of the elite justified Pakistan's nuclear response to India's tests.[46] The public survey from various sources indicated that there was strong support in favour of Pakistan's nuclear tests. Public opinion in the country played an effective part in shaping the policies of Pakistan's decision-makers in going for the tests and acquisition of nuclear weapons. In this environment of strong public demand and the predominant position of Pakistan's armed forces and other analysts from across the country ultimately convinced the then polity under the civilian leadership of Nawaz Sharif that there was no choice but to go for the bomb.

Nawaz Sharif announced that "we have settled scores with India...We have paid them back."[47] On 28 May, 1998, Chinese spokesman Zhu Bangzao, just hours before Pakistan's tests, was again asked if Beijing supported or opposed a nuclear test by Pakistan. He made it clear that China believed India was responsible for the nuclear crisis in South Asia. "The current situation in South Asia was created solely by India. India, in disregard of strong international opposition, brazenly conducted nuclear tests and threatened its neighbours." He reiterated that, "the most pressing matter for the international community now is to act together to immediately demand that India abandon its plan to develop nuclear weapons and change its mistaken stance. Only in this way can the security concerns of this region be fundamentally resolved."[48]

Pakistan finally adopted the long pursued *opponent-centric nuclear posture.* This was in the wake of long and controversial public debate in Pakistan and the US pressures to dissuade Pakistan from nuclear testing by providing Pakistan economic and military assistance. Pakistan remained determined to acquire nuclear weapons despite formidable constraints from both internal sources (opposition to Pakistan's policy of conducting nuclear weapons' tests) and external sources (pressure of international community and strict nuclear export control).[49]

There can be certain reasons why Pakistan's security epistemic community (SEC) shared ideas and beliefs that remained influential and successful. First, Pakistan considers and justifies its nuclear development programme as a response to India's. Both these states have fought more than three times and confronted several other limited crises. They have been rivals since their inception in 1947, and Kashmir and other outstanding issues have strained their relationship. Pakistan's SEC have propagated their shared ideas and beliefs that the country cannot deter its adversary with conventional means. If Pakistan desires to protect its territorial integrity and maintain its sovereignty, it needs to develop and acquire nuclear weapons to offset the conventional might of its rival. Due to this conflicting past, the shared ideas and beliefs in relation to state security were likely to be more successful, and hence institutionalised. In the words of John Ikenberry, "Particular historical moments can provide expert groups wielding new policy approaches and philosophies with opportunities to decisively shape a government's conception of the national interest."[50] So it was this defining situation that tilted Pakistan's decision in favour of the nuclear option. In the words of Foote, "Motivation refers to degree to which a human being, as a participant in the ongoing social process in which he necessarily finds himself, defines a problematic situation as calling for performance of a particular act..."[51]

Second, the shared opinion and expert advice of Pakistan's SEC were both credible and capable of influencing the state policy on security related matters. The success of diffusion, selection, and persistence of shared ideas and beliefs depends on their effectiveness, translation, and capability of popularisation. They should "be capable of being transmitted through a mechanism in a way that affects behaviour in a desirable way from the standpoint of the members of a community."[52] In addition to this, Pakistan's SEC remained accessible to Pakistan's nuclear management because majority of them were/are part of government officialdom. The epistemic community's access, as Haas argued, to main decision-makers in an issue-area is one of the reasons of success of the policy ideas.[53]

Third, for shared ideas and beliefs to be innovated, transmitted, and accepted, it is important that these shared ideas and beliefs converge with the state security interest. Both shared ideas and beliefs should be congruent to the state's political or strategic culture. Pakistan's state leadership and ideas and expert opinion from within its SEC merged together for the policy ideas to be selected and persisted. Any divergence of interests between the epistemic community and the state may not help the shared ideas to be selected and persisted. Had Zia's military regime not been interested in developing and acquiring nuclear weapons, the shared voices of Pakistan's nuclear family could not have been effective, and hence not institutionalised. Ayub's military regime's turning down Bhutto's stance for acquiring nuclear weapons is an example to this convergence-divergence approach of interest, that is, Bhutto's perception for acquiring nuclear weapons[54] at that particular time did not match with the pre-existing beliefs of Ayub's regime who was more interested in military forces rather than nuclear weapons.[55]

Finally, Pakistan's knowledge-based experts could better crystallise their set of opinions in respect of Pakistan's development and acquisition of nuclear weapons because, majority of the members of Pakistan's SEC had served Pakistan's government on various important fronts. Their ideational endeavours and shared beliefs built a 'winning coalition' within the Pakistan's government. They had an authoritative claim to setting up a security agenda for

Pakistan's security. Their shared voices in support of Pakistan's acquisition of nuclear weapons have not only resisted the internal[56] and external pressure, but also manipulated the public opinion in such a way that the latter could not deny the knowledge providers. The authoritative claim to their ideas helped the policies to be adopted and acted upon.

## Conclusion

Pakistan was looking for a concrete security guarantee from a major power visà-vis India's nuclear weapons capability, but the major power failed to convince Pakistan and its polity that in the event of any crisis with its adversary the security umbrella would be guaranteed. Due to the lack of security guarantee coupled with the discriminatory approach of the major power towards Pakistan, Pakistan felt more insecure, isolated, and unconvinced. Despite external and internal pressure, the only option left for Pakistan was to demonstrate its nuclear weapons capability. Cohen is quoted to have said, "Pakistan is a profoundly insecure state. It is a state that feels itself surrounded by enemies, beginning with Iran, a security problem. Afghanistan has turned out to be a terrible disaster for them. The Indians are as troublesome as ever. Their friends are not really friends. The US has moved out of the region, and the Chinese are cool. Add to that the domestic troubles."[57]

In a similar vein, in response to two articles titled "Against the Nuclear Apartheid" by Jaswant Singh, senior advisor on India's defence and foreign affairs (September/October 1998) and "Dealing with the Bomb in South Asia" by the former US Deputy Secretary of State, Strobe Talbott (March/April 1999) published in *Foreign Affairs Journal*, Pakistan's former Foreign Secretary Shamshad Ahmad stated that, "To restore strategic balance to South Asia, Pakistan was obliged to respond to India's May 1998 nuclear blasts. India already held an advantage in conventional weaponry, and it followed its underground tests with statements threatening nuclear blackmail. Pakistan's nuclear tests were undertaken in self-defence."[58] That said, Pakistan did not refrain from carrying out nuclear weapons tests despite internal and external pressure. Pakistan disclosed that its primary motivation of conducting nuclear weapon tests was to follow in the footsteps of India on the basis of nuclear deterrence and self defence. The claims by the proponents of Pakistan's nuclear weapons tests seemed stronger and convincing for Pakistan's government than that of the critics.

Keeping all these factors into consideration, the following assumptions could be made as to why Pakistan responded by retaliatory nuclear tests to India's in 1998. First, if Pakistan did not respond to nuclear tests in kind, India's statement on 'Pakistan's possession of nuclear weapons and their testing is a bluff' would prove correct not only to India but this would also assure the international community that, in fact, Pakistan was bluffing about its possession and testing of nuclear weapons. Second, Pakistan would lose its nuclear weapons capability and credibility if it showed restraint and kept its nuclear weapons' opacity. A nuclear India would have a greater and hegemonic say in the South Asian region finding Pakistan weak with no credible nuclear capability. It would plunge Pakistan's nuclear leadership into psychological confusion if the tests were not conducted to correct the balance of power disturbed by India's initiative. Third, Pakistan could not set aside the strong security rationale in favour of restraint for the sake of international guarantees in the background of the conflicts that have marred the relationship of the two countries since their inception. Signing the NPT/CTBT unilaterally and accepting the offers made by the international community for not conducting the nuclear weapons tests in 1998 would mean that Pakistan forget its long history of conflicts with India, leave aside all its endeavours and investments on Pakistan's nuclear weapons development programme, and overlook the contribution of those individuals who shaped the country's security rationale since its inception.

Taking these factors into consideration, it was not easy for anybody to summarily dismiss the plea for the nuclear weapons tests. The most effective option left – albeit a difficult option – for Pakistan in the 1998 scenario was testing the nuclear weapons and declaring Pakistan a nuclear-weapons state to boost state security and restore equilibrium in South Asia.

## References


1. Nawaz Sharif's Declaration to the Nation 1998, cited in Samina Ahmed, "Pakistan Nuclear Weapons Program: Turning Points and Nuclear Choices," *International Security,* Vol. 23, no. 4 (1999): 178-204.
2. Feroz Hassan Khan, "Nuclear Proliferation Motivations," *The Non-Proliferation Review,* Vol. 13, no. 3 (2006): 501-517.
3. Rai Muhammad Saleh Azam, "When Mountains Move: The Story of Chagai," *Defence Journal* (June 2000), http://www. defencejournal.com/2000/june/chagai.htm(accessed June 15, 2011).
4. *Ibid.*
5. Ayesha Khan and Zaffar Abbas, "Pakistan Joins the Club," *Bulletin of Atomic Scientists,* Vol. 54, no. 4 (July-August, 1998): 7.
6. For details see Rabia Akthar, "Nuclearlisation of Pakistan: Motivations and Intentions," *CCRP*, www.dodccrp.org/events/10th_ICCRTS/CD/track01.htm (accessed June 14, 2011).
7. Bhumitra Chakma, *Pakistan Nuclear Weapons* (London: Routledge Taylor and Francis Group Publications, 2009), 65.
8. Naeem Salik, *The Genesis of South Asian Nuclear Deterrence: Pakistan's Perspective* (London: Oxford University Press, 2009), 209-210.
9. *Ibid.*, 211-212.
10. For Pakistan's Foreign Minister's statement in response to India's May 11, 1998 nuclear test see, "May 1998 Pakistan Special Weapons News," *Federation of AmericanScientists* (FAS), http://www.fas.org/

news/pakistan/1998/05/index.html (accessed June 14, 2011). Other Pakistan's officials' statements against the Indian nuclear weapon tests can also be seen. Also see, "Pakistan's Foreign Minister Gohar Ayub Khan," *News International,* May 12, 1998.

11. For this quotation see for example, Rabia Akthar, "Nuclearlisation of Pakistan: Motivations and Intentions."

12. For these statements see, "Time Line: History of India-Pakistan Conflict," *Washington Post,* http://www.washingtonpost.com/wpsrv/inatl/longterm/southasia/timeline.htm (accessed July 14, 2011).

13. The former Pakistan's Prime Minister statement on *Pakistan's nuclear deterrence* posture, in Bhumitra Chakma, Pakistan Nuclear Weapons (London: Routledge, 2009), 48.

14. See for example, Cyril Almeida, "Uncontested Dominance," *Dawn,* 2010, http://www.dawn.com/wps/wcm/connect/dawn-content-library/dawn/thenewspaper/columnist (accessed September 2, 2010); Mario Esteban Carranza, *South Asian Security and International Nuclear Order: Creating a Robust Indo-Pakistan's Nuclear Arms Control Regime* (England: Ashgate Publishers, 2009), 63; Rodney W. Jones, *Minimum Nuclear Deterrence in South Asia: An overview* (US Defence Threat Reduction Agency: Advance Systems and Concepts Office, 2001), 36; Rizwan Zeb, "David Versus Goliath? Pakistan's Nuclear Doctrine: Motivations, Principles and Future," *Defence & Security Analysis* Vol. 22, no. 4 (2007): 387-408.

15. Hassan Askari Rizvi, "Pakistan's Nuclear Testing," *Asian Survey,* Vol. 41, no. 6 (2001): 941

16. For details of Chinese reactions to both India's and Pakistan's nuclear weapons tests see, "China and Nuclear Tests in South Asia," *Nuclear Threat Initiative* (NTI), http://www.nti.org/db/china/nsascris.htm (accessed June 13, 2011).

17. For interesting accounts on Pakistan-US relations when Pakistan was not given the military and economic assurances, Pakistan expected during the 1965 and 1971 wars with its adversary see for example, Dennis Kux, *The United States and Pakistan, 1947-2000: Disenchanted Allies* (Washington: Woodrow Wilson Centre Press, 2001); Howard Wriggins, "The Balancing Process in *Pakistan's Foreign Policy," in Pakistan: The Long Way,* ed. Lawrence Ziring, Ralph Braibanti & Howard Wriggins (Durham,N. C: Duke University Press, 1977), 301-339; Hassan Askari Rizvi, *"Pakistan*

*and the Geostrategic Environment: A Study of Foreign Policy,"* (New York: St. Martin Press, 1993); & A. Z Hilali, *US-Pakistan Relationship: Soviet Invasion of Afghanistan* (Burlington: Ashgate, 2005).

18. Shahid-ur-Rehman, *Long Road to Chagai* (Islamabad: Shahid-ur-Rehman Publishers, 1999), 116.
19. Pyongyang got US $4 billion to cap its nuclear weapons program whilst Pakistan was given vague promises that it might finally be given the 28 F-16 aircraft it bought and paid for almost a decade ago. See Barbara Crossette, "Nuclear Anxiety: The Rivalry; South Asian Arms Race: Reviving Dormant Fears of Nuclear War," *New York Times*, May 29, 1998, http://www.nytimes.com/1998/05/29/world/nuclear-anxiety rivalry-south-asian-arms-race-reviving-dormant-fears-nuclear-war.html (accessed June 13, 2011).
20. See Stephen Cohen Statement in Barbra Crossette, "Nuclear Anxiety: The Rivalry; South Asian Arms Race: Reviving Dormant Fears of Nuclear War."
21. *Ibid.*, 2.
22. Samina Yasmeen, "Pakistan's Nuclear Tests: Domestic Debate and International Determinants," *Australian Journal of International Affairs* 53 (1) (1998): 43-56.
23. Jyotsna Bakshi, "Russia's Post-Pokhran Dilemma," *Strategic Analysis* XXII, no. 5 (1998): 721-736.
24. "EU Sanctions Seem Unlikely," Dawn, May 14, 1998, http://www.fas.org/news/india/1998/05/index.html (accessed June 13, 2011)
25. Pervez Hoodbhoy, "Nuclear Myths and Realities," in *Pakistan's Atomic Bomb and the Search for Security*, ed. Zia Mian (Lahore: Gautam Publishers, 1995), 17.
26. Yasmeen, "Pakistan's Nuclear Tests: Domestic Debate and International Determinants," 53.
27. Samina Ahmad, "Pakistan Nuclear Weapons Program: Turning Points and Nuclear Choices," *International Security*, Vol. 23, no. 4 (1999): 200.
28. Talat Hussein, "Pakistan Hedged on Obvious Bet," *Nation*, May 29, 1998.

29. Yasmeen, "Pakistan's Nuclear Tests: Domestic Debate and International Determinants," 50; Hassan-Askari-Rizvi, "Pakistan in 1998: The Polity under Pressure," *Asian Survey* Vol. 39, no. 1 (1998): 181-183.
30. Talat Hussein, "Pakistan Hedged on Obvious Bet;" Asad Rehman, "Nuclear Escalation in South Asia," Nation, May 15, 1998; Farrukh Saleem, "Do Nukes Make Power?," *News*, May 24, 1998.
31. Sarfraz Iqbal, "Wazir-Azam Sey Ek Iltija Hey (A request to the Prime Minister)," *Awsaf* (Urdu Daily), 1998; Saeed Ahson Hasan, "Think Well before Testing," *Nation*, May 20, 1998.
32. Talat Hussein, "Pakistan Hedged on Obvious Bet."
33. Yusouf Qureshi, "To Test or Not to Test," *Nation*, May 20, 1998.
34. Ayesha Khan & Zaffar Abbas, "Pakistan Joins the Club," 7.
35. There are number of proponents who supported Pakistan acquisition of nuclear weapons in response to its adversarial nuclear weapons tests. Few are mentioned as: Abdul Qayyum, "Nuclear Power and the US Dual Standards," *Dawn*, April 26, 1979; Afzal Mahmood, "Priorities in Foreign Policy," *Dawn*, December 14, 1988; Anwar Shamim, "Pakistan's Security Concerns," *Dawn*, November 2, 1988; Mushahid Hussein, *Pakistan and the Changing Regional Scenario: Reflections of a Journalist* (Lahore:Progressive Publishers, 1988); K.M. Arif, "Expanding Indo-Israel Nexus," *Dawn*, June 17, 1993; Ghani Eirabi, "Blackmailing Can Backfire," *Dawn*, April 18, 1993; Jafar Wafa, "Our Security Option," *Dawn*, August 3, 1993; Muhammad Aslam Beg, "Who will Press the Button?," *News*, April 23, 1994; Gen. Mirza Aslam Beg (retd), *Development and Security: Thoughts and Reflections* (Rawalpindi: Foundation for Research on National Development and Security Press, 1994); Khurshid Ahmed, "Summation: Capping the Nation," in *Pakistan's Security and the Nuclear Option*, ed. Tariq Jan (Islamabad: Institute of Policy Studies, 1995), 145-158; Tahir Amin, "The Paradox of Civil-Military-US Triangle and Pakistan's Security," *ibid.*, 99-106; Agha Shahi, "Nuclear Non-Proliferation Treaty and the Security Dilemma," ibid., 39-53; Abdul Sattar, "Nuclear Issue in South Asia: A Pakistan's Perspective," *ibid.*, 55-90; K.M. Arif, "Retaining the Nuclear Option," *ibid.*, 121-129; S. M. Koreshi, "The Method in American Duplicity," ibid., 131-136; Syeda Hussein Abida, "Don't Give Up What is Yours and the World will Come Around," *ibid.*, 107-120; Zulfiqar Ali Khan, "Pakistan's Security and Nuclear

Option," *ibid.*, 137-144; Shireen M. Mizari, "NPT: An Unfair Treaty Pakistan Must Not Sign," *ibid.*, 29-38; Haider K. Nizamani, "Nuclear Weapons and Kashmir," Dawn, February 22, 1999; Nizamani, *The Roots of Rhetoric: Politics of Nuclear Weapons in India and Pakistan* (USA: Praeger Publications, 2000).

36. Tariq Jan, "Pakistan's Security and the Nuclear Option," 21.
37. *Ibid.*, 25.
38. Shahi, "Nuclear Non-Proliferation Treaty and the Security Dilemma," *ibid.*, 53.
39. Sattar, "Nuclear Issue in South Asia: A Pakistan's Perspective," *ibid.*, 59.
40. Arif, "Retaining the Nuclear Option," *ibid.*, 122.
41. Khan, "Pakistan's Security and Nuclear Option," *ibid.*, 140-144.
42. Munir Ahmed Khan, "Nuclearisation of South Asia and its Regional and Global Implications," *Regional Studies 26* (4) (1998): 3-58.
43. Tariq Butt, "Only Gohar, Mushahid Allowed to Speak on Foreign Policy," *Nation*, May 19, 1998.
44. Rana Qaiser, "Senate Supports Government against India," *Nation*, May 15, 1998.
45. The former Pakistan's Foreign Minister statement quoted in, Yasmeen, "Pakistan's Nuclear Tests: Domestic Debate and International Determinants," 52; Rizvi, "Pakistan's Nuclear Testing," 952.
46. Samina Ahmed & David Cortright, *Pakistan and the Bomb: Public Opinion and Nuclear Option*, ed. (Indiana: Notre Dame Publication, 1998), 15-23, 78, 92 & 111-131.
47. Nawaz Sharif's Speech to the Nation 1999, in Ahmed "Pakistan Nuclear Weapons Program: Turning Points and Nuclear Choices," 195.
48. For details of China's stance on the ultimate Pakistan's decision of conducting nuclear weapons, see http://www.nti.org/db/china/nsascris.htm (accessed June 13, 2011). It is interesting to note that China initially was in support of the policy that both India and Pakistan should not test their nuclear weapons rather should engage in resolving their outstanding issues including the core issue of Kashmir politically and peacefully. However, when

India went for nuclear tests, China seemed to be tacitly supporting Pakistan's policy of responding in kind.

49. Bhumitra Chakma, "Road to Chagai: Pakistan's Nuclear Programme: Its Sources and Motivations," *Modern Asian Studies,* Vol. 36, no. 4 (2002): 909.
50. G. John Ikenberry, (1993) "Creating Yesterday's New World Order: Keynesian 'New Thinking' and the Anglo-American Post-war Settlement," *in Ideas and Foreign Policy: Beliefs, Institutions, and Political Change,* eds. Judith Goldstein, and Robert O. Keohane (Ithaca and London: Cornell University Press, 1993), 57-86.
51. N. Foote Nelson, "Identification as the Basis for a Theory of Motivation," *American Sociological Review* 16 (1) (1951): 14-21.
52. Geoffrey Garrett and Barry R. Weingast, "Ideas, Interests, and Institutions: Constructing the European Community's Internal Market," in *"Ideas and Foreign Policy: Beliefs, Institutions, and Political Change,* 173-206.
53. Peter M. Haas, "Do Regimes Matter? Epistemic Communities and Mediterranean Pollution Control," *International Organisation* 43(3) (1989): 377-403; also see, Haas, "Introduction: Epistemic Communities and International Policy Coordination," *International Organisation* 46 (1) (1992): 1-35.
54. It is imperative to note that Zulfiqar Ali Bhutto was the first person in Pakistan's polity who had developed the perception for acquiring nuclear weapons out of Pakistan's nascent nuclear development programme. The desire for the acquisition of nuclear weapons exists in his discourses that later shaped the discourses of subsequent Pakistan's governments (civilian & military) in connection with acquisition of nuclear weapons. See, Zulfiqar Ali Bhutto, *The Myth of Independence* (London: Oxford University Press, 1969); Bhutto, *If I am Assassinated* (New Delhi: Vikas Publishers, 1979).
55. The perception for acquiring nuclear weapons is missing in Ayub Khan's discourse. There is no insight that Khan's military government was interested to acquire nuclear weapons as a deterring force vis-à-vis its adversary despite India's perception for going nuclear in the mid 1960s. See, Ayub Khan "Pakistan Perspective," *Foreign Affairs* Vol. 38, No. ¼ (1960): 547-556; Khan, *Friends, Not Masters: A Political Autobiography* (London: Oxford University Press, 1967).

56. Amongst the Pakistan's epistemic community who opposed the ideas and beliefs of acquiring nuclear weapons, Zia Mian, Pervez Hoodbhoy, Inayatullah, and Khalid Ahmed were at the forefront. This opposition to Pakistan's acquisition of nuclear weapons can be depicted through their writings in the Zia Mian edited volumes and other short pieces in the Pakistan's English news papers and magazines. See for example, Zia Mian, ed., *Pakistan's Atomic Bomb and the Search for Security* (Lahore: Gautam Publishers, 1995) and Smitu Kothari & Zia Mian, eds., *Out of Nuclear Shadow* (London: Zed Books, 2001). Also see, Khalid Ahmed, "Pakistan's America Problem: Crisis of Defiance," *Friday Times*, March 24-30, 1994; Ahmed, "NPT: More Troubles Ahead for Pakistan," *Friday Times*, December 1-7, 1994; Ahmed, "After Hiroshima: Why Do We Still Love the Bomb?," *Friday Times*, August 17-23, 1995).
57. Cohen's statement in, Barbra Crossette, "Nuclear Anxiety: The Rivalry; South Asian Arms Race."
58. Shamshad Ahmad, "The Nuclear Subcontinent: Bringing Stability to South Asia," *Foreign Affairs* (July/August, 1999): 1.

# 10

# Pakistan's Nuclearisation – Imperatives of National Security and Survival of a Smaller State

*Naeem Salik*

## Preamble

The decision by any state to go nuclear is not always easy to explain given the complexity of motivations and drivers behind such decisions. Similarly, Pakistan's imperatives for going nuclear are not simple to rationalise. An attempt will however be made to explain these to the extent possible through an examination and analysis of available literature and Pakistan's real or perceived threat perceptions. Of particular relevance for the purpose is Professor Scott Sagan's excellent exposition, "Why do States Build Nuclear Weapons? Three Models in Search of a Bomb" and an analysis based on the historical evolution of Pakistani security perceptions and its strategic culture by a prominent Pakistani security analyst, Feroz Hassan Khan, in his "Nuclear Proliferation Motivations–Lessons from Pakistan". The third source, of course, would be an analytical study of Pakistan's evolving attitudes towards nuclear weapons and understanding of the role and significance of nuclear weapons in resolving its security dilemmas. Additionally, the growing conventional imbalance, India's ever expanding nuclear prowess, failure of carefully crafted alliance relationships to underwrite Pakistan's security, and the preferences and persona of its leadership in influencing the direction of its nuclear endeavours, would also help in highlighting its compulsions for eventually deciding to take the nuclear path.

Nuclear technology is highly complex, sophisticated and cost prohibitive, involving not only cutting edge technologies and specialised machine tools but rare materials as well. These technologies and materials are not only expensive but are hard to procure. One has to carefully tread one's way through a labyrinth of technology control arrangements that have evolved, particularly after India's first nuclear test in May 1974. Over the years most of the advanced industrialised countries have also tightened and strengthened their export control laws and enforcement mechanisms. United Nations Security Council Resolution 1540 (2004) has made it obligatory for all member states to bring their national export control laws and implementation and enforcement mechanisms in line with the international standards. In addition to financial costs, efforts by any country to go nuclear under the prevailing international environment would entail serious politico-diplomatic and economic costs in the form of sanctions and international isolation. This is not to imply that procurement of nuclear materials, technology and know-how was easy at any given point of time in the past decades. It is, therefore, logical to assume that no state has taken or will ever take the decision to nuclearise without taking due cognisance of its serious repercussions. Unfortunately, though, the non-proliferation efforts usually lay too much emphasis on the supply side of proliferation to the virtual exclusion of the demand side. The tendency on the part of many analysts to rely on stereotypes to explain the causes of proliferation, results in overlooking the profundity of motives behind such decisions, and leads to shaping inappropriate and ineffectual policies.[1]

Pakistan's nuclear programme has always been at the centre of one controversy or another. Pakistan initiated its nuclear weapons programme in the early 1970s when the NPT was already in force; and when it started its efforts in earnest in the aftermath of the 1974 Indian test, technology control arrangements such as the London Suppliers Group, the precursor of the Nuclear Suppliers Group, and a series of other technology denial agreements were already evolving. Pakistan, therefore, not only had to negotiate a series of obstacles, but its nuclear programme was also unfairly labelled as the 'Islamic Bomb' which created sensitivity and political opposition amongst the pro-Israel lobbies in the United States. In such a hostile environment, Pakistan has had to pay a heavy price for attaining nuclear capability in terms of opportunity costs and political retributions in the form of layers of US sanctions. But Pakistan was willing to pay the cost since its very existence and survival was at stake. Pakistan's determination is epitomised in the famous statement made by Zulfikar Ali Bhutto in 1965 that, "If India makes an atomic bomb, then we will also do so, even if we have to eat grass or go hungry."[2]

Pakistan is erroneously regarded as a small state even by its own people. But such characterisation is probably unjustified. Precisely for this reason the expression 'smaller state' has been deliberately used here for Pakistan instead of a "small state" to highlight the fact that Pakistan is a country with a population of 170 to 180 million and an area of 0.8 million square kilometres, with the fifth largest armed forces in the world. A state with such physical attributes could be a major player in any region of the world. Pakistan also enjoys an important geo-strategic location at the crossroads of South, West and Central Asia and overlooks the entrance to the strategic Persian/Arabian Gulf. However, this very geo-strategic location, and especially the geographic configuration and orientation of the country, bring with it some serious disadvantages as well. Why then Pakistan is generally perceived as a small state has been very aptly explained by Thomas Perry Thornton:

> *When Pakistan became independent in 1947 it was the fifth most populous nation, but three of the four above it – China,India and the Soviet Union – were its nearby neighbours. Pakistanis came to think of themselves as a small country that had to shape its foreign and security policies accordingly. To make matters worse, Pakistan came into existence split in two and lacking strategic depth; its borders were ill-defined and indefensible, dividing ethnic groups. Thus from its very inception, Pakistan was an 'insecurity state' that perceived itself not only as small and disadvantaged but as on the defensive against a real and present threat, with its survival at stake.*[3]

Pakistan's decision to pursue a nuclear weapons capability is deeply rooted in its historical experience as a young nation. Faced with a much larger adversary and located in a difficult neighbourhood, Pakistan has been perpetually struggling for its survival. A brief overview of Pakistan's history is pertinent here to be able to understand the context of Pakistan's nuclearisation before we proceed to explain it in terms of the more immediate causes based on its security perceptions and other geo-strategic compulsions.

## A Brief Historical Background

Pakistan appeared on the world map as a newly independent state on 14th of August 1947 as a result of the British decision to grant independence to the new dominions of India and Pakistan by partitioning the South Asian subcontinent. Though the decision to allow the establishment of a Muslim state in the North Western and North Eastern parts of India had resulted from a long politico-legal and constitutional process, it was not accepted by the Indian leadership with good grace, while there was some opposition amongst segments of Muslim community as well, especially amongst the religious parties, some prominent Hindu leaders supported the partition.[4] Unfortunately, the partition which caused the largest mass migrations in history involving scores of millions was accompanied by widespread communal violence resulting in large scale loss of life and property. This bitter memory of partition has left deep and indelible marks on the psyche of the two nations and has continued to bedevil the relations of the two states and impeding development of good neighbourly relations between them. It took over five decades for an Indian leader to formally accept the reality of Pakistan when Prime Minister Vajpayee visited the site in Lahore in February 1999, where the historic resolution, which codified the aspirations of the Muslims of the subcontinent for a separate homeland, was passed in March 1940.[5] The gesture was reciprocated by President Musharraf when he paid his tributes at the Mausoleum of India's supreme leader Mahatma Gandhi during his visit to New Delhi in 2001.[6]

Pakistan was born with serious structural problems. Its two wings were separated by a thousand miles of hostile territory and the government machinery was virtually non-existent. The only solace was the presence of some experienced hands from the Indian Civil service but they were faced with the challenge of building up the administrative machinery virtually from a scratch in the face of severe resource constraints. The only other national institution with long established traditions of professionalism, institutional coherence, discipline and organisation was the military which Pakistan inherited from the erstwhile British Indian Armed Forces. Unfortunately, the Indian government held back the bulk of weapons, munitions and equipment that was due to be transferred to Pakistani armed forces. Additionally, the burden of rehabilitation of millions of refugees made the situation look very bleak with apparently insurmountable difficulties. Pakistan's founder Muhammad Ali Jinnah's untimely death in September 1948, just over a year after independence, came as a severe blow to a fledgling nation's morale and confidence. His closest lieutenant and the first Prime Minister of Pakistan also did not survive long enough to oversee the consolidation process when he was assassinated in Rawalpindi in October 1951. These setbacks and plethora of economic, political and administrative problems encouraged Indian leaders in their belief that this unique experiment in nation building was bound to fail sooner than later and Pakistan would one day fall back into the lap of mother India.

The unsatisfactory handling of the fate of the princely states by the last British Viceroy and his team created new sources of friction amongst the two newly independent states. Two such states came into prominence namely Hyderabad Deccan and Jammu and Kashmir. Whereas Hyderabad was a Hindu majority state with a Muslim ruler, Jammu and Kashmir was a predominantly Muslim majority state (about 80 per cent Muslims) with a Hindu ruler. India annexed Hyderabad with military force in September 1948. India supported the Maharaja of Kashmir's efforts to suppress an internal rebellion that tribesmen from Pakistan's North West Frontier Province had joined. It airlifted its forces to the state capital Srinagar and accepted the Maharaja's controversial instrument of accession to India.

The rivalry between India and Pakistan has been so deeply internalised in popular perceptions over the last six decades that it has come to be regarded as the obvious outcome of their creation. However, some prominent Pakistani analysts have argued that this was in fact an unexpected outcome in stark contrast to the vision of Pakistan's founding fathers who had seen in the creation of a separate homeland in their majority areas a solution to the communal mistrust, friction and hostility that had developed during the period of half a century preceding the independence.[7] According to Dr Hassan Askari Rizvi, "Pakistan's founders thought that the new state would protect, not threaten India."[8] He goes on to cite from Dr Muhammad Iqbal - the poetphilosopher who had propounded the idea of a separate Muslim homeland during the course of his address to the annual convention of the All India Muslim League at Allahabad in 1930 - as saying that, Pakistan should not worry India, for "the North-West Indian Muslims will prove the best defenders of India against a foreign invasion, be that invasion one of the ideas [an obvious reference to the Communist threat from the Soviet Union] or of the bayonets."[9] Similar sentiments were expressed by Muhammad Ali Jinnah in the early 1940s, when he stated, "We join together as good friends and neighbours and say to the world, 'Hands of India'."[10]

However, instead of becoming good neighbours somewhat like the United States and Canada, complementing each other's socio-economic development, Pakistan and India became staunch rivals and antagonists. Stephen Cohen, a noted South Asia expert, has thus observed that:

> *...India and Pakistan immediately clashed over three issues. The boundaries created through the partition were viewed as neither fair nor just. The division of civil and military assets was inequitable. Most importantly, the accession of the princely states was improper. The most glaring injustice was created by the accession into India of the state of Jammu and Kashmir - a Muslim majority state under a Hindu ruler or maharaja.*[11]

## Origins of Pakistan's Nuclear Development

Pakistan was a relatively late entrant in the nuclear arena. It was not until a touring nuclear exhibition came to Pakistan in 1954 under the auspices of President Eisenhower's 'Atoms for Peace' initiative that some interest in this new technology was generated. Pakistan Atomic Energy Commission (PAEC) decided to enter into an agreement with the United States for the provision of a 5 MW Research Reactor in 1957. It was hoped that the reactor would be functional by 1960, however, due to bureaucratic inertia, lack of funding and disinterested leadership it only went critical in 1965.[12] By that time India had established complete fuel cycle facilities including fuel fabrication and heavy water production plants, a plutonium production reactor built with Canadian and American assistance, a chemical reprocessing plant – the first of its kind in Asia[13] and a conversion plant needed to convert separated plutonium into metallic form. Only a few of the Indian nuclear facilities such as the Tarapur Power Plant were under IAEA safeguards, the rest were un-safeguarded leaving India free to do with whatever it wanted to do with the materials produced by these plants.

The focus of Pakistan's nuclear research and development in the first decade and a half was on peaceful applications of nuclear energy specifically in the fields of medical, agriculture and power generation. The first nuclear power plant, a 137 MW CANDU type reactor constructed at Karachi with Canadian assistance and under IAEA safeguards was inaugurated in 1972.[14] During the 1960s a large number of young scientists and engineers were sent abroad for specialised and advanced training. Some of those chose to stay back while many others returned to Pakistan. Many of these, helped train the coming generations of nuclear scientists and engineers at the Pakistan Institute of Nuclear Science and Technology (PINSTECH) which was co-located with the research reactor at Nilore near Islamabad. Uranium exploration, mining and processing skills and related infrastructural facilities were also being developed. When Mr Z.A. Bhutto joined President Ayub Khan's cabinet as Minister for Fuel, Power and Natural Resources, he found the nascent nuclear programme as part of his portfolio.[15] He tried to energise the programme but could not achieve much in the face of the powerful duo of Finance Minister and the Chairman of the Planning Commission. Neither did he find any support from President Ayub or the military top brass. The lack of interest amongst the military leadership was due to the fact that by the early 1960s the well trained Pakistani Armed Forces equipped with American military hardware were confident of their ability to deter, even defeat Indian military which had been badly mauled and humiliated in their border war with the Chinese in late 1962. Bhutto, then Foreign Minister, took serious note of the inauguration of India's first reprocessing plant in early 1964 and urged President Ayub Khan to allow the procurement of a similar plant which the French were willing to sell at that time, but was overruled by the financial bureaucracy.[16]

## How and Why Pakistan Went Nuclear?

### The Early Nuclear Discourse

Nuclear issues had never caught the imagination of the Pakistani public or its political elites. Neither the military leadership evince any interest in nuclear technology nor did the political leadership grasp the significance of the fast growing Indian nuclear programme for Pakistan's security, with the sole exception of Zulfikar Ali Bhutto. The Foreign Policy establishment with stalwarts like Agha Shahi was also well aware of the intricacies of the nuclear issues and showed good foresight in keeping Pakistan's options open once India decided to stay out of the NPT. There was no public debate over whether or not Pakistan should join the NPT and Pakistan's decision to stay out of the NPT was largely a bureaucratic decision. It is hard to find any serious nuclear discourse in Pakistan in either the media or academia during the 1960s and early 1970s except the statements made by Agha

Shahi in the Eighteen-Nation Disarmament Committee (ENDC) – the precursor to the present day Conference on Disarmament (CD) and United Nations General Assembly sessions. Mr Bhutto who had clearly discerned the linkage between India's nuclear ambitions and Pakistan's threat perceptions and had given expression to his feelings through the 'eating grass' statement in 1965, dilated upon nuclear issues in much greater detail in his book *The Myth of Independence* published in 1969. However, his statements are usually quoted out of context of the overall vision he had laid out for Pakistan's future security.

Although Bhutto realised that nothing can counter the strategic threat posed by the adversary's nuclear weapons than owning nuclear weapons of your own, this was not the only option in his mind to counter the Indian military threat to Pakistan. He argued that, "All wars of our age have become total wars;....and it will have to be assumed that a war waged against Pakistan is capable of becoming a total war. It would be dangerous to plan for less, and our plans should, therefore, include the nuclear deterrent."[17] He was critical of the NPT and cautioned his country not to be deceived by an unjust treaty which had legitimised the possession of nuclear weapons only for five countries. He was also closely following nuclear technological developments in India and was convinced that India would not let the major powers monopolise nuclear weapons. Bhutto predicted that sooner or later India would detonate its own nuclear weapon and if Pakistan restrained its nuclear development it would become vulnerable to nuclear blackmail by India.[18] Referring to the fact that India had received substantial technical assistance from foreign countries and was continuing to do so, he wanted Pakistan to embark on a similar effort. However, he was pragmatic enough to recognise the challenges such a programme would pose and the long gestation period before it would yield some results. He, therefore, viewed it as a long term objective and something that would not be of any practical value should there be a military confrontation with India in the short term.[19]

Given his socialist political philosophy and his fascination with Mao's People's War concept he also proposed a kind of 'Nation in Arms' concept wherein he was advocating training and arming the civilian population of the country so that even in case Indians were able to overcome regular Pakistani military they would face resistance at every step. This is evident from the following excerpt from his book:-

> *...A non-industrialised country, without even the basis of a heavy industry, cannot depend entirely on the traditional defence system of a small, though highly efficient, armed force equipped with conventional weapons.....The economic strains created by the expansion of a standing force would be great, and it would be unwise to think in terms of competing with India in size of forces and quantity of equipment.*[20]

Seeking inspiration from the Vietnamese people's struggle against the military might of the United States, he argued that the lesson Pakistan could learn from that war was that an armed and determined populace can successfully resist any foreign invader even if that invader was a global power. He proposed a 'national militia' led by professionally trained military officers to augment the standing army in the event of any war. He also advocated the introduction of compulsory military training in the universities besides training the rural population in the handling of small arms.[21]

He went on to add that, "Diffused warfare is extremely costly for the aggressor and offers no hope of a speedy victory. The knowledge that an attack upon Pakistan would lead to total warfare against a fully armed nation can be the only real deterrent"...... [22]

Parallel to the people's war concept he also invoked the religious injunctions about war as enunciated in the Quran quoting some verses which enjoin upon the Muslims that, "Fighting in the defence of Truth and Right is not to be undertaken light-heartedly, nor to be evaded as a duty.... Not all can be chosen to fight for God. It requires constancy, firmness and faith. Given these, large armies can be routed by those who battle for God."[23] Such references were obviously aimed at raising the morale of the people and to build their will and determination to fight a numerically superior enemy, trying to impress upon them that given the righteousness of their cause they were bound to be victorious as predicted by the Quran. He was in no doubt that if Pakistan gave in to the external pressures it would lose its sovereignty and independence.[24] In other words it would tantamount to a sort of 'Finlandisation' of Pakistan. It is, therefore, unfair to definitively conclude from the arguments in the book that Bhutto had already irrevocably made up his mind to pursue a nuclear weapons option as and when he will assume power in Pakistan, given the fact that his earlier advocacy had not made any headway due to an unresponsive President and active opposition of the finance minister.

## The Trauma of 1971 War

Bhutto took over power in Islamabad in the wake of the traumatic events of 1971 war, wherein, Pakistan had lost its Eastern wing through active Indian military intervention, which had further widened the military imbalance with India. Faced with the challenge of rebuilding a distraught and demoralised nation and hamstrung by resource constraints, he could not afford to experiment with fanciful, risky and alien concepts such as the people's war. He must also have realised that in a politically fragile country, like Pakistan, imparting military training and arming the populace could become a danger to the state authority and also encourage fissiparous tendencies. Pakistani leadership had seen the futility of dependence on allies who couldn't prevent the dismemberment of the country and had realised that in any future crisis Pakistan would have to fend for itself. Bhutto's search for a credible security mechanism to guard against any future Indian aggression and his desire to close the widening gap between the conventional military capabilities of the two countries, naturally led him to the nuclear weapons option. Pakistan's precarious security situation called for drastic measures and irrespective of Bhutto's past rhetoric, nuclear weapons' option was the only logical solution available at the time. Consequently, Bhutto convened a meeting of nuclear scientists in Multan. This was supposed to be a highly classified meeting where a very sensitive national security decision was to be taken. However, instead of holding it behind closed doors to ensure secrecy, the meeting was held under a tarpaulin roof in the lawn of the house of a ruling party politician, much in keeping with Mr Bhutto's dramatic populist style of politics.[25]

The senior scientists including the future Nobel Laureate Dr. Abdus Salam and the incumbent Chairman of PAEC, Dr. Ishrat Usmani, were not supportive of the nuclear weapons option and wanted to maintain the peaceful orientation of the programme. However, the younger scientists were far more enthusiastic and very vocal in their support of the weapons programme. They dominated the proceedings and Bhutto got what he wanted. He announced to the gathering his decision to replace Dr Usmani with Munir Ahmad Khan as the Chairman of PAEC,[26] a position he was to retain for the next 18 years. Munir Ahmad Khan had worked for over a decade in the IAEA as head of its nuclear power programme and was convinced of the need for Pakistan to develop a nuclear weapons option. His views had brought him closer to Mr. Bhutto when the latter was in political wilderness in Europe. Once the political decision had been taken, Munir Ahmad Khan set about preparing a road map for mastering the complete nuclear fuel cycle without which the nuclear dream could not be translated into reality. The next logical step was to set up a procurement network and start acquiring essential pieces of equipment and technology from Europe.

## The First Indian Nuclear Test in May 1974 and the Pakistani Response

The pace of development of the essential nuclear facilities and infrastructure however, remained sluggish, until in May 1974[27] the Indians shocked both the Pakistanis as well as the Western industrialised countries. Their resultant responses were, however, at cross purposes with each other. Whereas the Pakistanis were trying to speed up their procurement efforts, the Western suppliers were erecting a series of barriers in their way in the form of technology control and denial regimes.

After the Indian test, Bhutto convened a meeting of the Defence Committee of the Cabinet (DCC) on 15th of June 1974 and decided to initiate a nuclear weapons programme28, this time around in a more formal setting. Since the Indian test had further vitiated Pakistan's security environment, the acquisition of a nuclear weapons capability had now become unavoidable. It was decided to redouble the efforts to procure the necessary technology and equipment. As Feroz Hassan Khan has aptly remarked, India's maiden test in the Pokhran desert had turned 'a policy option' for Pakistan into an 'imperative'.[29] Bhutto's first reaction to the Indian test was to send his Foreign Minister Aziz Ahmed to Washington, Paris, London and Beijing to seek a collective or bilateral nuclear umbrella. At the declaratory level, Bhutto reacted very strongly to the Indian test both in his address to Pakistani parliament as well as in his exchange of letters with the Indian Prime Minister, Mrs. Indira Gandhi. While addressing the National

Assembly on 7th June 1974, Mr. Bhutto stated that, "a more grave and serious event...has not taken place in the history of Pakistan. The explosion has introduced a qualitative change in the situation (between the two countries)."[30] In his letter written on 6th June 1974 in response to Mrs. Gandhi's letter of 22nd May, 1974, Bhutto recalled the history of hostility between India and Pakistan since their independence which had resulted in major conflicts which took place in 1948, 1965 and again in 1971 and had left behind a legacy of unresolved disputes principally over the issue of Jammu and Kashmir. He argued that, "Pakistan has reason for unique anxiety because no two among the five nuclear weapon states have been involved in the kind of confrontation and unresolved disputes which have bedevilled India – Pakistan relations."[31] It is interesting to note that Bhutto's formulation in the above statement appears to be taking for granted India and Pakistan as nuclear weapon states.

Bhutto brushed aside the assurances given by the Indian Prime Minister that there would be no political or military implications of the test by commenting that the real issue was not of intentions but capabilities, adding that he did not see any technical difference between testing of a 'peaceful nuclear device' and that of a nuclear weapon.[32] He was also sceptical of the value of verbal assurances given by Mrs Gandhi explaining that these could not be of any value unless they were converted into binding international agreements, pointing out that in the past India had not lived up even to solemn international commitments – in relation to holding of a plebiscite in the state of Jammu and Kashmir.[33]

In an interview with Pakistani journalists on the occasion of the third anniversary of his government, Bhutto apparently made a strong plea for a Pakistani nuclear weapons programme though staying just short of making an unequivocal pronouncement of a decision to go down that path, saying that, "The US military embargo has not contributed to stability in South Asia. If conventional arms are not supplied to Pakistan under treaty obligations and the disparity reaches a stage where it threatens the stability of South Asia, Pakistan will be duty bound to take all measures to protect its integrity. Pakistan has no intention at this point of developing nuclear weapons, but the country may be forced into a military – nuclear programme....we are still examining the pros and cons of it."[34]

The Indian security analysts knowing the deficiencies in Pakistan's nuclear infrastructure remained sceptical and viewed Bhutto's statements as empty rhetoric. As *India Quarterly*, an International Affairs Journal, wrote in its issue of October-December 1974 that, "This threat to go nuclear should not be taken too seriously, because Pakistan has neither access to un-safeguarded plutonium, nor does it have a plutonium separation plant. He may be striking this posture to impress domestic public opinion and perhaps also to underline to the international community how strongly he feels on the subject."[35] Thomas Thornton, however, seems to be convinced of Bhutto's determination to respond to India's nuclear provocation saying that "once the Indians tested a nuclear device in 1974, Bhutto decided to give additional priority to Pakistan's nuclear weapons program, as a parallel way of dealing with the problem of Indian predominance through means independent of the goodwill of others."[36]

In August 1974, Pakistan made a proposal before the United Nations General Assembly for declaring South Asia as a Nuclear Weapons Free Zone (NWFZ). Though this proposal was approved by a large majority of votes it was opposed by India. It is clear that Bhutto was pursuing a three pronged strategy to deal with the situation. Firstly, while he was seeking nuclear guarantees from major powers, he had given a formal go ahead to his nuclear establishment to pursue a nuclear weapons programme. Secondly, he was maintaining an aggressive stance at the rhetorical level and was sending signals to both India and the international community that a nuclear weapons decision has become unavoidable for Pakistan. Thirdly, acutely aware of India's advances in nuclear technology and the long lead time needed for Pakistan to build its essential nuclear infrastructure, he made the NWFZ proposal at the UN to mobilise international pressure against India's nuclear programme in order to retard its further progress to gain for Pakistan some breathing space to do the catching up. From then onwards, Pakistan single-mindedly pursued the nuclear option irrespective of the costs and irrespective of changes of leadership and governments in the country. By the mid 1980s it had developed nuclear designs, tested their viability through "cold tests", prepared a nuclear test site in the Chaghai mountains in Balochistan and had commenced production of fissile material in the form of Highly Enriched Uranium.[37] But Pakistan refrained from testing to fulfil the commitment President Zia-ul-Haq had made to President Reagan that he would not embarrass him. By the late 1980s, in response to India's burgeoning ballistic missile programme, Pakistan had also started its own effort to produce missiles for its potential nuclear arsenal.

## Possible Explanations for the Pakistani Decision to Go Nuclear

Pakistan's achievements in the nuclear field are nothing less than a modern day miracle. The country had a poor industrial base, limited economic and financial resources and under-developed and weak institutions when it embarked on its nuclear journey in the face of strong non-proliferation pressures. Pakistanis, unlike the Germans, generally display a distaste for order, discipline and organisation and the chaotic nature of Pakistani society is most clearly manifest in the state of traffic on public highways and inner city roads alike. It, therefore, baffles many an observer as to how such a country succeeded in mastering a cutting edge technology requiring sophisticated skills in diverse fields of precision engineering and technology. However, more important than wondering as to how the Pakistanis were able to organise advanced industrial processes, would be the need to identify the motives behind Pakistan's pursuit of a military nuclear capability. An attempt would be made here to explain the rationale behind Pakistani nuclear decision in view of arguments offered by different scholars and to determine whether it fits neatly into a particular model or whether it would need a combination of two or more models to find a credible justification for it. Professor Thornton has for instance argued that, "...The nuclear programme is both a remarkable technological accomplishment and rational response to Pakistan's strategic situation. It gives Pakistan another type of 'equaliser' in its relationship with India – more reliable than the political support it has sought elsewhere and it has considerably increased Pakistan's capability of passive deterrence against India...it is a Pakistani, not an Islamic bomb."[38] In essence, his argument revolves around the security imperative.

Scott Sagan has developed a framework based on his three models namely 'the security model', 'the domestic politics model' and 'the norms model' to analyse the nuclear proliferation decisions by various countries.[39] Sagan believes that reliance on the security model alone is 'dangerously inadequate' since nuclear weapons have the potential to serve other important purposes as well, stating that, "Nuclear Weapons are more than tools of national security; they are political objects of considerable importance in domestic debates and internal bureaucratic struggles and can also serve as international normative symbols of modernity and identity."[40] Under the rubric of the 'Security Model' he explains that, "any state that seeks to maintain its national security must balance against any rival state that develops nuclear weapons by gaining access to a nuclear deterrent itself."[41] This variant of the security model appears to best fit Pakistan's case since it not only had to balance against India's development of nuclear weapons but, in fact, could have justifiably developed nuclear weapons capability as a means to neutralise the significant quantitative advantage India enjoyed in terms of conventional forces, even if India had not developed nuclear weapons. The other variant of the security model is seeking an alliance with a nuclear power. However, given the doubts about the credibility of extended deterrence, especially when the vital interests of the state providing extended deterrence are not involved, and failure of Pakistani efforts to secure a nuclear umbrella from one or more nuclear powers in the immediate aftermath of the Indian test in 1974, renders this as irrelevant to the Pakistani situation.

Quoting George Schultz' statement that, "proliferation begets proliferation", Sagan has argued that every time a state builds a nuclear arsenal to match its main antagonist, it triggers a chain reaction wherein it creates a threat to another regional state which in turn also exercises its nuclear option.[42] This argument is difficult to prove through an empirical analysis of the available evidence. For instance, even if it is accepted that India's nuclear weapons programme was in response to the Chinese nuclear test in 1964, (there is no logical explanation as to why India responded to the Chinese threat after a decade, given the fact that India's programme was technologically far more advanced than the Chinese programme in 1964), and in turn it led to Pakistan's decision to follow suit. There is no evidence to suggest that any other regional state felt threatened in turn by the Pakistani nuclear capability and initiated its own nuclear programme out of fear of a Pakistani nuclear threat. Similarly, Iraq may have started its nuclear weapons programme in response to the Israeli nuclear programme and Iran began its nuclear effort as a reaction to the Iraqi effort. How does one explain Iran's continued pursuit of a nuclear capability long after the Iraqi threat had disappeared? The Iraqi action cannot be logically explained in view of the fact that Egypt did not act in a similar manner despite common borders with Israel and having gone to war against that country in 1948, 1956, 1967 and 1973. It is, therefore, difficult to unconditionally accept the statement that, "...each time one state develops nuclear weapons it will increase the strategic incentives for neighbouring states to follow suit."[43] The same criterion is also not applicable to the Libyan case or indeed to the situation on the Korean peninsula.

While one can agree with Sagan's explanation of the joint decision by Brazil and Argentina in 1990 to give up their respective nuclear weapons programmes due to absence of mutual security threats, since the two countries had not fought a war since 1828, it is difficult to apply the same logic to the Soviet decision to go nuclear in response to US nuclearisation in 1945, since these two countries had also never fought a war against each other.

The 'Domestic Politics Model' does not seem to be relevant to the Pakistani decision, since the country's national nuclear programme is unique because of an almost complete national consensus as to its need for the country, despite a highly fractious political landscape. The programme has been pursued with the same vigour by leaders as diverse as Bhutto and Zia-ul-Haq to Benazir and Nawaz Sharif and irrespective of the military or democratic ruling dispensation in the country. This model, however, is more appropriate for the Iranian situation where, in addition to the external security imperatives, it is also actively employed as a tool in the domestic political competition. It also played a major part in Indira Gandhi's decision to authorise the May 1974 test as a means of overcoming her growing domestic challenges. Sagan too has argued that the Indian case best fits the 'Domestic Politics Model.'[44] In Pakistan's case neither the senior scientific leadership was in favour of pursuing a nuclear weapons programme, nor did the scientific establishment enjoy much influence until recently, while the military generally remained disinterested and, there is nothing to suggest, that it carried out any professional evaluation of the nuclear option. On the other hand, the financial managers were never favourably disposed towards it.

As for the 'Norms Model', again there is little evidence to suggest that the symbolic value of nuclear weapons was a factor leading to Pakistani nuclear weapons decision. Pakistan, unlike India, did not view nuclear weapons as status symbols or the means to propel itself as a major regional or global player. Nor has it staked a claim to a berth in the UNSC on the basis of its acquisition of a military nuclear capability. The display of life size models of Pakistani missiles and replicas of the Chaghai nuclear test site are more a function of the rivalry between the PAEC and Khan Research Laboratories (KRL) and their desire to attract public attention than any well thought out national policy to display nuclear muscles.

Professor Stephen Cohen has also corroborated the argument in favour of the "Security Model" as the raison d'etre for Pakistani nuclearisation arguing that:—

> *"Like Israel, Pakistan was founded by a people who felt persecuted when living as a minority, and even though they possess their own states (which are based on religious identity), both remain under threat from powerful enemies. In both cases, an original partition demonstrated the hostility of neighbours, and subsequent wars showed that these neighbours remained hostile. Pakistan and Israel have also followed parallel strategic policies. Both sought an entangling alliance with various outside powers (at various times, Britain, France, China, and the United States), both ultimately concluded that outsiders could not be trusted in a moment of extreme crisis, and this led them to develop nuclear weapons."*[45]

Feroz Khan and Peter Lavoy have taken a similar line saying that, "Pakistan's quest to acquire nuclear weapons arose from an urgent need to deter political coercion or outright military attack by its powerful rival India, especially when Pakistan could no longer count on an offsetting security relationship with the United States"[46]... They further argue that, "At the core of Pakistan's national identity and strategic culture is India's threat to Pakistan's survival. Since the early 1970s, Pakistan's leaders have consistently seen nuclear weapons as crucial to deterring the existential threat from India, which they believe is real."[47]

Sagan, however, is convinced that "multi-causality rather than measurement error lies at the heart of nuclear proliferation problem".[48] However, he concedes that most credible theories are the ones which can provide a rationale for the bulk of the cases and that the largest number of nuclearisation decisions of the past such as those of the US, the USSR, China, Israel and Pakistan can be most convincingly explained by the security model. Same applies to the more recent cases such as Iraq, Libya and possibly North Korea and Iran. One may, however, disagree with him on the inclusion of the Libyan case as the one that can be explained by the security model which is a bit hard to imagine since Libya was never faced with any existential threat, neither did Qaddafi – an autocratic ruler, face any domestic political pressures and therefore, Libya's motivations can probably be best explained by the norms model.[49]

Former Pakistan Foreign Minister Abdul Sattar has argued that the disastrous outcome of the 1971 War with India forced Pakistan to carry out what he calls a "painful reappraisal of its policy of nuclear abstinence". He explains that as a consequence Pakistan became acutely aware of the inadequacy of its conventional military capability and was left with no doubt about India's nefarious designs and the decision to go nuclear was a logical outcome of this reappraisal of its security environment.[50] Feroz Khan seems to concur to this line of argument stating that, "Humiliated by India in 1971 war, Pakistan wanted to acquire a nuclear capability quietly. But India's 1974 nuclear test turned a policy option into an imperative....."[51] He has also stressed the significance of a state's motivation to nuclearise and has ascribed the American failure to prevent Pakistan from going nuclear to its failure to grasp the depth and intensity of Pakistan's security concerns vis-à-vis India.[52] Feroz has carried the same argument further saying that:—

> *...Pakistan's case reveals that states that have experienced catastrophic defeats and face significant security concerns will gravitate towards nuclear weapons as their ultimate security guarantee. Insecure states that lack firm security commitments from allies and that fear for their survival are essentially 'orphan' in a nuclear armed world. Michael Mandelbaum has placed Pakistan and Israel in such a category.*[53]

Three points emerge from this statement namely, stigma of a humiliating defeat, lack of credible security guarantees by allies and existential threat, that have been used to explain the nuclearisation decisions by states. This may sound convincing as an argument but it only has a purely theoretical value since there are real practical challenges in the way of translating a 'wish' into a 'capability'. There is no gainsaying that development of nuclear capability is an extremely demanding enterprise. There are five essential ingredients all of which are critical for attaining a nuclear weapons capability. First, the requirement of highly skilled manpower trained in many technology areas such as theoretical physics, mechanical engineering, electronics, geophysics, chemical engineering including explosives chemistry and metallurgy. Second, the availability of requisite materials and components including raw materials in the form of Uranium mines, specialised metals and alloys and scores of electronic and mechanical components.

Third,manufacturing facilities to convert these materials and components into a workable device. Fourth, is the ability to design a deliverable nuclear device. Fifth, is the expertise needed in preparing nuclear test sites and availability of diagnostic equipment and a team of experts for conducting not only the nuclear explosive tests but cold tests as well, to validate the theoretical designs. If any one or more of these essentials are missing no country can achieve nuclear capability irrespective of the intensity of its motivation to go nuclear.

In Pakistan's case, time was also at premium and it had to procure necessary equipment from abroad before all loopholes in the export control regime were plugged, while at the same time, developing indigenous capabilities to design, manufacture and reverse engineering components which were not available in the international market. By the time Pakistan embarked on its nuclear weapons enterprise there was no dearth of skilled manpower. It was also endowed with adequate domestic uranium reserves. A research reactor was operating at Pakistan Institute of Nuclear Science & Technology (PINSTECH), the premier training institution in the country in the field of nuclear engineering. Pakistan started moving simultaneously on multiple routes. It began negotiating with France to procure a reprocessing plant while a team of scientists was put together to experiment with enrichment technology. Simultaneously, a weapon design team was set up in the mid 1970s to start work on producing workable nuclear devices. When the reprocessing deal with France appeared to be falling through, it quietly decided to pursue the enrichment route based on the gas centrifuge technology. It was clear after the cancellation of the reprocessing deal that it would not be possible to import complete plants from abroad and therefore through a network of procurement agents, middlemen and front companies, components of key technologies were procured. Many other countries with similar motivations are not endowed with the advantages Pakistan had and therefore, their efforts did not make any headway. A typical example is that of Libya which had acquired an almost complete centrifuge enrichment plant. However, it could not even unpack and assemble the machines due to lack of skilled manpower and was also unable to domestically produce some minor yet critical missing components.

Elsewhere, Feroz has, like Sagan, argued that no single factor can satisfactorily rationalise Pakistan's decision to nuclearise and has identified six factors which in his opinion have driven Pakistan's Nuclear Weapons effort including ineffectiveness of conventional forces to prevent 1971 disaster, loss of faith in the efficacy of alliances, introduction of the nuclear factor in South Asia by India's 1974 nuclear test, Bhutto's longstanding nuclear ambitions and the nature of civil-military relations, a sense of betrayal by the US, and concerns about the growing strategic imbalance with India.

One can of course take issue with Khan's comment about Bhutto's predisposition for acquiring a nuclear capability because his ambition cannot be taken as an independent variant. His final decision was influenced by the outcome of the 1971 war and reinforced by the May 1974 nuclear test by India. One can argue that despite Bhutto's fascination with nuclear weapons, he might have acted differently had there been no war and dismemberment of Pakistan in 1971 and especially if India had not forced his hand by its test in 1974. The second issue is with regard to civil-military relations in Pakistan. Some analysts have argued that wary of military interventionism in Pakistan, Bhutto had found an opportunity to put down a discredited and demoralised military in the aftermath of the disastrous war in 1971, as is evident from his summary dismissal of a dozen or so generals. He might also have seen in nuclear weapons instruments of national security which would reduce the salience of conventional weapons and by extension the importance and influence of the military. With his finger on the nuclear button, he would be wielding all the power with the military having to play a secondary role. This factor is hard to prove empirically and its logic has not been proven by later events. As it turned out, it is the military which has become the custodian of the nuclear arsenal, though the civilian leadership has a major say in the nuclear decision making. In the final analysis, however, all the six factors listed by Feroz are derivatives of the national security imperative. One can, therefore, safely conclude that Pakistan's case is best explained by the 'Security Model' and its decision to go nuclear emerged from the national security imperatives of a 'smaller nation' faced with a clear and present threatboth conventional as well as nuclear- to its national security and sovereignty by a larger and more powerful adversary.

## References

1. Feroz Hassan Khan, "Nuclear Proliferation Motivations – Lessons from Pakistan," *Non-Proliferation Review* 13, no.3 (November, 2006): 502.
2. Abdul Sattar, *Pakistan's Foreign Policy* 1947-2005 – *A Concise History* (Karachi, Oxford University Press, 2007), 144.
3. Thomas Perry Thornton, "Pakistan : Fifty Years of Insecurity" *in India and Pakistan – The First Fifty Years,* ed. Selig S. Harrison, Paul H. Kreisberg and Dennis Kux (The Woodrow Wilson Center for International Scholars, 1999), 171.
4. Hafeez Malik, *Dilemmas of National Security and Cooperation* (London, Macmillan, 1993), 10-15.
5. Indian Prime Minister Vajpayee visited the Minar-e-Pakistan (the Pakistan Monument) at Lahore during his historic bus journey to Lahore in February, 1999. See Owen Bennet Jones, Pakistan: *Eye of the Storm* (London, Yale University Press & New Haven, 2002), xiv.
6. "First Pak Head of State to Visit Rajghat," *The Tribune* (Chandigarh), July 15, 2001.

7. Feroz Hassan Khan, "Pakistan's Security Perspectives," *Force Magazine* (New Delhi, April 2005).
8. Hassan Askari Rizvi, "Pakistan's Strategic Culture," "South Asia in 2020: Future Strategic Balances and Alliances," Michael R. Chambers, ed., (Carlisle, Penn: US Army War College, November, 2002), 309 as quoted in Feroz Hassan Khan, "Pakistan's Security Perspectives."
9. *Ibid.*
10. *Ibid.*
11. Stephen P. Cohen, *The Idea of Pakistan* (Washington D.C., Brookings Institution Press, 2004), 46-47.
12. P.B. Sinha and R.R. Subramanium, *Nuclear Pakistan- Atomic Threat to South Asia* (New Delhi, Vision Books, 1980), 30.
13. US Department of State, "Inauguration of Indian Plutonium Separation Plant," *Airgram* No, A-253, April 29, 1964 from American Consulate, Bombay to the Department of State.
14. Sinha and Subramanium, *Nuclear Pakistan- Atomic Threat to South Asia* (New Delhi: Vision Books, 1980), 33.
15. *Ibid.*, 31-32.
16. Jozef Goldblat and Peter Lomas, "The Threshold Countries and the Future of the Non-proliferation Regime," in John Simpson ed., *Nuclear Non-proliferation: An Agenda for the 1960s* (Cambridge: Cambridge University Press, 1987), 309.
17. Zulfikar Ali Bhutto, *The Myth of Independence* (Karachi, Oxford University Press 1969), 153.
18. *Ibid.*
19. *Ibid.*
20. *Ibid.*, 152.
21. *Ibid.*, 154.
22. *Ibid.*
23. *Ibid.*, 156.
24. *Ibid.*, 157.
25. The account of this meeting is based on an interview with the late Khalid Hassan, an eminent Pakistani Journalist, who at the time was Bhutto's Press Secretary.

26. Sinha, "Nuclear Pakistan- Atomic Threat to South Asia," 35.
27. Charles K. Ebinger, *Pakistan Energy Planning in a Strategic Vortex* (Bloomington: Indiana University Press, 1981), 84.
28. Feroz Hassan Khan, "Nuclear Proliferation Motivations," 503.
29. *Ibid.*, 501.
30. *India Quarterly* xxx, no.4 (October-December 1974): 262.
31. *Ibid.*
32. *Ibid.*
33. *India Quarterly*, 263.
34. *Ibid.*, 265.
35. *Ibid.*, 266.
36. Thornton, "Pakistan : Fifty Years of Insecurity," 178.
37. Abdul Sattar, "Pakistan's Foreign Policy 1947-2005 – A Concise History," 147-150.
38. Thornton, "Pakistan : Fifty Years of Insecurity," 182.
39. Scott D. Sagan, "Why Do States Build Nuclear Weapons? Three Models in Search of a Bomb," *International Security* 21, no.3 (Winter 1996-97): 54-86.
40. *Ibid.*, 55.
41. *Ibid.*, 57.
42. *Ibid.*, 57-58.
43. *Ibid.*, 62.
44. *Ibid.*, 65.
45. Stephen P. Cohen, *India: Emerging Power* (Washington D.C., Brookings Institution Press, 2001), 204.
46. Feroz Hassan Khan & Peter Lavoy, "Pakistan: the Dilemma of Deterrence," in Muttiah Alagappa ed., *The Long Shadow: Nuclear Weapons and Security in 21st Century Asia* (Stanford University Press, 2008), 215.
47. *Ibid.*, 218.
48. Sagan, "Why Do States Build Nuclear Weapons? Three Models in Search of a Bomb," 85.
49. *Ibid.*

50. Sattar, "Pakistan's Foreign Policy 1947-2005 – A Concise History," 145.
51. Feroz Khan, "Nuclear Proliferation Motivations," 501.
52. *Ibid.*
53. *Ibid.*, 502.

■■■

# 11

# The Indian Undersea Nuclear Deterrence and Pakistan Navy

*Muhammad Azam Khan*

At around noon on July 26, 2009, Gurushuran Kaur, the wife of Indian Prime Minister broke a single coconut on the hull of a submarine in a 15 meter deep Matsya dry dock at Visakhapatnam (Vizag). The port on India's eastern seaboard in the Bay of Bengal has a disconcerting significance for Pakistan Navy. It is the site where PNS Ghazi after having effectively curtailed the Indian Carrier operations during the 1971 war had met a tragic end. But this July ceremony was no traditional naval ritual; neither was the Indian vessel an ordinary one. It was the unprecedented occasion that marked the formal launch of India's first indigenously-built 6000-ton nuclear powered submarine S-2,[1] more commonly, the Advanced Technology Vessel (ATV) or INS Arihant (destroyer of enemy), an SSBN.[2] The launch ended India's journey stretching over three decades since the inauguration of what is said to be India's worst kept secrets,[3] the ATV programme. It was also the last event in the 11-year construction period[4] of INS Arihant.

Described by Indian scientists as historic and challenging achievement, the first of the three submarines developed under the ATV project was christened as 'technology demonstrator'—a test bed for developing operational 'nuclear capabilities'.[5] S-2 will now validate its equipment and systems before commencing extensive harbour trials. Later on, it would be subjected to sea trials successful completion of which would pave the way for the boat to be commissioned as an operationally integrated unit of the Indian Navy, sometimes in 2012. The rolling out of the first ATV makes India the world's sixth country to construct and field a nuclear submarine.

S-2 is intended to form a crucial pillar of India's strategic deterrence. Its successful trials and integration will conclude India's final leg of the nuclear weapons delivery TRIAD as articulated in the Indian Maritime Doctrine (IMD) and substantiated in Indian Maritime Military Strategy Doctrine (IMMS). The launch is an extraordinary development for the littorals washing the shores of the Indian Ocean Region (IOR), particularly Pakistan. It is germane to the military nuclearisation of the Indian Ocean (IO) and noticeably dents the strategic balance with the potential to trigger a nuclear arms race.[6] It would also enhance India's outreach and allow it a comprehensive domination of the Arabian Sea, the Indian Ocean littoral and even beyond.[7] The stability and security in the IOR may never be the same again.

## The Technology and the Achilles Heel

Costing US $ 2.9 billion,[8] the ATV project was a joint effort involving several government and private organisations. These included BARC (Bhabha Atomic Research Center), DRDO (Defence Research and Development Organisation), L&T (Larsen and Toubro); a Mumbai based private defence contractor[9] along with some major contributions by the Indian Navy.

India's nuclear propelled ballistic missile submarine

is the world's smallest yet will pack a mega ton punch. The boat is driven by a single seven- bladed highly skewed propeller. Special anechoic rubber tiles (the anti sonar protection tiles to reduce the risk of detection)[10] coat the steel hull to reduce noise. A similar technology was previously used in the Soviet Kilo class submarines.[11]

The Russian help in designing the ATV has long been an open secret. But more than design or fabrication of hull, it was the downsizing and mating of the 90 MW (120,000 horsepower) low-enriched uranium (LEU) fuel pressurised light water reactor (PWR), meant to propel the vessel, that took almost a decade for the submarine to finally roll out of the dock. The development of nuclear propulsion for ATV remained the most ill-managed as well as challenging part of the programme.[12]

Unlike civilian power reactors which operate at a steady state, a naval reactor has to respond instantly to repeated variations in power for ship manoeuvring. Nuclear safety, radiation, shock, quieting and operating performance requirements, in addition to operation in close proximity to the crew, demand exceptionally high standards of design, manufacturing and quality assurance. Once on patrol, a submarine's reactor remains inaccessible for inspection or replacement throughout its core life – unlike a typical commercial nuclear reactor which can be shut down for refuelling or repairs as required.[13]

For the Indian scientists used to designing shore-based natural uranium/heavy water reactors spread over a couple of football fields, miniaturising reactor components to fit inside a 20x20 foot (8 menclosure[14]) compartment (with the entire assembly weighing no more than 300-400 tons) posed an insurmountable challenge.[15] The reactor and containment vessel was initially consuming one tenth (nearly 600 tons) of the vessel's total displacement. The hydrodynamics of a vessel with such enormous weight concentrated in one place was indeed a formidable naval engineering challenge. No wonder the design and slimming down of the reactor and its containment plants for the propulsion system[16] persistently plagued and delayed the programme.

After the BARC reactor designs failed, India turned to Russia for two 90 MW PWR's and related parts. Still, there were integration problems. Accordingly, there are reports of some Israeli, French and German imprints too on the project.[17] Another critical benchmark was conducting the land test of the reactor at Kalpakkam for which ground and technical facilities had been established. The test was eventually carried out in 2000-2001.[18] All in all, by 2004 the reactor had been built, tested on land and had gone critical.[19]

## Testing the Technology Demonstrator

Before attaining the status of a ballistic missile nuclear submarine and becoming the Indian Navy's first locally constructed SSBN (INS Arihant), S-2 is likely to remain a "technology demonstrator" for a considerable period. The submarine will have to seek 'fitting certification' in three crucial areas. These include the affirmation of stealth features, inadequacy if any, in the reactor design and confirmation of the missile's range.

A primary reason why nations invest and place a significant part of their nuclear arsenal on board nuclear submarines is the purported stealth features or the undetectability associated with these platforms. Once on station and submerged, an SSBN with her lethal cargo of ballistic missiles ready for launch at instant notice, is considered safe from surveillance satellites and consequently secure from threat of attack by the adversary. The only way to detect the SSBN (or for that matter any submarine) is through the passive/ active listening devices[20] mounted on ships, submarines and helicopters of the challenger that can readily pick up any acoustic signatures (across the full spectrum of frequencies) including those generated by a submarine's hull, reactor, machinery, propeller and even her crew.[21]

In the case of S-2 the first crucial test will be the meticulous calibration of her underwater noise signature, which will determine the degree of her invulnerability and suitability as a Ballistic Missile carrying platform. This may necessitate extensive trials involving adjustments and design modifications – if not for S-2, certainly for successor versions.[22] 'The refuelling cycle or replacing of the reactor's fuel rods is a complex dockyard operation which may require a submarine to be placed out of operational cycle for a significant period of time (exceeding 18-24 months). Being a first or second generation technology with shorter fuel cycle, the S-2 reactor places a premium on the boat's performance as an instrument of deterrence.[23] The net result would be that either the submarine's patrol areas will have to remain close to home base or else the vessel's endurance (deployment period) will be curtailed. In either case there would be long gaps unless a large pool of SSBN is available for recycling.

Lastly, S-2 currently configured to launch a Pakistan specific SLBM, will have to accommodate missiles of not only greater range (ICBM) but in greater number if the platform is to have a deterrent value against China. This will require further underwater launches and flight trials for the next Arihant class of SSBN.

## Sea Based Strategic Missiles Development

Capable of carrying 12 tube launched ballistic missiles and achieving a top speed of 44km (24 knot)[24], S-2 is planned to be initially armed with the 700 km Sagarika[25] (K-15) ballistic missiles that can carry a payload of 500 kg.[26] The follow up versions of the submarine are expected to carry 3500 km K-X (IRBM) missile with multiple warheads while the ultimate goal is to arm these submarines with the three-stage, 5000 km Agni - III SL (the submarine launched version of Agni - III IRBM).[27]

Submarine-based nuclear weapons are regarded as the safest, particularly if the submarines are powered by nuclear generators that provide them months of undetected submerged operations.[28] Sealaunched nuclear missiles are accordingly central to second strike capability which acts as a stabiliser in the context of nuclear strategy since it reduces the imperatives for a first strike.[29] Indian defence planners had long bemoaned the absence of nuclear powered submarines armed with nuclear tipped missiles, considered the most reliable, survivable and deadly nuclear weapons delivery platforms.[30]

In order to enhance the credibility of strategic deterrence, New Delhi is currently executing an ambitious plan for development of the ballistic cruise missile.[31] Besides modifications of surface ships to launch nuclear capable ballistic missiles and the ongoing construction of nuclear powered submarines,[32] India is engaged in developing two missile systems that will constitute the naval leg of its planned triad of nuclear forces. The first is the Dhanush (Bow), a modified Prithvi II ballistic missile launched from a stabilisation platform mounted on surface ships.[33] The liquid fuel 28-foot long missile with a launch weight of four tons has a range of 350 km[34] and can deliver a payload of up to one ton.[35]

The naval ships usually carry cruise missiles and their top decks have to be reinforced to sustain the powerful thrust generated by the launch of a ballistic missile. Arrangements have also to be made to provide a stable launch platform because of the ship's continuous movement in both axes.[36] On 13 December 2009, Dhanush was reportedly fired from INS Subhadra[37] off the Chandigarh coast in Orissa state. Jointly conducted by the IN team and scientists from DRDO, the successful test was stated to have met all the mission objectives.[38]

The other naval system, Sagarika (Oceanic),[39] a two-stage ballistic missile, is expected to become operational after 2010.[40] The missile can be launched from a submerged submarine using a gas booster. The nuclearcapable missile powered by solid propellants is a light miniaturised system which is about 6.5 meters long and weighs sevcn tons.[41] A product of DRDO missile complex in Hyderabad, Sagarika has the latest technologies in aerodynamics, control and guidance as well as navigation.[42] The DRDO complex consists of the Defence Research and Development Laboratory (DRDL), the Advanced Systems Laboratory (ASL) and the Research Center, Imarat (RCI). While the missile was designed and developed by the DRDL, the ASL provided the motors and propulsion systems. The RCI's contribution was in avionics, including control and guidance systems and inertial navigation systems. On 26 February, 2008, the missile was test launched for the first time from a submerged pontoon near Visakhaptanam.[43] The trial was declared successful.[44]

## The Indian Nuclear Doctrine and IN

"All neighbouring countries are actual or potential enemies."

—Chanakya Kautaliya, 350-283BC, (*Arthashastra*)

The Indian Navy strongly began supporting nuclear related programmes at sea in the wake of the 1998 tests for valid and legitimate reasons - that of an invulnerable nuclear capability in support of a posture of 'no first use'. At a press conference in 2002, the Indian Navy Chief said,

> *any country that espouses a no first use policy (as India does) must have an assured second strike capability. All such countries have a triad of weapons, one of them at sea. It is significant that the Standing Committee on Defence of the twelfth Lok Sabha had advised the government to review and accelerate its nuclear policy for fabricating or for acquiring nuclear submarines to add to the (nation's) deterrent potential.*[45]

When in January 2003 the major elements of India's official nuclear doctrine were brought into the public domain,[46] the Indian government stressed on the building and maintenance of a 'credible minimum deterrent' alongwith a posture of 'no first use'. Nuclear retaliation to a first strike was expressed to be "massive and designed to inflict unacceptable damage". Significantly, however, the 2003 statement did not reiterate the 1999 draft nuclear doctrine's aim of building a nuclear triad, although all the three armed services were keen to deploy nuclear capable weapon systems.[47]

Whereas the Indian Navy was disappointed at the lack of official sanction for its submarine-based nuclear deterrent, it tried hard not to show it. While the ATV project was underway with the funding and guaranteed political support from the government, this notable absence was possibly motivated by an attempt at not alarming the international community about India's multidimensional nuclear programme.[48]

## Deterrence Described

In accounting for deterrence, the Indian Maritime Doctrine, IMD (INBR 8) articulates that "the aggressor must be convinced that the cost benefit ratio of aggression is to his detriment". This, it maintains, could be done either by raising the costs or by denying the gains. The former, according to the doctrine, is known as 'deterrence by punishment', while the latter is termed as 'deterrence by denial'. It further states that 'deterrence by punishment' requires a strong retaliatory capability and a politicomilitary posture that assures the potential aggressor of unacceptably high costs. On the other hand, 'deterrence by denial', entails the ability and intent to deny victory to the enemy regardless of the cost.[49]

The Indian Navy document titled, *'The Freedom to Use the Seas: Indian Maritime Military Strategy'* (IMMS) is juxtaposed with the IMD and the Joint Doctrine of the Indian Armed Forces. The IMMS describes nuclear deterrence as a subset of strategic deterrence. It explicates that the sea-based leg of the nuclear triad enables a survivable second strike capability and is therefore, a critical enabler for the doctrine of 'no first use' to attain credibility.[50]

According to the IMMS, nuclear stability is divided into crisis stability and arms control stability. The former is achieved by a mutual readiness to give up the ambition of attaining escalation dominance through early manoeuvring. In this context IMMS deems the nuclear submarine to be an ideal platform. The stealth characteristics of a ballistic missile submarine ensure that no advantage can accrue to the other side from positioning, escalating and manoeuvring. The second factor, arms control stability, it states, is best achieved at the lowest arsenal levels. Here again, the most credible of all arsenals in a second strike is the nuclear armed missile submarine. On both counts, therefore, the nuclear submarine option has been exemplified as the preferred arsenal for small nuclear forces.[51]

## India's Monroe Doctrine

India today demonstrates an ever increasing thirst for regional eminence. A former Indian Navy Chief, Arun

Prakash, accordingly pleads with the Indians to keep it etched in their minds that should a clash of interests arise between India and any other power, regional or extra-regional, the use of coercive power and even conflict remains a distinct possibility. Such Kautilyan-sounding statements lend credence to the notion of a forward-leaning India that will increasingly incline on hard power solutions to regional challenges.[52]

Indian strategists phrase their analyses of India's maritime surroundings – and the proper responses to those surroundings – in decidedly geopolitical terms. The declaration by the Indian Naval Chief in the foreword of 2007 IMMS[53] is a lucid demonstration of a strategic thought process that aims at making India a strongman– a Naval 'Constable' in the Indian Ocean.[54]

In their nation's novel bid for great sea power, Indians look for inspiration to the Monroe Doctrine, the 19th century US policy declaration that purported to place the New World off-limits to new European territorial acquisitions or a reintroduction of the European political system. An identical philosophy for India was first purported by PM Jawahar Lal Nehru in a speech in 1961 justifying the use of force to evict Portugal from Goa, "...any attempt by a foreign power to interfere in any way with India is a thing which India cannot tolerate, and which, subject to her strength, she will oppose. That is the broad doctrine I lay down".[55]

While the success or otherwise of India's Monroe Doctrine could be debated, it has remained an "article of faith for many in the Indian strategic community"[56] till it now seems to have entered into the Indian foreign policy lexicon. And since the Monroe Doctrine was and remains very much a maritime concept,[57] India has made huge strides in recent times to develop and expand its sea power. In the process, New Delhi has also largely shed its continental way of thinking to a great extent.[58]

## The Force Structure

The long term force structure of a hegemonic Indian Navy will have 'reach, endurance and sustenance' created through indigenous design and industrial effort.[59] The IN may feature six to nine carrier task forces, four to six SSBNs, and a fleet of SSN. At least three carrier groups may thus be available for expeditious deployment.[60] In the short-term however, a navy accruing advantage of the presence of USN would imply two to three carrier battle groups organized into single fleet depending on New Delhi's tolerance for risk and the IN's ability to maintain the fleet in top operational state. During the period, the IN is also likely to continue developing and expanding the undersea nuclear deterrent manifest in a fleet of ballistic-missile submarines (SSBNs) with Nuclear Attack Submarines, SSN's (able to operate throughout the IO basin and beyond) taking low priority.[61]

## In Perspective - Pakistan's Nuclear Policy

> *Any future threat scenario against Pakistan shall most probably have complex multidimensional facts, i.e., sub - conventional and unconventional actors, too. Therefore, to cover such a large spectrum of threat dimensions, a reappraisal of Pakistan's nuclear capabilities as well as policy is urgently required.*[62]

In a recent expose, the former US Secretary of State and National Security Adviser, Henry Kissinger argues that, "the persistence of unresolved regional conflicts makes nuclear weapons a powerful lure in many parts of the world—to intimidate neighbours and to serve as a deterrent to great powers who might otherwise intervene in a regional conflict".[63]

Unlike India,[64] Pakistan's nuclear policy is entirely security driven and is India-centric. Islamabad's threat perceptions are seen as stemming primarily from India both at the level of all-out conventional war, limited war and low intensity conflict (LIC). Within the nuclear framework, Pakistan seeks to establish deterrence against all-out conventional war.[65] In other words, Pakistan's nuclear deterrence is not only against a possible Indian nuclear attack, but a conventional one as well.[66] The discourse on the direction, aims and objectives of the nuclear policy is however veiled and mainly confined to official circles. Accordingly, public debate is very generic; much in contrast to India's voluminous print material on the subject.[67] The decision not to publicly enunciate a comprehensive nuclear doctrine is partly because Pakistan does not see a political/ status utility for the nuclear capability - rather, it envisages the nuclear capability as having a purely defensive, security related purpose.

## PN and the Economic Security

Pakistan Navy falls in the category of a small navy also called coastal or brown water navy. By definition a small navy is one that has "no ship bigger than a destroyer in its inventory".[68] A small or coastal navy operates relatively close to base at all times.[69] But with the advancement in technology, diverse weapon systems and the intrinsic value of information age throwing up newer challenges, navies are increasingly categorized as global, blue water, regional or coastal. In US parlance a coastal navy is termed as brown water navy.[70]

Like India, Pakistan's commerce too is intrinsically sea borne. More than 95 per cent of Pakistan's trade by volume and 88 per cent by value is transported via sea.[71] Three sea-lines of communication (SLOC) support Pakistan's maritime trade viz, the Far East, Red Sea and the Gulf. These sea arteries transport the country's imports as well as exports. In the former are included edible oil, tea, sugar and wheat and other value added food stuff. During the first eleven months of the last fiscal year, $ 3.662 billion was spent on food imports.[72]

Much of Pakistan's oil too has to come over the sea. The Gulf sea artery ships the country's annual oil imports and constitutes a strategic energy lifeline. With a 5 per cent annual growth rate, Pakistan's oil import is likely to reach 22.2 million tons during FY 2010-11.[73]

During FY 2008-09, the ports of Karachi and Qasim collectively handled 24.4 million tons of dry cargo imports and 20.9 million tons of liquid bulk cargo totalling some 45.3 million tons. The overall tonnage of exports at these ports during the same period was 18.3 million tons. In addition the ports handled 1.9 million TEUs[74] worth of containerised cargo.[75] All in all, Pakistan's critical overall dependence on sea-based imports is a good deal greater than India's. With India's superiority over Pakistan, most pronounced in the maritime field, a blockade of Karachi or national sea lines can seriously impinge on the country's economic security as well as war efforts within two to three weeks.[76] A compelling situation may well lead to crossing the nuclear Rubicon. Given the value and quantum of Pakistan's sea-based commerce and its correlation with the country's economic security, PN's role in the overall national security calculus is all too important to be set aside easily.

## The Task amid Growing Imbalances

The tasks performed by Pakistan Navy are traditional and involve protection of maritime interests including preservation of SLOCs and seaward defence of Pakistan.[77] Also included is the complex challenge of coastal security now magnified following 26/11 Mumbai attacks. On the other hand, the Sir Creek maritime boundary dispute has resulted in numerous unpleasant incidents at sea. In the wake of the Kargil conflict, the cold blooded shooting down of PN Atlantic maritime reconnaissance aircraft by the IAF fighters while the former was on a routine training mission had its origin in the dispute. The conventional force ratio hugely favouring the IN has been persistently enlarging over the past three decades much to the detriment of PN. The latest addition (nuclear submarine) will now tip this balance further in good deed for IN. In an extended stand-off, INS Arihant may play a crucial role in enforcing a protracted blockade against Pakistan.

## The Choices

Pakistan's situation, both internally as well as externally, is precarious. The gulf between Washington and Islamabad also continues to widen and is now beginning to irk and anger the latter.[78] With its strategic interests now 'exactly aligned' with Washington,[79] New Delhi is drawing extensive mileage out of Pakistan's current predicament. Islamabad's choices to address this strategic asymmetry and to ensure survivability of its nuclear forces are seemingly fewer. But China's signal that it will try and win Islamabad a concession similar to the July 2005 Indo-US nuclear initiative that granted a special exemption to India from global nuclear rules[80] is indeed reassuring.

That fact aside, the currently available means of delivering nuclear strikes are susceptible to air and missile attacks. The Indian Air Defence system including efforts to build PAD (Prithvi Air Defence) capability,[81] acquire the Israeli AWACS as well as the upcoming US-Israeli-Russian Ballistic Missile Shield,[82] together reduce the possibility of penetration by either missiles or the fighters. The option of missiles with multiple warheads too is open to debate. For now, the dispersal of the nuclear arsenal also becomes questionable. The cutting edge technology, the surveillance means like IRS satellites/MiG25 or the day-night capable Israeli surveillance satellite RISAT, along with platforms like Phalcon AWACS, SU 30 aircraft etc., in the Indian inventory raises questions about the value of asset dispersal by Pakistan. To compound matters further, the volatile situation prevalent in the country's two provinces, i.e. Khyber-Pakhtunkhwa (KPK) and Baluchistan further limits geographic spreading of strategic weapons, at least for now.

For the moment, the recent negotiations in the Conference on Disarmament (CD) in Geneva on a Fissile Material Cut-off Treaty (FMCT) threaten to freeze the stocks' imbalance between Pakistan and India, which is to the distinct advantage of the latter. New Delhi gains further through the Indo-US nuclear deal and the consequent NSG waiver that has allowed India to conclude agreements with countries including Russia and France to supply it with nuclear fuel.[83] Pakistan's resource imbalance as well as geographic disproportion (landmass)[84] with the latest inclusion of the nuclear submarine in its arsenal provides India a convincing capacity to strike all over Pakistan from Deep South alongside ensuring survivability of its own forces. While Pakistan does not have the potential to deliver a nuclear riposte, an economic threshold could certainly reach in days if Pakistan's sea lines particularly that of Gulf, were to be blocked.

## Second Strike on Board Conventional Submarines

In October 2008, the Chief of Staff of Pakistan Navy claimed that Pakistan Navy was capable of deploying strategic weapons at sea.[85] The details on how the strategic or nuclear weapons would be deployed and if Pakistan has developed a capability to launch missiles from submarines were not disclosed. But it is widely speculated that work on arming PN's conventional submarines with nuclear tipped missiles has now been going on for quite sometime. A sea version of cruise missile Babur is thought to have been developed by the country's strategic organisations. If true, Pakistan would not be the first country to arm its conventional submarines with such a capability. Israel's 1,900-ton Dolphin class German origin submarines are believed to be part of the country's second strike capability. It provides Tel Aviv the crucial third pillar of nuclear defence complementing the country's much vaunted land and air ramparts.[86]

## The Agosta 90Bs

Pakistan Navy's Agosta 90 B or Khalid class attack submarines (SSK) carry a team of highly skilled and professionally trained officers and men. The submarines designed by DCN (now DCNS) of France are an improved version of the Agosta series featuring superior performance and a new combat system. A higher level of automation has resulted in a reduced crew from original 54 to 36. Improvements also include a new battery for increased range, a deeper diving capability of 320 m resulting from the use of new materials including HLES 80 steel as well as a reduced acoustic signature through the installation of a new suspension and isolation system.[87]

Three Agosta 90Bs were ordered by Pakistan in 1994. The first, Khalid (1999) was constructed in France, the second Saad (2003) was assembled at Karachi Naval Dockyard and the third Hamza (2008) was constructed and assembled at Karachi. These submarines are equipped with a diesel electric propulsion system and the MESMA Air Independent Propulsion system.[88] The diesel electric system consists of two SEMTPielstick 16 PA 4 V185 VG diesels providing 3,600 hp and a 2,200kw electric motor driving a single propeller.

Pakistan is the only country bordering the Indian Ocean to have acquired Air Independent Propulsion (AIP) submarines. The 200 kw MESMA liquid oxygen AIP system significantly increases the submerged endurance of the submarine at 4 knot.[89] The system consists essentially of a turbine receiving high pressure steam from a boiler using hot gases from a combustion chamber, burning a gaseous mixture of ethanol and liquid oxygen (LOX).[90] While Agosta 90 Bs' performance remains the same in all other respects, the system (AIP) causes an 8.6 m extension to the original

67.6 m long hull increasing the boat's submerged displacement from 1,760 tons to 1,980 tons.[91]

*SUBTICS (Submarine Tactical Integrated Combat System)*

## Command and Control system

Agosta 90-B is equipped with SUBTICS fully integrated combat system. SUBTICS processes signals from submarine sensors, determines the tactical situation by track association, fusion, synthesis, trajectory plotting and management. This track management allows the Command in appreciating the surface picture and consequent handling of weapons related commands and control functions.

## Weapons System

The Agosta 90 B submarine has four bow 533 mm diameter 1Q63A Mod 2 Torpedo tubes with the capacity to carry a mixed load of 16 torpedoes and missiles. The boat can further fire tube launched SM-39 Exocet subsurface to surface missile, capable of hitting targets out to 27 nm (50 km). The sea skimming missile has inertial guidance and active radar homing system and travels at a speed of 0.9 Mach.[92] The target range and bearing data is down loaded into Exocet's computer via SUBTICS. The boat has also acquired the capacity to launch DM2A4 wire guided active/passive wake homing torpedo adding a new dimension to its firepower. Targets upto 45 km can now be engaged.

## Short-Term (within 5 Years)

Since S-2 is not likely to be formally integrated into the Indian Navy until at least 2012, PN must obtain the most out of the available time. With their cutting edge technology, Pakistan Navy Khalid class submarines could be armed to carry nuclear tipped cruise missiles. Several formidable challenges will however have to be overcome. The missile installation and subsequent integration with on-board combat system[93] as well as with the nuclear command and control infrastructure (C-4I network) could be a daunting task. The combat system, meant for conventional weapon system may also require major changes to accommodate a non-conventional weapon. During operational deployments and as opposed to the existing practice, a PN submarine carrying nuclear weapons will no longer remain under the operational control of the Commander Pakistan Fleet. Such a control will shift to the National Command Authority (NCA).

Perhaps a greater challenge would be ensuring foolproof communication between the submerged submarine and the shore-based command. An EMP (Electro Magnetic Pulse) following a nuclear cloud burst disrupts the earth's Electro-Magnetic (EM) spectrum. This results in either a partial or else complete breakdown of communications (shoresubmarine). The problem gets compounded in the absence of any domestic communications satellite. A VLF communications system can however provide an answer to some extent.[94] The platform will have to be subjected to a sustained period of tests and trials to develop a robust communication system to meet such a contingency.

The submarine crew, obviously amongst the specially selected,[95] will also require extensive training in handling all kinds of unforeseen events, developing SOP's and minimising situations where, in the absence of communications, confusion may occur on board. Test firings of missiles too will be required to ensure crew confidence as well as weapon system's credibility.

Numerous issues, both of technical as well as operational nature, will thus have to be addressed at each tier to fully integrate the vessel as part of the national strategic forces. Close cooperation and coordination between Development and Employment Control Committees under the NCA (National Command Authority), strategic organisations like KRL (Kahuta Research Laboratories), NESCOM (National

Engineering and Scientific Commission), SUPARCO (Space and Upper Atmosphere Research Organisation), PAEC (Pakistan Atomic Energy Commission), MTC (Maritime Technology Complex) and NDC (National Development Complex) too will be essential all along. More importantly, these organisations will have to rise above intra establishment rivalries and jealousies that might come in the way of smooth and timely achievement of various objectives.

A word of caution may be in order here. Pakistan Navy had previously enjoyed a sharp edge over the Indian Navy's conventional submarines like Foxtrot, Kilos etc., which were relatively noisier compared to the French submarines. The Indian Navy has not only been catching up on this lately but is now on the verge of surpassing Pakistani submarines. The French Scorpenes are supposedly a generation ahead of the Agosta 90-B.[96] On a positive note however, the recent induction of advance platforms like the *SAAB AEW&C Erieye* system and IL-78 refuellers by PAF, besides bolstering Pakistan's strategic capability, both on land and at sea, would significantly strengthen Pakistan's air defence landscape.[97]

## Employing Strategic Weapons on P3-C's

The P-3C Orion LRMPs have a proven maritime surveillance and reconnaissance record that dates back to the Cold War period. Several old and new versions of the aircraft continue to provide service in more than 18 countries including the US. It is a turbo prop, multidimensional aircraft, known to the naval community as 'Air Borne Destroyer'.

PN first acquired P3Cs in 1991. The present inventory is suitably modernised and equipped with cutting edge sensors and weapons suite to track, identify and hunt surface as well as subsurface targets. The aircraft can carry a mixed pay load of 8 Harpoon, 6 Torpedoes, besides mines and bombs. It has endurance in excess of 12 hours and can fly as low as 300 feet, thus making its detection quite difficult.

A fresh deal for eight additional refurbished P3Cs was recently concluded between Pakistan Navy and the US. In addition to improved sensors, like the digitalised tracking system, electro-optical IR, chaff dispenser, ESM suite as well as the sonobuoy detection system, the new batch of P3Cs is also due to be fitted with Inverse Synthetic Aperture Radar (ISAR). The ISAR is a state of the art radar that provides dual advantage. It eases the identification problem by projecting target's silhouette (physical image) which in turn improves the overall accuracy of tracking and attacking. Its other advantage is the variable power output that renders ISAR difficult to detect on an ESM.

Following 26/11 Mumbai attacks, the Indian Navy too has concluded a deal with the US for acquisition of 8xMMAs (Multi Mission Aircraft), the successor to P-3Cs, also called Poseidon. The Indian Navy is currently operating an old generation of Russian IL-38 and TU-142 LRMPs while the jet driven Poseidon will be a multi-mission maritime reconnaissance aircraft suitably converted for maritime ASV/ ASW roles. The first prototype of MMA is however not expected to roll out anytime before 2012, following which its true capabilities would be known.

The P-3Cs are the main stay of the PN's offensive arm. Given the advanced outfit onboard P-3Cs, Pakistan Navy, at least for now, maintains a clear qualitative edge over the Indian Navy's LRMPcapability. PN could arm its P-3Cs with a suitably modified version of Babur missile to serve as a back up to the undersea second strike on-board Agosta 90Bs. A careful employment strategy may then transform P-3Cs to a potent constituent in the nuclear triad.

## Medium and Long Term (Beyond 5 years)

The prolonged and sustained Russian assistance to India for developing a nuclear submarine that will now provide the latter with a sea-based nuclear deterrence potential was patently marked by absence of any opposition by the US or the rest of the international community. This is not all; the 2005 Indo-US nuclear deal never caused any uproar in the West or by the NSG (Nuclear Suppliers Group). Besides raising concerns on proliferation, the deal significantly undercut the efficacy of the NPT.[98] This provides Pakistan enough justification to go for both the lease of nuclear submarines and (or) eventual development of the technology for production of such a platform.[99] It is not about matching India's nuclear weapon for a nuclear weapon but about preserving stability and ensuring survivability of the deterrence forces. The national maritime objectives or the task assigned to PN may not merit a nuclear submarine. Nonetheless, preservation and credibility of deterrence value obligates such a consideration particularly in the evolving geo-politics in the IOR.

The gradually expanding civil-military ties between Beijing and Islamabad have now matured into a strategic partnership. This is distinctly evident from the ongoing efforts between the two sides to meet Islamabad's demand for additional nuclear reactors (Chashma-III and IV) despite tremendous international pressure on Beijing not to go ahead with the deal. Besides, the local production of PAF's JF-17 Thunder multi-role fighter, Al-Khalid tank and Pakistan Navy's F-22P frigates are all living symbols of an enduring partnership. PLAN's regular participation in large scale multinational AMAN series of exercises hosted by Pakistan Navy also certifies the mutually shared strategic interests.

Pakistan's strategic community and Beijing can now put a plan on the drawing board for training and later lease of a nuclear powered submarine. The PLAN Xia class submarine could be an appropriate starter. A pool of selected PN officers may be trained to operate an SSBN. The scheme may appear to be rather ambitious. But given the fact that PLAN SSBNs rarely prowl around,[100] it could serve the strategic interests of both sides fairly well. With PLAN now certain to field an aircraft carrier in near future and project power beyond its shores, nuclear submarines will become an integral part of carrier task force. Like the USN-IN, the two navies (PLAN-PN) could eventually conduct exercises in different theatres (Indian or Pacific Ocean) to solidify interoperability procedures and doctrines. A two tiered training with first phase (ashore) involving theoretical/academic part could be followed by operational training at sea with the final phase devoted to strategic deployment training.

## Conclusion

Deterrence is not a dormant concept; it must be stepped up proportionate to the adversary's increase in arsenal or delivery means. The international community will react sharply were Pakistan to field a sea based nuclear deterrence. The timing in this case is perhaps crucial. Pakistan is currently too dependent on the US and multilateral financial institutions for keeping its economy afloat. The situation is not likely to alter for next few years. The country's security situation and fears of radicalisation (real or imaginary) in western minds reinforces the possibility of a strong reaction.[101] Nonetheless, Beijing understands very well the enduring geographic significance and perennial value of Pakistan as a valuable trip switch to cap India's great power ambitions. China's decision to expand its nuclear cooperation with Pakistan in defiance of the international norms underlines an irreplaceable value the former attaches to its relations with Islamabad. Such a relation must then be exploited to the mutual benefit of both sides. If not addressed, Pakistan's hard earned nuclear stability may erode beyond recovery. In the early periods the role of the armed forces was to win a war once diplomacy had failed and in the nuclear age their role is to prevent a war from breaking out.[102] In this scenario, Pakistan has no option but to take some hard decisions.

## References

1. The correct current designation of Advance Technology Vessel is S-2 according to a former Indian Navy Chief. The vessel will become INS Arihant only upon commissioning in due course. See Admiral Arun Parkash, "A Step Before the Leap: Putting India's ATV Project in Perspective," *Force* (September 2009), http://www.maritimeindia.org/pdfs/AP-FORCE1.pdf
2. "Deep Impact", *India Today,* August 3, 2009, 48 and *Jane's Defence Weekly,* August 5, 2009, 6. ATV (S-2) is a fleet ballistic missile submarine, known in US parlance as SSBN.
3. Admiral Arun Prakash, "A Step before the Leap: Putting India's ATV Project in Perspective," *Force* (September 2009).
4. "India Finally Launches ATV," *Jane's Defence Weekly,* August 5, 2009, 6.
5. "India Confirms Plans for Nuclear Submarines," *Jane's Defence Weekly,* December 12, 2007, 12 and Vijainder K. Thakur, "INS Arihant: A Technology Demonstrator and Testbed", http://flareout.blogspot.com/2009/07/insarihant-technology-demonstrator-and.html
6. "India N-Sub to Trigger Arms Race," *Nation* (Lahore), July 28, 2009.
7. "Second Strike Challenges," *Daily Times* (Lahore), September 11, 2009.
8. $ 1 billion was spent in 2005 alone. See Eric Margolis, "India Rules the Waves," *Proceedings,* March 2005, 66.
9. "India's Top Secret N- Submarine Project," *Defence Journal* (April 2009): 27.
10. "SSK Kilo Class Attack Submarine, Russia," Naval technology.com,http://www.naval-technology.com/projects/kilo877/
11. See, "The Secret Undersea Weapon," *India Today*, January 28, 2008, 52.
12. "Arihant - Advanced Technology Vessel (ATV)," www.globalsecurity.org/military/world/atv
13. Admiral Arun Prakash, "A Step before the Leap".
14. "The Secret under Sea Weapon," *India Today*, January 28, 2008, 55 and "India's Top Secret N-Submarine Project," *Defence Journal* (April 2009): 28.

15. Admiral Arun Prakash, "A Step before the Leap".
16. "India's Top Secret N-Submarine Project," *Defence Journal* (April 2009): 28.
17. "India's nuclear sub," *Nation* (Lahore), March 28, 2007.
18. Lowell Dittmer, "South Asia's Nuclear Security Dilemma," *Pentagon Press*, Rahul Roy Chaudhury, "India and Pakistan Nuclear Related Programs and Aspirations at Sea," Chapter 4, 88.
19. The submarine reactor uranium is enriched to 45 percent as against civilian nuclear reactors that require less than 5 per cent enrichment.
20. Sonar, LOFAR (Low Frequency Acoustic Ranging/ Recording and Analysis), and other similar devices can pick up submarine acoustic signals from tens of miles and pinpoint the position in minutes.
21. Admiral Arun Parkash, "A Step before the Leap".
22. *Ibid.*
23. The US Navy has 25 different types of submarine reactors and is running the 9th generation since the first was developed and put in use in 1954 onboard USS Nautilus. See Admiral Arun Parkash, "A Step before the Leap".
24. "Pakistan Hits out at Detrimental Indian Nuclear Sub," *News* (Rawalpindi), July 29, 2009. Some sources claim the submarine will be able to achieve up to 25knots.
25. Also called K-15, Sagarika has been variously described as SLBM or a SLCM. See Naeem Salik, *The Genesis of South Asian Nuclear Deterrence* (Karachi: Oxford University Press), 199.
26. *Jane's Defence Weekly*, August 5, 2009, 6. According to other estimates, K-15 a short range ballistic missile can carry 1 ton nuclear warhead. See *India Today*, August 3, 2009, 48. Certain sources also claim that ATV can carry up to 16 Brahmos Supersonic anti-ship missiles.
27. "The Secret Undersea Weapon," *India Today*, January 28, 2008, 55.
28. Gulshan Luthra, "India Test Fires New Supersonic Missile," *India Strategic* Vol. 3, issue 11 (November 2008): 17.
29. Shireen M. Mazari, "India's Arihant - Upping the Psychological Ante," *News* (Rawalpindi), July 29, 2009.

30. "Going Ballistic: India Looks to Join Elite Missile Club', *Times* (London), May 13, 2008. See Gaurav Kampani, "Stakeholders in the Indian Strategic Missile Program," *The Nonproliferation Review* (Fall-Winter 2003): 65.
31. See "India's Missile Program," *Weekly Pulse*, December 11-17, 2009, 15.
32. Indian Navy is currently involved in seven major nuclear related programs at sea. These include acquisition and operation of nuclear powered subs, the ATV project, the modification of surface ships to launch ballistic missiles, the Dhanush ballistic missile, the Sagarika missile and BrahMos supersonic cruise missile and the modification of ex-Russian conventionally armed Klub antiship cruise missile to a nuclear capability.
33. According to some Indian sources, Dhanush is a cruise missile and could be carried on ATV as well. See Eric S. Margolis, "India Rules the Waves," *Proceedings,* March 2005, 67. Other sources maintain that Dhanush being too large cannot be placed on-board submarines.
34. Rahul Roy Chaudhury, "India and Pakistan Nuclear Related Programs and Aspirations at Sea," in Lowell Dittmer, South Asia's Nuclear Security Dilemma: *India, Pakistan, and China* (New York: M.E. Sharpe, 2005), 89.
35. According to Indian MoD, Dhanush will be capable of carrying both conventional and nuclear warheads. The system's operational utility may be limited by its relatively short maximum range—350 km.
36. Naeem Salik, "The Genesis of South Asian Nuclear Deterrence," 196.
37. Subhadra a 1,890 ton OPV, Offshore Patrol Vessel, was selected by the IN in the late 1990's to be converted for launch of ballistic missiles. The modification was done at the Naval dockyard Bombay with assistance from Larsen & Toubro L&T. The OPV had limited sea going capabilities and its helicopter deck was strengthened and converted into launch pad.
38. "India Test-Fires Short Range Dhanush Missile" *Daily Times,* December 14, 2009. See Janes Defence Weekly, December 23, 2009, 12.
39. Indian MoD statements designate the missile as the K-15, though other sources refer to it as Sagarika.

40. "Ballistic and Cruise Missile Threat," a paper prepared by the *US National Air and Space Intelligence,* Wright Patterson Air Force Base, April 2009, 23.
41. "Sagarika Missile Test-Fired Successfully," *Hindu* (Delhi), February 27, 2008.
42. *Ibid.*
43. *Ibid.*
44. "World Nuclear Forces," *SIPRI Year Book,* 2009, 371.
45. Arpit Rajain, "Nuclear Deterrence in Southern Asia: China, India and Pakistan," SAGE Publications, 243-244.
46. See Indian press release, January 4, 2002, titled "Cabinet Committee on Security's Review of the Operationalisation of India's nuclear doctrine".
47. Rahul Roy Chaudhury, "India's Nuclear Doctrine: A Critical Analysis," *Strategic Analysis*, vol. 33, issue 3 (May 2009): 409.
48. Lowell Dittmer, "South Asia's Nuclear Security Dilemma: India, Pakistan, and China," *Pentagon Press,* Rahul Roy Chaudhury, "India and Pakistan: Nuclear Related Programs and Aspirations at Sea," 82.
49. "Concepts of War," Chapter 3, *INBR* 8 (Revised Edition), 26.
50. "Strategy for Employment in Peace, Freedom to Use the Seas: India's Maritime Military Strategy," Chapter 6, 76.
51. *Ibid.*
52. James R. Holmes, Andrew C. Winner and Toshi Yoshihara, *Indian Naval Strategy in the Twenty First Century'* (Taylor & Francis Routledge), 36.
53. The foreword states: "our primary maritime military interest is to ensure national security, provide insulation from external interference so that the vital task of fostering economic growth and undertaking developmental activities, can take place in a secure environment".
54. James R Holmes and Toshi Yoshihara, "Indian's Monroe Doctrine and Asia's Maritime Future," *Strategic Analysis,* Vol. 32, no 6 (November 2008): 997-998.
55. *Ibid.*
56. *Ibid.,* 1000.
57. The influential sea-power theorist Alfred Thayer Mahan was an outspoken disciple of Monroeism.

58. James R Holmes and Toshi Yoshihara, "Indian's Monroe Doctrine and Asia's Maritime Future," 1001.
59. See Admiral Arun Parkash, "Maritime Challenges," *Indian Defence Review,* Vol. 21 (1) (Jan-Mar 2006): 52.
60. James R Holmes and Toshi Yoshihara, "Indian's Monroe Doctrine and Asia's Maritime Future," 1005.
61. *Ibid.,* 1003-1004.
62. "Nuclear Pakistan: Ten Years On: Foreword," *Margalla Papers,* Special Edition (2008).
63. Henry A. Kissinger, "Our Nuclear Nightmare," Newsweek, February 16, 2009, 30.
64. India's nuclear program is believed to be status driven.
65. Dr Shireen M. Mazari, "Understanding Pakistan's Nuclear Doctrine," *Strategic Studies,* Vol. XXIV, no. 3 (Autumn 2004): 5.
66. Ken Berry, "The Security of Pakistan's Nuclear Facilities," a research paper commissioned by the International Commission on Nuclear Non-Proliferation and Disarmament, August 2009, 12.
67. Naeem Salik, *The Genesis of South Asian Nuclear Deterrence,* 230.
68. Commodore Muhammad Anwar, "Role of Smaller Navies," *Army Press,* Rawalpindi, 2.
69. The bases are also always situated on home territory and are thus secure in a sense that their availability is not influenced by the political restraints in other countries that the Naval Powers sometimes encounter. See Jacob Borresen, "The Sea Power of the Coastal State," *Journal of Strategic Studies* (Special Issue on Sea Power Theory and Practice), Vol. 17, no. 1 (March 1994): 150.
70. The development in weapons technology has made it possible to pack enough firepower even into the smallest craft, so that small vessels or craft of minor navies may be in a position to threaten even the strongest naval units of a Naval Power.
71. PNSCs limited number of national flag carriers' transport 45 per cent of liquid and 5 per cent of the country's dry cargo. Rear Admiral Mohammad Shafi, "Formulation of Maritime Strategy," talk delivered at *Pakistan Navy War College,* September 25, 2006.
72. "Agriculture Productivity and Food Security," News (Rawalpindi), February 1, 2010.

73. Ministry of Petroleum and Natural Resources.
74. "Tons Equivalent Unit," a twenty foot equivalent unit is a standard measurement of volume in container shipping. The majority of containers are either 20 or 40 in length. A 20 container is one TEU; a 40 container is two TEUs. One TEU refers to a 20 ft long container 8 ft wide and 8.6 ft in height.
75. "Cargo Handling at KPT&PQA," data obtained from *KPT*.
76. Verghese Koithara, "Coercion and Risk Taking in Nuclear South Asia," *CISAC Working Paper,* March 2003, 10.
77. Rear Admiral Mohammad Shafi, Deputy Chief of Naval Staff, "Maritime Strategy," talk delivered at Pakistan Navy War College, Lahore, September 25, 2006.
78. "Rebuffing US, Pakistan Balks at Crackdown," *New York Times*, December 15, 2009.
79. Fareed Zakaria, "The Prize is India," *Newsweek*, November 30, 2009, 5.
80. "The battle for Pakistan," *Indian Express,* June 21, 2010.
81. Dr Maleeha Lodhi, "India's Provocative Military Doctrine," *News* (Rawalpindi), January 5, 2010.
82. "Meeting India's Military Challenge," News (Rawalpindi), January 28, 2010.
83. Dr Maleeha Lodhi, "FMCT and Strategic Stability," News (Rawalpindi), *January* 26, 2010.
84. Verghese Koithara, "Coercion and Risk Taking in Nuclear South Asia," *CISAC Working Paper,* March 2003, 16.
85. *Dawn (Lahore),* October 15, 2008 and Defence Related News, Articles and Different Topics, October 19, 2008 at www.defence007.blogspot.com/2008/10/pak-navy
86. "Israel Makes Nuclear Waves with Submarine Missile Test," *Sunday Times* (London), June 18, 2000.
87. SSK Agosta 90B Class Attack Submarine, France, www.naval-technology.com/projects/agosta
88. Both the diesel generators as well as MESMA charge the submarine batteries that drive the propulsion motors while the vessel is submerged.
89. "Pakistan Commissions AIP-equipped Agosta," *Janes Defence Weekly*, October 8, 2008, 31.

90. SSK Agosta 90B Class Attack Submarine, France, www.naval-technology.com/projects/agosta

91. "Pakistan commissions AIP-equipped Agosta," *Janes Defence Weekly,* October 8, 2008, 31.

92. Jyotirmoy Banerjee, "Readying The Indian Navy for the Twenty First Century," *Asian Affairs,* V/ol. 26, no. 1 (January-March, 2004): 9.

93. Integration will be required unless it is a "stand alone system in itself" like the Harpoon missile system onboard.

94. In VLF communications set up, a submarine tows a long reception antenna while a huge shore based antenna transmits messages. Such a shore based antenna is nonetheless a vulnerable target for air strikes. Currently no such arrangement exists in PN.

95. The elite crew onboard Israel Navy Dolphin submarine is a specially selected lot. Nicknamed "force 700" because of the average 700 points (equivalent to an IQ of 130-140) they scored in psychological tests devised by the Israelis, the vessel is supplemented with another five specially selected officers solely responsible for the missile warheads. See "Israel Makes Nuclear Waves with Submarine Missile Test," *Sunday Times* (London), June 18, 2000.

96. Jyotirmoy Banerjee, "Readying The Indian Navy for the Twenty First Century," 9.

97. *Nation* (Lahore), December 30, 2009.

98. On 29 November 2009, the Indian PM announced that India is willing to join the NPT as a nuclear weapons state. The move is seen as a ploy to deflect arguments that New Delhi must accept CTBT, an agreement that would ban all testing of nuclear weapons. See *Newsweek,* December 14, 2009, 18.

99. "Strategic Stability in South Asia," *News* (Rawalpindi), August 1, 2009.

100. Jyotirmoy Banerjee, "Readying The Indian Navy for the Twenty First Century," 14.

101. Views of Lt. Gen. Talat Masood, Pakistan Army (retired).

102. K. Subrahmanyam, "Generally Speaking," *Yahoo India News,* www.in.news.yahoo.com (accessed January 8, 2010).

# Index

## H



## I



## J